CONSTRUCTION FOR LANDSCAPE ARCHITECTURE

TO JOHN OUTRAM

Published in 2011
by Laurence King Publishing Ltd
361–373 City Road
London EC1V 1LR
Tel +44 20 7841 6900
Fax +44 20 7841 6910
E enquiries@laurenceking.com
www.laurenceking.com

A catalog record for this book is available from the British Library

ISBN 978 185669 708 8
Designed by John Round Design
Printed in China

ROBERT HOLDEN AND JAMIE LIVERSEDGE

CONSTRUCTION FOR LANDSCAPE ARCHITECTURE

Laurence King Publishing

Contents

Related study material is available on the Laurence King website at
www.laurenceking.com

Introduction

"Each nation, in short, has its own way of building, according to the materials afforded and the habits of the country."
Marcus Vitruvius Pollio, *De Architectura*, Book II, Chapter 1

The vernacular tradition and globalization

Traditionally, building materials were those found locally—so in forest areas, timber was used. When forests were cleared stone was quarried or clay was dug to make bricks or earth was used to make dried mud structures. This tradition of using locally available materials continues in many areas today. In mountain regions, such as the Lake District or North Wales, the whole built environment can be made predominantly of one material – such as slate, which could be used for walls, paving, roofs and, in crushed form, as roadstone. Slate was even occasionally used for coffins.

However, prestigious structures tended to be built of imported materials: a process seen in the use of limestone in London both for churches and major institutions, and until the end of the eighteenth century for paving.

An understanding of vernacular tradition is important when working in existing cities and settlements, and is evidently vital when undertaking conservation work. For that reason, we have included here something of the history of the development of materials. However, an understanding of the vernacular is also a key to sustainable forms of construction. For example, the current revival in the use of green oak has promoted a market for this form of timber.

Industrialization

The Industrial Revolution and globalization led to moves away from the use of local building materials. The nineteenth century saw the introduction of new materials such as wrought iron (used in the Eiffel Tower) and then steel in structures,

Above
Japanese temples, such as this example, feature beautiful craftsmanship both in the stone paving and the carpentry of the temple building.

Top right
A traditional Middle Eastern, sun-baked mud-brick building at the Dubai Museum.

Above
This farm at Cefnmaesmawr, Wales, includes examples of drystone walls, limewash, slate-slab paving, slate roofs, a loose gravel road, a cattle grid of old railroad lines, and mid-twentieth-century corrugated iron.

while railroads and cheaper shipping costs made long-distance transportation of bricks and stone affordable. The nineteenth century therefore saw London's streets paved in granite from the Channel Islands, and the use of brick for most buildings and walls, while the twentieth century saw the use of asphalt for roads. The tar was a by-product of coal-gas manufacture and ceased to be available with the decline of coal gas in the 1960s following the introduction of natural gas, so there was a further change to bitumen-based asphalt binders.

New materials: High tech and low tech

The twentieth century saw the widespread introduction of metal alloys such as stainless steel and of aluminum, polymers, and new ways of using glass. The past few decades have seen a rise in the cost of lumber and new and economic ways of using wood, such as in laminated structures and the use of green forest roundwood thinnings as a structural material.

Reinforcement of materials produces composites. GRP is glass-reinforced plastic and GRC is glass-reinforced concrete, while CFRP is carbon-fiber-reinforced polymer. However, along with new forms of materials, new ways of manufacturing older materials have also appeared—witness the current interest in "ecoconcrete." Polymers or plastics are the most recently developed material in widespread use, and are largely a twentieth-century development. However, polymers are subject to concern about the energy costs of their manufacture, and the challenge of how to dispose or recycle something that does not normally biodegrade.

Renewed interest in old materials and traditional forms of construction

Alongside such new developments, there is, conversely, an interest in reviving old forms of construction—and not only in conservation projects. Use of lime mortar, hemp mortar and rammed earth construction owes as much to their sustainability and concern about the production of global-warming gases during manufacture as to their historical precedents. Lime mortar absorbs carbon dioxide and is self-repairing. Similarly, concerns about sustainability have led to the development of self-cleaning photocatalytic concrete that can "fix" pollutants from the atmosphere. This is a new development of an older material.

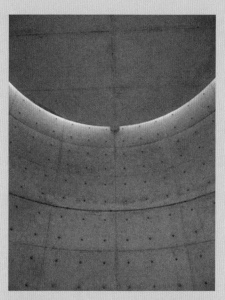

Far left
Portland stone has been the classic building material for important public and commercial buildings in London since the Great Fire of 1666.

Left
Fair-faced, cast-in-place concrete at the Place for Contemplation, UNESCO headquarters, Paris, designed by Tadao Ando.

Below left
Purbeck limestone setts were the normal paving in London in the eighteenth century.

National construction techniques and globalization

Historically, there have tended to be national construction materials, which were a product of supply conditions and, partly, of custom. For instance, brick is characteristic of the Netherlands. Lowland England was a lumber-construction region until the seventeenth or eighteenth century, as evidenced by its many half-timbered buildings, but the clearance of forests led to the use of brick. As a result, sophisticated timber-construction skills are uncommon in England today compared with the USA or Scandinavia. In the USA, road curbs are usually built of cast-in-place concrete while in much of Europe precast concrete is used.

Each city traditionally tended to have its own set of paving materials. In London, granite setts and curbs were the standard nineteenth-century street paving, while footpaths were sandstone. Amsterdam is still a city of narrow brick pavers. In historic towns in northern Russia, such as Suzdal, you can still find wooden boardwalks, as in a Wild West town. Denmark is a country of granite-paved streets. The material, however, does not occur in peninsular Denmark, rather it comes from the relatively distant Danish island of Bornholm in the Baltic (and today more often from China).

In many cities, such traditions are continued. For instance, in Paris there is a city-wide range of building materials, and footpaths are paved with granite slabs and cheaper mastic asphalt. Similarly, in reunified Berlin large traditional granite paving blocks are being reintroduced in areas where similarly sized, but cheaper precast concrete blocks had been laid in the 1950s and 1960s. In the British capital, it is only in the City of London, and to some extent in Westminster, that there is an overall policy of maintaining the use of sandstone sidewalks. Elsewhere, each of London's 32 boroughs follows its own differing paving policies; the result is an ill-coordinated patchwork of different materials.[1]

By globalization, we mean the increasingly integrated and complex global system of production and exchange—linked with cheap labor and low shipping costs. This has led to the supply of stone from China and India.

Top
Stainless-steel pool at the Plaza Tower and Town Center, Costa Mesa, California, designed by Peter Walker.

Above left
Laminated wood at the Kourion Amphitheatre Visitor Centre, near Episkopi, Cyprus.

Above right
Old street with cobble paving, sett edging, and granite curbs, Kraków, Poland.

Sustainability

Concern about humankind's impact on the planet leads to consideration of the sustainable sourcing of materials, as well as the amount of energy required to make and transport a material and the pollution consequent on its manufacture.

Sustainability and economic concerns favor recycling of materials. Responses to these concerns in construction suggest the following courses of action:

- **use resources efficiently and economically**; e.g. do not waste materials—for example: recycle any waste used in manufacturing; recycle materials already on site; specify paving stones of a range of sizes, so as to avoid wastage; source naturally occurring boulders from construction sites where they will be disturbed anyway, rather than from the wild; and clean and recycle waste water used in manufacturing.
- **use renewable resources**; e.g. lumber from renewable forests, not from virgin forest; consider use of compressed earth for wall construction; favor use of organic materials.
- **maintain natural supplies of materials and maintain natural diversity**; e.g. use lumber from sustainable sources.
- **beware of using man-made materials which do not biodegrade**; e.g. avoid plastics produced from petroleum and toxic preservatives.
- **beware (and be aware) when using finite resources from the earth's crust**; e.g. stone, clays, and metals, and polymers based on hydrocarbons.

Life-cycle analysis

In sustainability terms, it can help to evaluate the life cycle of building materials. Life-cycle analysis (or life-cycle assessment) involves the measurement of six different components: weighted resource use, embodied energy inputs, global-warming potential, solid-waste emission, and air and water toxicity, where:

- **resource use** is a measure of all the natural materials used to create a material—in the case of concrete for instance, the materials used to make the formwork of cast-in-place concrete and any scaffolding required to access it;

Above left
Aberllefenni slate quarry (technically a mine), Wales, which closed in 2003.

Top right
Demolition materials sorted for reuse: in the foreground are setts, and to the right is concrete ready for crushing.

Above right
Second World War blitz material including concrete, bricks, and setts was reused to build this random-rubble retaining wall in London.

- **embodied energy** is that required to extract, process, transport, install, maintain, and dispose of a product;
- **global-warming potential** can be measured by estimating the equivalent amount of carbon dioxide released into the atmosphere by the manufacture, transport, installation, and maintenance of a component: other global-warming gases, such as methane or nitrous oxide, are estimated as "carbon dioxide equivalents;"
- **solid-waste emissions** are the total impact of landfill consequent on a product or material; and
- **air and water toxicity** are measured by quantifying the health effects of toxic emissions through the lifetime of the product or component.

There are various life-cycle software tools which measure these components, including those produced by the Athena Sustainable Materials Institute[2] and the Building Research Establishment (they also refer to environmental profiles).[3] Such software tools are covered by ISO 14001, which is the international specification for environmental management systems (ISO is the International Organization for Standardization).

Energy-efficiency in manufacture and embodied energy

In the command economy of the former Soviet Union, cutlery was often made of aluminum because the electricity was free for the factory despite the high energy usage involved—and even though the knives and forks often bent. Where there is a free market the costs of manufacture should reflect energy costs but concern about employment often leads to distortions in the market.

Energy required to produce one ton of product[4]

Aluminium	20,169 kWh/ton
Steel	3,780 kWh/ton
Concrete	1,250 kWh/ton
Timber	435 kWh/ton

However, the energy tied up in the use of a construction material is more than just that used in its manufacture. Embodied energy is all the energy needed to transform the raw material, i.e. to extract it from the ground, process and manufacture it, and transport and assemble it on the ground. Generally, the more stages of manufacture the greater the embodied energy will be; for example, tongued-and-grooved lumber board has a higher embodied energy than rough-sawn lumber (*for a table of embodied energy, see Table 1, Appendix, page 225*).

As can be seen, embodied-energy findings vary but a useful way of looking at them is to rank embodied energy by construction material:

- aggregates – low embodied energy;
- cement – moderate embodied energy;
- brick and clay products – moderate embodied energy;
- wood – moderate embodied energy (depending on source);
- glass – relatively high embodied energy;
- steel – relatively high embodied energy; and
- plastics – very high embodied energy.

There are some software tools that model materials, though the application tends to be towards building construction rather than landscape construction. Examples include ECO-BAT (Eco Balance Assessment Tool), with a menu of 60 construction materials, produced by the Solar Energy and Building Physics Laboratory of the Haute Ecole d'Ingénierie et de Gestion du Canton de Vaud in Switzerland.[5]

Greenhouse gases

Here the concern is anthropogenic or man-made gas production and its global-warming effects. Therefore it is important to look at the embodied carbon dioxide used in manufacture, and so compare the global-warming effect of materials. For example, concrete made with PFA (pulverized fly ash—a by-product of coal-burning power stations) and GGB (ground granulated blast-furnace slag—a by-product of steel manufacture) compare favourably in terms of embodied carbon dioxide with conventional Portland cement concrete, while clay bricks and lumber are largely more economical and steel, polymers, and aluminum clearly have high levels of embodied carbon dioxide (*for a table of embodied carbon dioxide, see Table 2, Appendix, page 226*).

However, when considering carbon dioxide it is important to remember that it is just one global-warming gas. The Kyoto Protocol (1997) to the UN Climate Change Convention is concerned with six greenhouse gases and groups of gases—carbon dioxide, methane, nitrous oxide, sulphur hexafluoride, hydrofluorocarbons (HFCs), and perfluorocarbons (PFCs). Construction is a significant producer of carbon dioxide (as above), and consumer of methane. Methane is a major constituent of natural gas, and therefore products which use natural gas in their manufacture consume methane and produce carbon dioxide. The other global-warming gases are little used in landscape construction. In consequence, concern for global warming in construction should be particularly focused on carbon dioxide emission and the choice of materials.

Heat-island effect and reflectivity

Heat islands are built-up areas with higher temperatures than surrounding rural zones. Their temperatures can be between 33.8 and 37.4°F higher in the morning and up to 53.6°F greater in the evening in summer.[6] As cities develop, permeable vegetated areas are removed and buildings and

Top
Light brick paving with a high reflectivity or albedo at Colchester Business Park, England.

Above left
Newly laid Yorkstone (a sandstone) paving, London, 2008.

Above
The Noguchi garden at the UNESCO headquarters, Paris (1956–58), built by Japanese gardeners.

roads are built. It is the impermeability and low reflectivity of urban surfaces, together with the waste heat emitted by cities and the reduction of winds in urban areas, that leads to the heat-island effect. In short, towns and cities absorb more heat from the sun than rural areas and give off more heat from buildings and industry. In consequence, both surface and air temperatures rise in urban zones.

The US Environmental Protection Agency (EPA) argues that the heat-island effect, and its associated atmospheric pollution, leads to a rise in mortality among the more vulnerable, the old, the sick, and the young. However, it can be reduced by:
• minimizing the area of paving, and the area of built form;
• using permeable paving;
• using reflective paving surfaces;
• using low-thermal-conductivity materials, e.g. avoiding metal paving (high thermal conductivity) and favoring timber paving (low thermal conductivity);
• avoiding smooth surfaces with a high thermal conductivity and preferring rough surfaces such as gravel or small-unit paving, or preferring split setts to sawn setts;
• changing the form of the development (avoid high-rise and the 'urban canyon' effect);

• avoiding thick pavements with a higher thermal-storage capacity: e.g. don't lay concrete bases to stone paving;
• increasing vegetation, including parks and gardens, street trees and roof gardens;
• reducing waste-heat emissions from buildings.

This all constitutes an argument for using light rather than dark surfaces, and for specifying permeable materials. "Albedo" is a term for the measurement of reflectivity: dark materials absorb heat; white or light materials tend to reflect it.

Solar reflectance (albedo) of construction materials on a scale of 0 (dark) to 1 (light):

Material surface [7] [8] [9] [10]

black acrylic paint	0.05
new asphalt	0.05
aged asphalt	0.1
white asphalt shingle	0.2
aged concrete	0.2 to 0.3
new concrete (traditional)	0.4 to 0.5
new concrete with white Portland cement	0.7 to 0.8
white acrylic paint	0.8

Air and water

This book is about, landscape construction and materials. However, it should never been forgotten that air and water are also raw materials—basic to human existence and vital to our survival. Clean air and pure water are limited resources; much of our groundwater in intensively farmed areas is contaminated with nitrates and air in urban areas is polluted with hydrocarbons and particulates. We therefore need to ensure that construction does not contaminate air or water.

The water that is used in construction should also be relatively pure. Water with a high organic content produces poor concrete; high acidity in water dissolves mortar and limestone; water from marshland can be highly corrosive and sea water easily corrodes iron.

Freeze–thaw and water penetration must to designed for. When water freezes, it increases in volume by 9 per cent —and so stone or brickwork penetrated with freezing water will split and break up. Water penetration is a consequence of rain driven by prevailing winds. Prior to its recent reconstruction, the brickwork on the west side of St Pancras railroad station in London was severely eroded while that on the east was intact; conservation work therefore involved extensive replacement of the facing bricks on the west walls, which are open to the prevailing westerly wind in London.

Ground frost has to be designed for—typically by ensuring that foundations are buried a minimum of 18 in in a temperate climate, but deeper down, to 24 in, in colder climates and deeper on shrinkable clays. The depth should be as determined by the relevant building code. Walls should be protected from water penetration by copings or cappings. Water can be cast away from the face of a wall by the use of a string-course, and groundwater penetration can be limited by the use of a moisture-proof course. The lateral loading that groundwater can place on a retaining wall may be relieved by installing weep holes, which permit the water to drain away.

Air, whether polluted or clean, can attack construction materials. Metals combine with oxygen in the atmosphere to produce oxides, a process known as "rusting;" airborne sulphur dioxide can produce a dilute sulphuric acid in rain, which attacks buildings and other structures. Historically, carbon deposits from coal fires also turned many buildings black.

Far left
A dissolving limestone arch, Old West Station, Bexhill-on-Sea, England.

Left
Carved marble water trough showing signs of water erosion and manual abrasion in Carrara, Italy.

Bottom left
This building in Gordon Square, London, is blackened with soot that dates from the time before smoke-control laws came into effect in the mid-1950s. The buildings in most industrial cities turned black when coal fires were the main form of heating.

Attitudes to materials

Fashion also plays a part in landscape design. In post-war England, the fashion was for brick walls with thin precast-concrete copings and precast concrete and asphalt paving (except for cobbles or brick in special areas), while stone walls were built of broken paving stones. Cost constraints led to the construction of walls of fused brick from bomb-damaged buildings, while broken paving stones were also used for "crazy paving." In the 1950s, Mien Ruys, the Dutch garden designer, introduced the use of recycled lumber railroad ties for retaining walls, which the Danish landscape architect Preben Jakobsen later helped popularize in England in the 1960s.

Also in the 1960s, some countries were known for their board-marked concrete owing to the enthusiasm of architects for the work of Le Corbusier. Corbusier himself used board-marked concrete because it was a cheap and readily available material, often built with relatively unskilled labor. Many public works bodies adopted it, and made it a much more carefully constructed (and expensive) material.

In the 1980s, the trend was for herringbone-pattern concrete-block paving and textured concrete paving slabs. By the 1990s, fashion favored the use of Corten steel (trademark COR-TEN®), colored crushed glass, and granite for paving.

The past 20 years have seen a widespread reintroduction of stone for landscaping, supplied locally and from cheap Chinese and Indian quarries. The low prices of Asian stone are possible because of much cheaper labor costs (sometimes including child labor) and cheap shipping rates. In contrast to obtaining stone from such distant sources, in recent years Foster + Partners has favoured the use of long, thin, flexibly laid paving of dark Kilkenny blue limestone for its London projects, and its influence has spread the use of this material.

Top left
Characteristic undifferentiated 1950s precast concrete paving and vertical bar rails at the Shell Centre, London. The red band of textured tactile paving at the foot of the steps is a 1990s addition.

Bottom left
A 1936 rose garden at Peckham Rye Park, London, with typical 1930s construction: mortar-jointed crazy paving made of broken sandstone paving slabs, and piers similarly constructed from broken paving slabs.

Bottom right
Metal stretchers from the Second World War were reused as fences on some London social housing developments.

A note on standards

This is not a book about construction specification—it is an introductory text—and though we quote from some standards and refer to building codes we trust that it is understandable without a detailed knowledge of the subject. It is meant to be an introductory text. However, given that we refer to ANSI, ASTM, and so forth, we should explain what they mean so that readers can develop a knowledge of building specification.

Typically, construction work is designed using graphics (drawings), text (specifications), and figures (measured quantities in a bill of quantities). Referring to specifications assists the succinct description of a piece of construction and permits a commonly understood, detailed standard of work to be quantified by the building contractor.

The American National Standards Institute (ANSI) promotes and facilitates voluntary consensus standards and conformity assessment systems. ANSI is also actively engaged in accrediting programs that assess conformance to standards—including globally-recognized cross-sector programs such as the ISO (International Organization for Standardization) 9000 (quality) and ISO 14000 (environmental) management systems.

Somewhat confusingly, there is also ASTM International, formerly known as the American Society for Testing and Materials (ASTM), a globally recognized body that develops international voluntary consensus standards. Today, some 12,000 ASTM standards are used around the world and are developed following the principles of the World Trade Organization. In addition to standards development, ASTM International also offers training, testing, and certification programs.

The American Concrete Institute (ACI) publishes information on concrete and its applications and provides a standard cerfification program for the industry.

The American Association of State Highway and Transportation Officials (AASHTO) sets standards for specifications, test protocols, and guidelines for highway design and construction throughout the United States. The AASHTO Materials Reference Laboratory (AMRL) accredits laboratories, and AMRL accreditation is often required to submit test results to State DOTs.

Mention should also be made of the US Army Corps of Engineers' specifications, which are particularly useful for earthworks.

The text also refers to the various sustainable lumber certification systems; these may be summarized as follows:

ATFS   American Tree Farm System
FSC   Forestry Stewardship Council
PEFC   Pan European Forest Certification System
SFI   Sustainable Forestry Initiative

Left
An example of a well-crafted design: crazy paving at Les Bois des Moutiers, Varengeville-sur-Mer, France, designed by Edwin Lutyens in 1898.

About this book

This book surveys the basic principles of landscape construction and is an introductory text for those involved in the design, specification, and construction of landscape. It aims to be of interest to architects, engineers, urban designers, planners, landscape architects, garden designers, and contractors, and it is written from the point of view of two landscape architects who have been practicing since the 1970s. It began as a set of construction courses taught by Jamie Liversedge at Hadlow College, Kent, and the University of Greenwich, London, to undergraduate and graduate landscape architecture and garden design students since 1995.

Fundamental to good hard-landscape design is a knowledge of the chemical and physical characteristics of materials and the forces that work on them. For example, lumber posts for a pergola are commonly laid in concrete foundations where the groundwater will rot them: better by far to separate the post from the ground by using a steel pin or plate to connect post and foundation, or to set the post on a plinth or low wall.

The authors have worked in southeast Asia, the Middle East, and Europe as well as Britain. While the book is written from a British standpoint the authors realize that there are often ways of constructing landscapes other than those commonly practiced in Britain. Fashion and national practice play a part in much construction work and it is necessasry to see beyond the conventional in order to understand why. The book, perhaps unfashionably, argues for appreciating the aesthetic value of concrete and deals with the use of "newer"materials such as plastics while there is also appreciation of older materials such as wood, cast iron, stone, and brick. The basic premise is that good construction is good design. Well-designed landscape construction depends on a thorough understanding of materials (including their formation or manufacture, chemistry, and physical characteristics) and practical construction. Good design is not necessarily easy or cheap. Often, what is most elegant or longest lasting, the most sustainable, and the best value for money, is not the easiest to build.

The book begins with a survey of overall themes and what influences choice of construction material and method, including vernacular construction techniques, industrialization and globalization, and issues of sustainability and climate change. "General Principles" outlines the properties of materials, and of structures and mechanics. "Building Materials" introduces the materials used in building: stone, concrete, brick, metals, lumber, glass, plastics, and some non-conventional materials old and new. "Elements" looks at built elements ranging from earthworks and topsoil (a vital resource), retaining structures, walls, paving, and water bodies. "Assembly" describes the assembly of built components, and the final fifth chapter, "Protection and Finishes" is a survey of ways of finishing and protecting materials. At the end of the book there are appendices with tables of further information.

Above
An understanding of earthworks and retaining structures is necessary for good landscape design: Adobe wall, Harlemmermeer Floriade, the Netherlands, 2002.

Above right
Use of locally sourced materials is an aspect of good landscape design and slate is used extensively in areas close to quarries. Slate fence in Aberllefenni, Wales.

GENERAL PRINCIPLES

Properties of materials

"I shall now proceed to treat, in an intelligible manner, of the materials which are appropriate for building, how they are formed by nature, and of the analysis of their component parts. For there is no material nor body of any sort whatever which is not composed of various elementary particles; and if their primary composition be not duly understood, no law of physics will explain their nature to our satisfaction."

Marcus Vitruvius Pollio, *De Architectura*, Book II, Chapter 1

It is necessary to understand something of the physics, structural performance and indeed the chemistry of materials in order to understand how they work. This is not a scientific text book so we touch lightly on these subjects, but they are fundamental. The main properties of materials may be listed as follows:
- density;
- specific gravity;
- size;
- strength;
- optical characteristics;
- electrical conductivity;
- color and texture;
- thermal properties;
- acoustic properties;
- deformation; and
- deterioration, weathering, and life span.

A Sandstone clad wall, Belfast Shopping Centre, Northern Ireland.

B Precast concrete planters with inset ceramic tiles, La Défense, Paris.

C Finely crafted brickwork at Folly Farm, Berkshire, England, an Arts and Crafts style country house designed by Edwin Lutyens in 1906.

D Corten steel signage by Michael van Gessel, Grebbeberg, The Netherlands.

E Sustainably sourced teak decking at the Intercontinental Hotel, Aphrodite Hills Resort, near Paphos, Cyprus.

F

TIP BUILDING WITH ICE

It is worth noting that ice can be a construction material—and not just for igloos. Permafrost engineering is the study of semi-permanent ice roads and bridges in permafrost areas where the soil is permanently frozen.

F The National Police Memorial, St James's Park, London. This 24 foot 3 inch high glass wall consists of 633 sheets of annealed glass stacked flat.

G *WD Spiral Part 1*, a sculpture in polyester sheet by Hermann Maier Neustadt at the Kröller-Müller Museum Sculpture Park, Hoge Veluwe National Park, the Netherlands.

H A rammed earth (pisé) building in Corsica.

Density is the mass of a given unit of volume, and in building-construction materials (and in ISO convention) it is usually measured in lbs/ft³ (*see table of densities of construction materials, Table 3, Appendix, page 227*).

Note that the density of lumber will vary with moisture content, and all materials should be compared with water—which has a density of 62.4 lbs/ft³ at 39.2°F. Materials less dense than water will float; denser materials will sink. Bear in mind that density varies with temperature and pressure—hence, ice is less dense than, and so floats in, water. Most adult human beings just about float in water, but this varies dependent on how much air we hold in our lungs; expel it all and we sink.

Materials vary in density with temperature; for instance, water is densest at 39.2°F. Unlike many substances, it expands on freezing—by about 9 per cent. This is because it crystallizes on freezing into an open hexagonal form, which is less dense than liquid water.

G

H

Specific gravity

This is the ratio of the density of a material at a given temperature and pressure to the density of distilled water at 39.2°F—and so the specific gravity of water is expressed as "1." Note that specific gravity is a dimensionless unit; by comparison with water, iron has a specific gravity of 7.85. It is dense!

Size

This is a measure of physical magnitude and may be measured as follows:
- length in in (inches) or ft (feet);
- area in in^2 (square inches) or ft^2 (square feet);
- volume in in^3 (cubic inches) or ft^3 (cubic feet).

Strength

The strength of a material is based on the ability to carry its own weight and any applied loads without undue distortion. There are three particular forms of strength that we are concerned about in construction materials:
- **tension** strength on being stretched;
- **compression** strength on being squeezed; and
- **torsion** strength on being twisted.

However, the strength of a material also has various properties itself, namely:
- elasticity;
- stiffness or rigidity;
- plasticity; and
- ductile properties.

Elasticity is the property of reverting to original shape; a stiff or rigid structure will maintain and support a load without significantly changing shape. Plasticity is the ability to be molded (usually when heated) and ductility is the ability to be able to be drawn out or extruded (again, usually on heating).

Below left
A metal railing twisted by ivy, Hampton Court, England.

Below centre
Tree roots disrupting asphalt paving and curb.

Below right
Bowed iron bridge, Vaux-le-Vicomte, France. The iron structure has been overloaded and lacks elasticity, resulting in deformation.

Optical characteristics

These include transparency, translucency, and opaqueness, which are significant in glass and transparent or translucent plastics (and could be significant in paper if used as a building material—as it is in Japan).

Electrical conductivity

This is important in insulators; for example, slate slab is used for electrical switchboard mountings because of its electrical resistance. But it is also especially significant in metals because different metals have different electrical conductivity properties and rusting may result if they touch; therefore they should be separated by an inert buffer. Thus, a fundamental facet of designing with metals is: avoid non-compatible metals touching.

Color and texture

These are visual properties, with color encompassing three distinct concepts:
• hue;
• chromacity; and
• value.

Hue is the characteristic which distinguishes red from yellow from blue. Chromacity is the purity of the hue —the extent to which it contains white or gray. Value describes how light or dark a color is. In addition, saturation refers to a color's brightness or dullness. We are also concerned about how fixed and unchanging colors are: "fugitive" colors such as reds and blues soon fade when exposed to natural light—especially sunlight.

   Texture can vary from rough brick or stone to smooth metals, glass, or plastic.

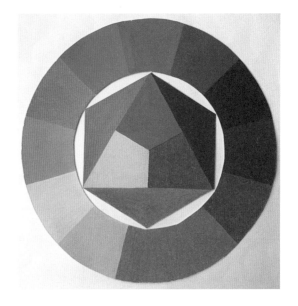

Above
The term hue describes the red, yellow, and blue color quality and the intermediate colors formed from them, as illustrated by this color circle.

Right
Red paint fading to pink, Borneo Bridge, Amsterdam, the Netherlands.

Thermal properties

Materials that conduct heat readily, such as metals or stone, feel colder in cold weather and warmer in the sunlight than do less-conducting materials such as timber. Therefore, one should design surfaces intended to be touched by people or plants—such as rails, seats, or pergolas—accordingly.

Acoustic properties

Hard materials with a short reverberation time sound hard—while softer, more absorbent materials, such as wood, give a "warmer" sound. This is most noticeable in enclosed spaces such as streets, squares, and town gardens. Loose fastenings tend to rattle, and noise is one of the challenges of designing in towns. However, gardens and squares can provide a refuge from the sound of city streets (but not so much from aircraft noise).

Deformation

This is caused by applied loads, changes in moisture content, or changes in temperature—any of which may cause expansion and contraction. Such change, therefore, should be designed for—for example, tubular steel handrails should have sleeve joints (aka "sprig joints") so they can expand and contract; while stone, brick, and concrete should be designed to avoid freeze–thaw and shrinkable clay damage, and to cope with variations in weather or climate (for example, snow can add a variable or "live load" to a structure).

A A clay plant pot cracked due to root growth stress.

B Icelandic style drystone wall with sod serving as a coping, at Barnes Wetland, London.

C The color in concrete blocks quickly fades as a result of exposure to ultraviolet light—as has happened with this gray example —unless the aggregate is strongly colored. Clay brick pavers hold their color.

D World War II concrete bunker on the Atlantic Wall near Sangatte, France. Built from reinforced concrete to withstand attack, the bunker has since moved because it was built on sand.

E A marble bust of Sir Thomas Hanbury at the Hanbury Botanic Gardens, La Mortola, Ventimiglia, Italy. The affect of wind exposure and the prevailing southwesterly winds have cleaned the right side of the bust.

F Teak fading to silver, Parc des Cormailles, Ivry-sur-Seine, France.

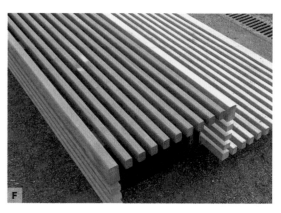

G Rusting at Duisburg Nord Landschaftspark, Germany.

H Rusting sheet piling, Aberdyfi harbour, Gwynedd, Wales. Salt water is especially corrosive.

I Corten steel pool edge at the Barcelona Botanic Garden, Spain. Corten delaminates on contact with water.

J Thirty years of city rain separate the wall on the right from the rebuilt, bright orange wall on the left, the soft facing brick has absorbed damp and air-borne dirt and dust.

K Due to inadequate depth of concrete coverage (the original thin layer of concrete has spalled off), the reinforcement is rusting in this concrete bunker at Duisburg Nord Landschaftspark.

L Black soot mold on Western Red Cedar, Parc de Bercy, Paris.

M A wrought-iron strapped limestone bollard has been placed to protect this balustrade from damage by carts bumping into it at Vaux-le-Vicomte, France.

N The corner on the left side of the wall has been knocked and the soft bricks damaged, while on the right the corner is protected by a bollard.

O This limestone bollard has been eroded by more than 300 years of acidic dogs' urine.

Below
These diagrams illustrate the effect of forces upon and internal stresses in a structure of Newton's Third Law of Motion. Mass is the structural object. Whether a beam or column or wall, the integrity of a structural object depends on the strength of its mass. Tensile forces lead to stresses consequent on the outward pull of the forces,

which tend to elongate and lengthen the mass. Compressive forces tend to crush a mass. Shear stress is a response to a shear force acting parallel to the surface of the mass and so the response is a sliding apart of the object. Finally, bending stress leads to a curving or bending of the structural mass, whether a column or a beam.

Principles of assembly

Fundamental to structural design is the study of mechanics: the action of a force on a mass. The study of statics is that branch of mechanics which studies the forces that hold a mass in a state of equilibrium. A force is an "agency," which tends to change the condition of rest of a rigid body; such agencies can be considered as push or pull forces, which do not produce motion. In short, statics is the structural design of motionless objects.

Newton's Third Law of Motion (described in his *Principia Mathematica Philosophiae Naturalis* of 1687) is the law of action and reaction:
Whenever a particle A exerts a force on another particle B, B simultaneously exerts a force on A with the same magnitude in the opposite direction.

This is paraphrased as:
For every action, there is an equal and opposite reaction.

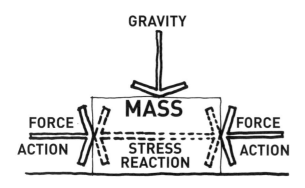

Force, mass, reaction, and gravity

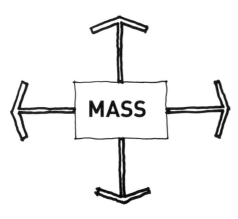

Tensile forces

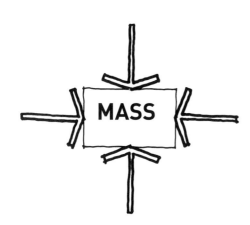

Compressive forces

Shear stress

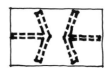

Tensile stress

Compressive stress

Bending stress

Loads and reactions

Consider the example of a book on a table:

Live load is the load of the book on the table, and may be removed or replaced. In landscape construction, illustrations of such live loads on a structure include wind, water, and earth pressure, snow, and people or vehicles on a sidewalk or road;

Dead load is an immovable load, such as paint or varnish on a table. Being permanent, these are not removable—hence the term "dead." Examples of dead loads include finishes and fittings, or fixed planters on a deck or patio;

Superimposed load is the live load and the dead load together: book and table (or car and road, for instance);

Self-weight is the weight of the structure itself, i.e. the weight of the table or the structure—e.g. a wall or roadway;

Aggressive forces are the live load, dead load, and self-weight all together, i.e. the book, varnish, and table together;

Reactions are the opposing forces of a structure and its foundations. These are caused by the aggressive forces and adjust themselves constantly to the tendency to motion of those aggressive forces;

Free body is an abstraction of the structure—e.g. the table with all loads, self-weight, and reactions is called a "free body," and this concept allows the subdivision of large composite structures into smaller free bodies, which permit structural calculation; and

Properties of force Forces have magnitude (measured in lbs) and direction towards or away from a fixed reference point following a line of action. Force is measured by weight/area e.g. pounds per square inch (lbs/in²). Thus:

$$f = P/A$$

where: f = unit of force
P = magnitude of forces in units of weight
A = area over which force is distributed.

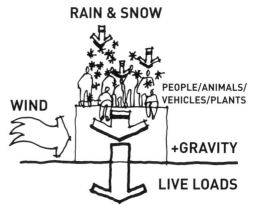

Superimposed load = dead load + live load

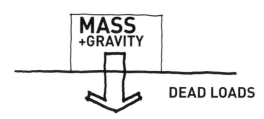

Mass + gravity = dead loads

Below
A worked example of elementary structural analysis

1700 lb table with four posts / hardwood deck with four 6 x 6 in timber posts

Each table leg or post carries one quarter of the weight of the structure. If the deck weighs 1700 lb and the area of each post is 6 x 6 in = 36 in², then the unit force exerted by the table on the floor (or the deck on the ground) at each leg or post is:

f = P/A   P = (1700 ÷ 4 posts) = 425 lbs
A = 6 x 6 in = 36 in²

therefore: f = 11.8 lbs/in²

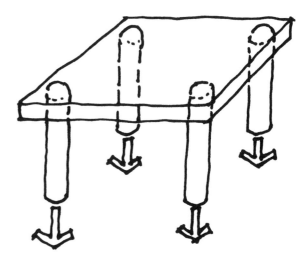

Properties of force

BEAMS

Beams—horizontal structural members also known as joists, girders, stringers, and plates

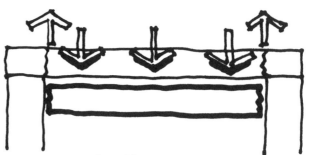

Beam failure—vertical shear

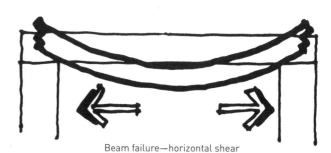

Beam failure—horizontal shear

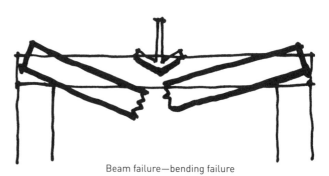

Beam failure—bending failure

Left
A simple beam and column structure: a pergola at Villa Hanbury, La Mortola, Italy.

Above
These diagrams show the basic categories of beam and also how beams and columns fail. Such simple construction is obvious when applied to a beam and column structure such as Stonehenge or a lumber pergola, but the principles can also be applied more generally in landscape structure. Good construction designers develop a feel for how structures perform, so they are well equipped to discuss alternatives with a structural or civil engineer.

Beam classification

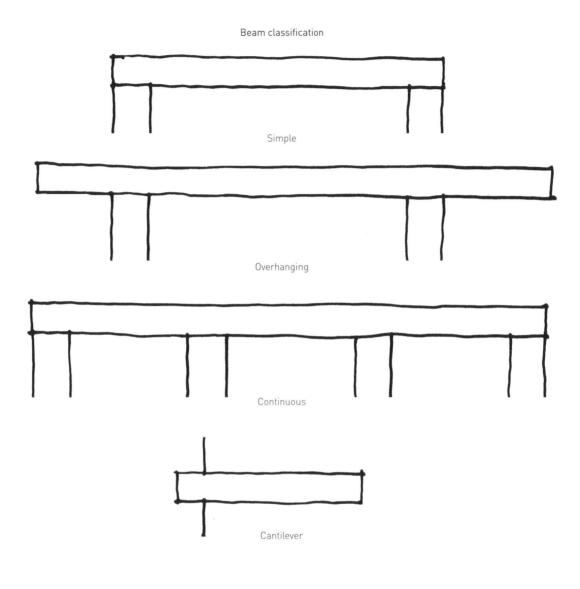

Simple

Overhanging

Continuous

Cantilever

Column failure

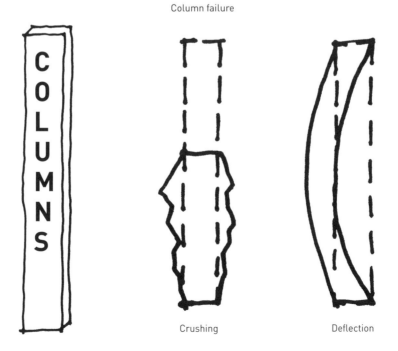

COLUMNS

Crushing

Deflection

BUILDING MATERIALS

"Since, therefore, all bodies consist of and spring from these elements, and in the great variety of bodies the quantity of each element entering into their composition is different, I think it right to investigate the nature of their variety, and explain how it affects the quality of each in the materials used for building, so that those about to build may avoid mistakes, and be, moreover, enabled to make a proper choice of such materials as they may want."

Marcus Vitruvius Pollio, *De Architectura*, Book II, Chapter 1

This chapter deals with building materials, their physical and chemical characteristics and the history of their use—and describes instances of ways of using them.

Stone

"The ideal building stone is one which embodies good weathering properties and agreeable colour and texture, with a consistency fine enough to admit of smooth surfaces and crisply carved details. Such a combination of qualities is not common…"

Alec Clifton-Taylor, *The Pattern of English Building*[1]

Traditionally, stone is the usual building material for paving and walls in upland areas where the material is easily accessible. Often, the process of constructing a house or farm building began with digging a quarry nearby. The stone was of the locality, providing it could be used for forming blocks or slabs.

However, when transport costs are small stone can become easily available in areas where it does not occur naturally. For example, as previously mentioned (in the Introduction), granite from the Baltic island of Bornholm

Right
Traditional pitching pavement in Llanidloes, Wales. Pitching is a kind of cobbling that uses long river-slate stones laid flexibly.

Far right
Cornish granite paving in Penzance, England. The old paving is on the right, the new on the left.

Far left
Kilkenny blue limestone paving and rill, laid flexibly on granite dust.

Left
The sandstone slabs in this sidewalk vary in length and width, which minimizes stone wastage. Note how the continuous joint is across the direction of travel.

Below left
Pentelikon quarry in Attica, north of Athens, was the source of the marble used to build the Parthenon.

is the classic paving material for all peninsular Denmark, where there is no granite; this is because Bornholm granite is easily transported by ship. The largest building-stone (as opposed to crushed-roadstone) exporting countries are China, Italy, India, Iran, and Spain.[2]

Choice of building stone depends on a variety of factors, including price and availability. There is no point in specifying something to be used next week if it has to be shipped from China; note, however, that Chinese supplies might be one-quarter the price of those from a comparable US supplier. Stone is also a finite material, and it is wise to be careful in its use. For instance, specify paving stones with a variable length; this wastes less stone and is therefore cheaper than using stones of the same length, and produces a visually more pleasing effect.

Local quarries close down. For example, the Pentelikon quarries north of Athens, the source of the marble for the Parthenon, closed for many hundreds of years until they were reopened in the 1860s to provide stone for the new royal palace in Athens.

It is best to examine samples of a favored stone which have been subject to weathering for some years —better still, visit the quarry to see how it is quarried and worked, and to understand which stone to specify and from which bed or strata. When specifying stone it is necessary to understand the difference between a freestone—which is even textured and not strongly stratified, and can be squared up or worked in all directions—and a layered stone like slate, which can only be worked along its layers.

Stone is categorized by how it is formed, as follows:
• *igneous* – e.g. granite;
• *sedimentary* – e.g. sandstone and limestone;
• *metamorphic* – e.g. slate, marble, and quartzite.

A Igneous stone: granite paving and wall, Amarante, Douro Valley, Portugal.

B Sedimentary stone: Indian Khatu rainbow sandstone at the Intercontinental Hotel, Aphrodite Hills Resort, Cyprus.

C Metamorphic stone at the Guildhall, London: the dark bands of slabs and setts are of Diamant granulite, a rock metamorphosed from sandstone from Namaqualand, South Africa.

D Contrasting paving of local metamorphic slate and white marble, Porto Vecchio, Corsica.

Igneous rocks

"Igneous" comes from the Latin *ignis*, meaning "fire." Igneous rocks are formed by cooling magma, which is the molten rock in the Earth's crust and consists of liquids, crystals, and gases. They therefore cannot include shells or fossils, which are classic markers of many sedimentary rocks.

Igneous rocks themselves may be subdivided, depending on how rapidly they cool when solidifying. The slowest-cooling rock forms the larger crystals, while quickly cooling rock forms small crystals, thus:
- *volcanic or extrusive* rock, i.e. very fine grained (with small crystals) and the result of quick-cooling eruptions —for example lava;
- *hypabyssal*, fine-grained igneous rock, which solidifies before reaching the earth's surface in a minor intrusion —for example dolerite and quartz porphyry;
- *plutonic*, also known as "intrusive," is a coarse-grained rock formed deep under the earth's surface, which cools slowly—for example granite.

The main constituents of igneous rocks are:
- *red or white feldspars*, which are aluminosilicates containing varying amounts of calcium, potassium, or sodium;
- *quartz*, which is a crystalline form of silica;
- *mica*, which embraces iron, magnesium, and aluminum silicates which crystallize in thin, easily separated layers;
- *augite*, which is calcium magnesium iron silicate;
- *iron pyrites*, which is crystalline iron sulphide; and
- *olivine*, an olive-green, silicate mineral, rich in magnesium and iron.

The building trade, however, uses terminology more loosely than do geologists, and often many igneous rocks are broadly termed "granites."

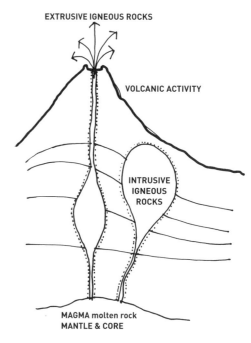

Volcanic activity and magma cooling

Above
Black diorite, a fine-grained igneous stone, used for the main steps of St Paul's Cathedral, London.

Above
The polished Shap granite bollards at St Paul's Cathedral are made of porphyritic granite (a plutonic rock) with large pink feldspar crystals.

M
A
G
M
A
Volcanic, e.g. basalt or pumice
Very fine-grained small crystals, often not visible to the human eye: glassy, difficult to work and can be unattractive—e.g. gray pumice stone. Used for concrete aggregate

Hypabyssal, e.g. porphyry
Medium-sized crystals, which can be polished. Used for setts and roadstone

Plutonic, e.g granite
Cools slowly at depth and forms large, crystalline rock structure

Fast　　　　　　　　　　　　　　　　　**Slow**

Structure of igneous stone is dependent on the rate of cooling

Sedimentary rocks

These may be either particles of older rocks broken down by natural forces such as frost action, or wind or wave erosion—or depositions of organic origin such as vegetable matter and bacteria, shells and coral formation, or precipitation of organically formed calcareous matter. They are rocks that have been laid down or deposited and the word "sedimentary" comes from the Latin *sedimentum* meaning "to settle" or "sink down." Typically, they may be thought of as solidified sandy beaches and sand dunes or coral reefs. Sedimentary rocks account for the majority of building stone because they are very common, forming up to 75 per cent of the earth's surface, and are characterized by:

- the natural grain showing as a consequence of the form of deposition, so that the beds of sand may have a ripple pattern like a beach;
- having been laid down in horizontal layers as bedding planes, though geological movement may have subsequently tilted them.

The two main sedimentary stones used in construction are limestone and sandstone.

Left
Bedding patterns formed by wind-blown sand in red sandstone.

Below
Horizontal stripes of bedding planes in chalk, a sedimentary rock, at Dover cliffs, England.

Sandstone consists of particles of feldspar, quartz, and mica, bound together by a natural cement or "matrix." This matrix cement determines the strength, durability, and color of the stone. Sandstone is classed according to the nature of the matrix as follows:

- *siliceous sandstone* is the strongest, bound with silica cement. It is extremely acid-resistant and also difficult to work;
- *calcareous sandstone* is cemented with calcite crystals of calcium carbonate ($CaCO_3$). It is easy to work, but less durable than siliceous sandstone.

TIP SANDSTONES

Fine sandstone wears very comfortably, does not polish and is resistant to slip. Gritstones, by contrast, are a much coarser sandstone, which makes them easy to climb and suitable for use as millstones.

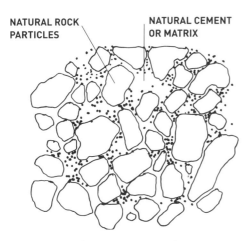

NATURAL ROCK PARTICLES

NATURAL CEMENT OR MATRIX

Sandstone cross-section

Left
Mansfield Red sandstone slabs with white squares of Portland stone, at Trafalgar Square, London.

Right
Sandstone paving with brown ferrous (iron) pattern markings.

Below right
Kentish ragstone, a form of limestone, with a brick top wall, Paddock Wood, England.

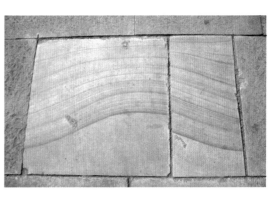

Limestone consists mainly of calcite or calcium carbonate ($CaCO_3$) and is formed in seas or lakes. Limestone rocks are made up of the skeletons or shells of sea creatures, or by the chemically induced precipitation of calcium carbonate. There are three main types:

- oolitic, with a cod roe-like texture formed of concentric rings of calcite – e.g. Indiana limestone, Nittany dolomite;
- organically formed accumulations of shells and animals or bacteria – e.g. chalk;
- crystalline formed from a solution when the water evaporates – e.g. travertine.

Note that travertine is not a marble, which is a metamorphic stone (see opposite).

Limestone varies in hardness, but generally it is softer and easier to work than sandstone. Because it tends to be soluble in slightly acid rainwater, it tends to be self-cleaning. Chalk is a poorly or loosely compacted form of limestone, and is not good as a building stone; it is good as a raw material for cement and concrete manufacture. Flints are nodules of silica found in chalk deposits, and can be used as building stones.

Table of the rock strata forming Portland stone quarry beds (beneath the soil and clay overburden)

Thickness	Types	Uses
5–6½ ft	Cap	used in white concrete
3 ft	Roach	oolitic limestone; full of shells, high resistance to weathering, used as ashlar or for rustication
3–5 ft	Whitbed	very strong, close-grained, contains shells in layers, less hard than Roach
3 ft	Curf	shelly limestone and sandy beds of chert (a flint-like material), not suitable for building
up to 5 ft	Base bed	fine-grained, contains shells in layers—less hard than Roach
up to 100 ft	Cherty Series	interspersed limestone and beds of chert; used, crushed, as roadstone

Right
Smooth white Whitbed Portland stone (left) contrasted with the rougher cavity-rich Roach bed (right).

Below right
Unfilled oolitic limestone, the Economist Building, London (1959–64). This is an early use of Roach bed Portland.

Far right
Grotto walls and ceiling at Painshill Park, Surrey, England, made of tufa embedded with chips of calcite, fulorite, and gypsum; tufa limestone is formed around hot calcareous springs.

Above left
Slate roof in Corsica.

Above
Marble mosaic paving in Porto, Portugal.

Metamorphic stone

The word "metamorphic" comes from the Greek *meta* meaning "to change" and *morphe* meaning "form." Geologically, it denotes a rock (whether sedimentary, igneous or pre-existing metamorphic rock) which has been changed in form, and therefore in structure, by heat, pressure, or a combination of the two. The heat and pressure are not sufficient to liquefy the material (so forming an igneous rock), but are sufficient to change it chemically. During this change, bedding planes and fossils are lost. Examples of metamorphic processes are:

• clay changing to slate;
• limestone changing to marble; and
• sandstone changing to quartzite.

Metamorphic rocks include:

Slate A very durable rock which is impervious, acid—and alkali – resistant, and also resistant to electricity. It is a good insulator. It is marked by cleavage planes, which may be thin or thick (suitable for slab slate).

Marble A finely crystalline rock, white and colored by veins of minerals. It is hard, dense and resistant to abrasion, but is vulnerable to acid rain.

Quartzite A sandstone transformed by heat so that re-crystallization occurs. It is 96 per cent silica, harder than granite, and available in a range of colors.

TIP METAMORPHIC ROCKS

Different temperatures change a rock in different ways. For example, when clay is heated and pressed it becomes slate, which is dense, smooth, and does not reveal visible minerals. If heated more intensely it becomes schist, which has visible layers of minerals. Heated even more it becomes gneiss, with light and dark layers of minerals.

STONE FINISHES AND FORMS

Stone is available in blacks, whites, grays, reds, pinks, oranges, greens, and blues. How the stone is finished is key to its appearance, while there is a major difference between wet and dry stone. A polished stone will generally reveal the strongest color and pattern

Steps with rock-faced risers and sawn treads.

Tooled finish

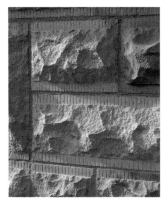

Rock-faced with drafted margins

Vermiculated (worm-like) finish

Table of stone finishes

Rough	rock-faced/pitch-faced	natural, rough, quarried rock-face finish
	rough-punched	roughly hewn with high points chiseled off
	fair-picked	smoother chiseled surface
	fine-picked/bush-hammered	a finely textured surface
	axed	worked with masonry tools to give a smooth, broad, chisel-marked finish
	flame-textured	surface is heated to give an undulating finish which is non-slip
	split/cleft	split applies mainly to slate, which has natural cleavage lines
	tooled	various finishes, patterned using masonry tools
	batted	a fine, straight, strong chisel pattern vertically across the stone
	sparrow-pecked	an even finish using a fine chisel
	saw-pulled	similar to a batted finish but using a saw, and so more regular, and machine-finished
	sawn	similar to a batted finish but using a saw, and so more regular, and machine-finished
	sandblasted	a dull non-glossy finish, made by blasting air and sand across the surface
	shot-sawn	a rough, gangsaw finish, made by sawing with chilled steel shots
	fine-rubbed	mechanically rubbed for smoother finish
	gritted	a smooth finish, which lacks the gloss of honed or polished surfaces
	eggshell/honed	a factory finish using abrasives; produces a smooth, matte finish
Smooth	polished	similar to honing—but using finer abrasives to produce a high gloss, which reveals natural pattern and color; suitable for stones with a high mineral content and tight structure.

Shot-blasted stone finish

Flame-textured finish

Tooled, blasted finish

Contrast of rock-faced (right) and sawn stone (left)

Split slate paving, Musée du Quai Branly, Paris

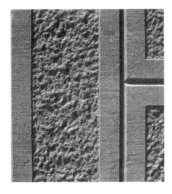

Rough-punched with draft margins

Honed sandstone

Saw-pulling; a fine saw-cut line was drawn across the stone, creating a non-slip surface on slate paving

Rough-punched stone finish, roughly hewn with the high points chiseled off, and edged with batted stone (top)

Manually split Chert paving, Cyprus

Contrast between polished (left) and flame-textured (right) red granite cladding

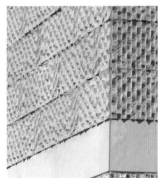

Saw lines cut vertically into the stone face have been mechanically chiseled off to create a regular dash pattern

Sparrow-pecked nameplate (top left) and rough-punched rusticated stone wall, Royal Geological Society, London

Flame-textured granite paving in Paris, laid rigidly and butt jointed. Traffic has caused chipping

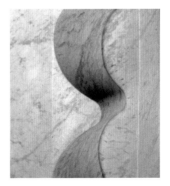

Honed stone-finished marble

Sawn stone finish

Concrete

"Concrete is an artificial conglomerate or pudding stone, in which the pebbles which make up the greater part of the bulk are cemented together by lime mortar"

E. Dobson, *A Rudimentary Treatise on Foundations and Concrete Works*

Concrete is a manufactured stone and is made with water, aggregate, and cement in different proportions and often with chemical admixtures. Concrete is usually a mixture of 10–15 per cent cement; 15–20 per cent water; about 60–75 per cent aggregates, such as gravel, sand and limestone filler; about 5 per cent entrained air (trapped air bubbles); and less than 0.1 per cent chemical admixtures. Aggregates are often quarried stone or gravel—but may be natural (like stone and gravel), recycled (like crushed brick or concrete), or manufactured material (like furnace clinker). Cement binds together the aggregate.

It is often said concrete has a relatively short history as a building material; however, forms of cement and concrete were used by ancient Egyptian and early Chinese builders, and certainly the Romans used concrete construction in the dome of the Pantheon.[3] Concrete is described by Vitruvius in his *De Architectura* and in standard architectural manuals of the Renaissance by Alberti and Palladio. Later, it fell out of favor in Europe largely owing to the problem of obtaining good cement. Curiously, it was experience with pisé (rammed earth) construction in France (see "Compressed earth, cob and pisé," page 95) which led to its being used again at the end of the eighteenth century.[4]

Above
An early form of concrete: Roman lime mortar and rubble fill from the late fourth century AD, Pevensey Castle, England.

Right
Early concrete gate pier of 1873, London, built by Charles Drake's London Patent Concrete Company.

Far right
Concrete is a freeform sculptural material, as used in this 1930s acoustic mirror, Dungeness, England.

Today, concrete is globally one of the most widely used materials in terms of tonnage[5] and cement production contributes some 5 per cent of global greenhouse gases.[6]

Concrete is strong in compression, but not in tension; however, it may be reinforced with steel to increase its tensile strength. Steel is some ten times stronger than concrete in compression, but at least 100 times stronger in tension. Unreinforced concrete is also termed "mass concrete." Concrete is long lasting: the Pantheon in Rome was rebuilt for Hadrian in the early second century AD using concrete in the dome. It is stable; more widely available than, say, stone; and adaptable—that is to say, its form is determined by the mould—and it can be low cost. It may also be produced from materials local to the site and from recycled materials.

Concrete is alkaline, which can be an advantage—for instance, it helps protect steel reinforcement from rusting. However, it does mean that, when liquid, concrete can burn the skin. It should be handled with care.

As concrete moves from a liquid to a solid state, the strength of the material develops over time; this process is called "hydration." Generally, the finer the cement particles the more rapid the setting and hardening, and hence the development of strength. Initially, the liquid cement stiffens then hardens to develop an initial structural strength (generally determined as being reached after 28 days). The rate of this initial stiffening is controlled by the addition of gypsum. Gypsum is a natural cooling mineral, a calcium sulphate dihydrate; it is familiar to many as plaster of Paris, used for casts.

Concrete construction is determined by:
- the quality of cement, aggregate, and water;
- the ratio of coarse to fine aggregate; and
- the type and amount of admixture; but also
  by how it is made, in terms of:
- placing;
- consolidating;
- finishing; and
- curing.

The advantages and disadvantages of concrete may be summarized as in the table below:

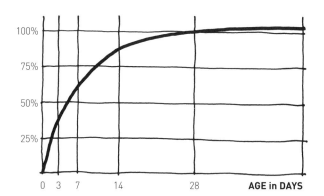

28-day strength development of concrete
Source: http://www.superformicf.ca/concretestrength.htm

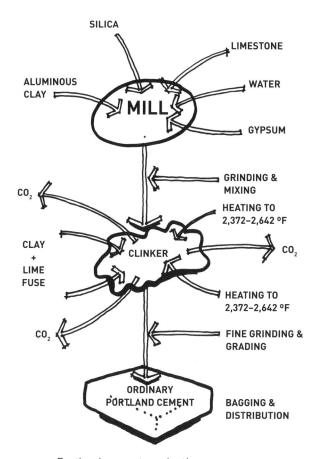

Portland cement production sequence

Advantages	Disadvantages
adaptable to any shape or form	requires formwork
high compressive strength	low tensile strength
durable, resilient surface	takes time to develop strength
wide choice of finishes and textures	reputation for being gray and of a "boring" appearance
low maintenance costs	reinforcement can rust
resistant to freeze–thaw process	requires movement and construction joints
relatively low embodied-energy costs	carbon dioxide produced during manufacture

Table of AASHTO designations for stone particle sizes

AASHTO designation	Maximum particle size (inches)	Nominal size
1	4	2½
3	2½	1½
467	2	1
5	1½	¾
57	1½	¾
67	1	½
7	¾	⅜
8	½	¼
10	⅜	⅛

Cement The binder that holds the other materials together, cement is made by grinding calcinated limestone and clay to a fine powder, and then adding water. Calcination is the heating of crushed limestone without air in order to change it chemically, and takes place in limekilns. By this process, calcium carbonate (the limestone) is heated to form calcium oxide (quicklime, caustic lime or burnt lime) and, as a consequence, carbon dioxide is released (the chemical equation for this process is $CaCO_3 = CaO + CO_2$). Calcination can also occur naturally under layers of hot ash.

Portland cement is now a generic name, and is the common form of cement used worldwide. It was first developed by Joseph Aspdin, a British bricklayer, in 1824 and so named because of its similarity in appearance to Portland limestone. In 1858 Aspdin's son, William, moved to Germany and popularized the name generally. The first German standard was issued in 1878. Now the material is covered by the American standard, ASTM C150.

Water is added to the cement powder, in a ratio of 0.45–0.60 water: 1.0 cement powder, i.e. the weight of water is 45–60 per cent of the weight of the cement powder, so 40–60 lbs of water is added to 100 lbs of dry cement. With the addition of water, the calcium oxide (CaO) in the cement hydrates to form calcium hydroxide: $Ca(OH)_2$.

White Portland cement is characterized by its color and is used either in combination with white aggregate to produce a brilliant white concrete, or with the addition of pigments to make brighter-colored concretes.

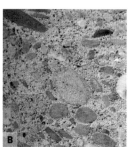

A Brilliant white Portland cement concrete construction, Jumeirah Beach Hotel, Dubai.

B Cross-section of concrete aggregate.

C Poorly graded concrete voids —the lines of different concrete pours are clearly visible—in the bunker section at Duisburg Nord Landchaftspark, Germany.

D A masterly use of precast concrete in various colors and textures by John Outram at a private house in Sussex, England. 'Blitzcrete' with red brick aggregate was used on the corner columns with black precast concrete colored with carbon. For the green lintels copper filings were added to the concrete.

Aggregates These may be natural rock, sands, or gravels, or recycled construction materials such as crushed stone, brick, or concrete. The choice of aggregate depends on its weight, size, and shape as well as the physical properties of the material. Angular aggregates bind better, but require more water. The most economical mix is one in which fine and coarse aggregates are evenly graded, so that the minimum amount of cement is required.

Sand The third element in a concrete mix is sand; the type depends on location and local availability; method of extraction; and grading.

Sharp sand has angular grains, and is used in concrete; soft sand is called "building sand," and has smaller, rounded grains. Both should be free of salts. Sand is determined by size.

Aggregates and sand The aim usually is to a have a wide range of grades of stone and sand in order to ensure a strong, consistent structure. However, "no-fines" concrete is made with a crushed rock or gravel of ¾ in single-size aggregate (⅜–¾ in), coated in cement slurry with no fine aggregate addition. Its strength is between 725 and 2175 lbs/in² at 28 days. The ratio of aggregate to cement by volume is 8:1. Formwork pressures are lower than for normal concrete, so forms can be lighter and pour-height "lifts" greater. No-fines concrete is used in highway construction.

Water Potable water is the only water allowed for concrete and masonry mixes, as specified in ACI 318/318R. Salt water will also result in efflorescence or the deposition of salt on the surface, which is unsightly. Therefore, it is avoided—as is any highly acidic water or water containing organic matter.

Concrete mixes These are determined by the following methods:
- *designated concrete*, the simplest approach, in which the producer demonstrates conformity with a standard. ACI 318/318R "Building Code Requirements for Structural Concrete" is the reference for materials and mix designs for concrete. ASTM C33 and ASTM C144 is the reference for concrete and masonry aggregates respectively;
- *designed mix*, in which the specifier lays down the properties and performance, and the producer determines the mix. This tends to be used when the criteria are outside those on "designated" concrete—e.g. for use in a maritime situation with salt water, or where there is extreme exposure;

(The above two methods are "performance options.")

TIP CONCRETE EXPOSURE

Specification of concrete should take into account exposure, such as whether the concrete is going to be permanently wet (e.g. in a swimming pool), is cyclically wet and dry (e.g. on sidewalks or bridge abutments exposed to road salt) or in a coastal situation where it will be exposed to salt water. Concrete can also be vulnerable to chemical damage, such as that from excessive alkalinity or acidity (high or low pH), chlorides or sulphates in the soil.

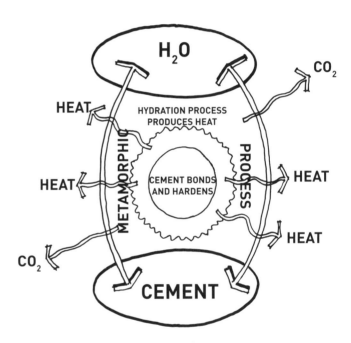

Cement hydration process

- *prescribed mix*, in which the purchaser determines the composition, usually because of a wish for a special effect or a uniformity of appearance (as in exposed aggregate finishes);
- *standardized prescribed mix*, based on published standards, and in cases in which the concrete is mixed on site; or
- *proprietary concrete*.

Strength classes

Strength classifications are based on compressive strength (pounds per square in) at 28 days of age. Requirements for design strength are specified in ACI 318. Common strengths are 2500, 3000, 3500, 4000, 4500. Classes can vary according to State DOTs guidelines.

Concrete may be site-mixed (most simply using a bucket and spade) or mixed off site in a concrete plant and delivered ready-mixed. Components can also be precast, meaning made and formed in a factory, or cast *in situ*. The material may be laid as mass concrete, without reinforcement, or be reinforced, most usually with steel rods or mesh.

ASTM C 150 standard specifications for Portland cement

Type I	Normal
Type II	Moderate sulfate resistance
Type III	High early strength
Type IV	Low heat of hydration
Type V	High sulfate resistance

STEP BY STEP CONSTRUCTING A CURVED CAST-IN-PLACE CONCRETE RETAINING WALL

This curved retaining wall was built around an existing tree (see page 96 for a view of the tree taken from a higher angle). The sequence of images shows how, once the foundation slab was cast and the vertical steel reinforcement bars were erected, the area was excavated and the soil protected by blue sheeting. Next, formwork was erected, which was supported by posts, gradually working along each section of the curved wall. The wall was then backfilled and cast-in-place concrete steps were added to the outer side. Once the wall was complete, it was grit-blasted to reveal the texture of the aggregate (not illustrated).

1 The concrete foundation has been laid and steel reinforcement is being put in position.

2 Formwork is placed and liquid concrete poured inside to fill the mold.

3 After the shuttering has been removed the area immediately behind the wall is backfilled with subsoil and an aggregate.

4 The steps are cast in place at the base of the soil.

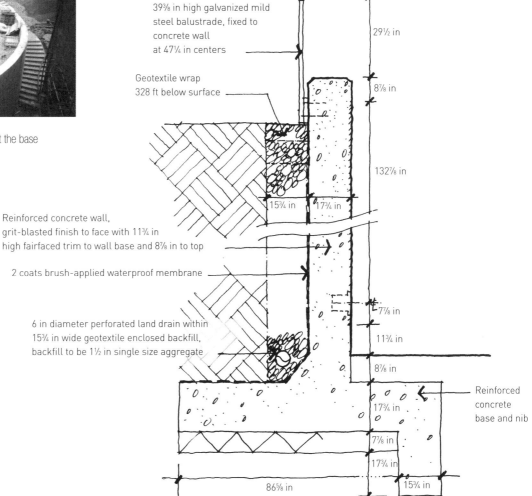

39⅜ in high galvanized mild steel balustrade, fixed to concrete wall at 47¼ in centers

Geotextile wrap 328 ft below surface

Reinforced concrete wall, grit-blasted finish to face with 11¾ in high fairfaced trim to wall base and 8⅞ in to top

2 coats brush-applied waterproof membrane

6 in diameter perforated land drain within 15¾ in wide geotextile enclosed backfill, backfill to be 1½ in single size aggregate

29½ in

8⅞ in

132⅞ in

15¾ in   17¾ in

7⅞ in

11¾ in

8⅞ in

17¾ in

7⅞ in

17¾ in

86⅝ in

15¾ in

Reinforced concrete base and nib

Admixtures These may be added to a batch of concrete during, or immediately before, its mixing. However, good concrete can be made without admixtures. Furthermore, as they can adversely affect the performance of concrete admixtures should only be used if the modification cannot be achieved by adjusting the basic constituents of sand, aggregate, water, and cement. (*For table of basic admixtures see Table 4, Appendix, page 227.*)

Examples of pigments
- Blacks and greys: black iron oxide, mineral black, and carbon black;
- Browns and reds: red iron oxide, raw and burnt umber;
- Blues: cobalt blue, ultramarine blue, phthalocyanine blue;
- Greens: chromium oxide, phtalocyanine green, copper filings (i.e. copper oxide);
- Ivory, cream, or buff: yellow iron oxide.

However, note that most pigments fade and that a strong-colored concrete effect is best achieved using exposed colored aggregate—e.g. red using bright-red brick aggregate, or black or gray using granite.

Waterproof concrete

No concrete is totally waterproof. The material contains fine capillary pores and voids—and ordinary concrete tends to act as a sponge, so it absorbs water. This can result in dampness, and promote staining and bacterial growth. Hence, concrete should be detailed to cast off rainwater, i.e. paving should be laid to fall to drains, and facing walls should be detailed to throw off water and avoid puddling. Tops of walls and steps should be 'canted', or laid to drain. This is particularly important in the case of reinforced concrete, because otherwise the steel reinforcement can rust.

If designing pools or tanks, the aim should be to avoid cracks and joints which would leak. Usually, it is therefore prudent to coat, line or otherwise protect the concrete. Even ordinary concrete can be made to hold water, but it will leak and so should be constantly fed with water. However, bear in mind that cracks in concrete are difficult to identify and to repair; therefore, for ornamental pools it is advisable to specify a liner to the concrete. For cheap structures such as water tanks, you can work with ordinary concrete specified in accordance with ASTM D5295-00 (2006) Standard Guide for Preparation of Concrete Surfaces for Adhered (Bonded) Membrane Waterproofing Systems. Water and sulfate resistant concrete is commonly achieved by use of admixures to concrete, application of sealers, and use of type II or type V portland cement (ASTM C150). ACI is a good source for reference documents.

Left
Black, precast concrete capitals at the top of multicolored ceramic tile-faced pillars. Oude Stadhuis, The Hague, The Netherlands, designed by John Outram.

Top right
Berthold Lubetkin's Penguin Pool at London Zoo, under construction in 1933.

Bottom right
The Penguin Pool, photographed 75 years later.

Below left
Foundation mesh reinforcement
and cast-in-place bolt plates, prior
to pouring concrete.

Below centre
Exposed wall reinforcement in the
bridge link between the towers of
the church of the Sagrada Familia,
Barcelona, Spain.

Below right
The concrete of this precast
fence post has crumbled where
the stresses of the strainer post
have caused cracking and water
penetration.

Ecoconcrete

Ordinary Portland cement requires a kiln temperature of 2,642°F. In order to reduce energy use, ecocement uses magnesia (magnesium oxide) in its mix in order to reduce the firing temperature to 1,382°F. Another technique is to produce calcium carbonate by using the waste-flue heat and carbon dioxide from other processes. In addition, recycled aggregate such as fly ash (a by-product of coal-fuelled power stations) can be used, which further reduces the concrete's embodied energy. Furthermore, ecoconcrete, like lime mortar, takes up carbon dioxide from the atmosphere.

Photocatalytic (depolluting) concrete

This is based on the addition of the white pigment titanium dioxide (TiO_2) in a water-based binder, which promotes oxidization of pollutants—notably nitrous oxide. In consequence, the manufacturers advise that their concrete and cement are self-cleaning and can also help deal with atmospheric pollutants. When ultraviolet light hits the surface of the concrete it causes electrons in the titanium oxide molecules to detach, so leaving positive "holes" which take on hydroxide (OH) ions from water vapour. The OH radical is unstable and attracts an electron from a nearby compound (which may well be a pollutant, such as nitrous oxide or carbon monoxide), which leads to the decomposition of the compound. This is a fairly new technique and has been applied by Italcementi to structural concrete, while Mitsubishi make a photocatalytic precast concrete unit paving.

Reinforced concrete

Concrete is strong in compression; in order to make it strong in tension, it is necessary to reinforce it by adding materials such as steel that have a strong tensile strength. It is the incorporation of reinforcing steel that permits concrete to be used for long structural spans, such as bridges, and for roadways or airplane runways when laid in large unit slabs. The main forms of steel reinforcement are steel bars or welded wire mesh, but it is also possible to use wire fibers. Other forms of reinforcement are fibers of glass and plastic, such as monofilament polypropylene and carbon fibre. GRC is glass-reinforced concrete, and is easily and finely molded (with a latex mold, it is used to make imitation rock faces). It is also much lighter than conventional reinforced concrete, and can be used to make reproductions of stucco details.

STEP BY STEP CONSTRUCTING GRC ROCKWORK

Factory-made glass-reinforced concrete (GRC) cast from a real rock face was chosen for this artificial rockwork at the Intercontinental Hotel, Aphrodite Hills Resort in Cyprus because it is more convincing than attempting to create a rock face effect in stone, and a precast product is easier to control in terms of quality. GRC permits fine molding and also a fairly lightweight cladding unit. This approach combines a fairly simple and inexpensive supporting structure (the cast-in-place concrete wall) with a more expensive, factory-quality cladding finish using a composite material (GRC).

1 A cast-in-place concrete wall provides the structure.

2 The ready-made GRC panels stacked ready for erection.

3 The GRC panels are supported by a welded rectangular hollow section (RHS) mild-steel frame attached to the wall.

4 The completed GRC panels with pool awaiting filling.

5 The completed project with the pool filled.

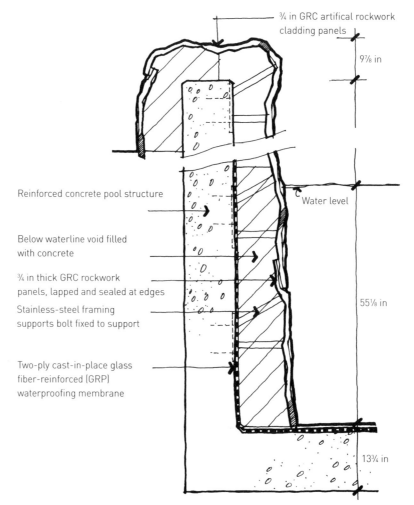

¾ in GRC artifical rockwork cladding panels

9⅞ in

Reinforced concrete pool structure

Water level

Below waterline void filled with concrete

¾ in thick GRC rockwork panels, lapped and sealed at edges

Stainless-steel framing supports bolt fixed to support

55⅛ in

Two-ply cast-in-place glass fiber-reinforced (GRP) waterproofing membrane

13¾ in

Concrete finishes

"Stamped" concrete is cast-in-place concrete in which a pattern has been made by placing a mold over it before it has cured. In this process, the concrete needs to be a wet mix with an air-entraining agent in order to ease leveling. Once placed, the wet concrete is worked over with a pierced tamper, to ensure a good cover of cement over the aggregate, and is screeded and leveled. At this stage, a coloring admixture can be added along with a chemical hardener. The pattern is imprinted using plastic or alloy texture mats, which may be to a regular pattern or can approximate a texture such as a slate or stone finish. The mats can vary in size from a small-pattern module of 11¾ x 11¾ in to larger texture mats of up to 5 ft 10 x 5 ft 10 in.

Between 24 and 96 hours later (depending on the weather), the patterned concrete is washed down and a sealant may be added in order to protect the color from fading owing to ultraviolet light. Typical sealants are acrylic, although urethane or epoxy-resin wearing coats can also be used. This gives a glossy, artificial appearance. Usually, an acrylic sealant would have a life of 25 years. An American firm, Bomanite, has given a generic name to this sort of cast-in-place concrete finish. Its patterns usually imitate setts, stone paving, or brickwork.

Other finishes are made by tooling, such as bush-hammering, by sandblasting, or by exposing the aggregate using a setting retardant.

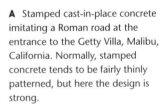

A Stamped cast-in-place concrete imitating a Roman road at the entrance to the Getty Villa, Malibu, California. Normally, stamped concrete tends to be fairly thinly patterned, but here the design is strong.

B Grit-blasted, cast-in-place concrete steps, Canon headquarters, Reigate, England.

C Bush-hammered ribs with reinforcement bar pattern, Parc Diderot, La Défense, Paris.

D Cast-in-place exposed aggregate path at Jardin Atlantique, Gare Montparnasse, Paris.

E Fine, exposed-aggregate precast wall panels at the London Zoological Society.

F Vertical board-marked cast-in-place concrete at the London Zoological Society.

Stucco

Stucco finishes on walls are of three basic types: a 'fat' lime-and-sand mix, sometimes with animal hair as reinforcement; a hydraulic mix, containing either hydraulic lime and sand or fat lime with a pozzolanic additive and sand; and various forms of mastic. Fat lime is a pure lime with a high calcium content. Stucco became a popular material in eighteenth-century London because it makes brick buildings look as though they are made from stone. However, its use is more traditionally common in the Mediterranean region. It is vital that stucco be repainted regularly, in order to avoid frost and root penetration.

Harling

Harling is very similar to stucco, and is a lime-based wall finish used in Scotland and Ireland. The lime cement and small-aggregate mix is usually applied in two layers, each ⅜–⅝ in thick, and then limewashed—often requiring several coats. Like stucco, harling has to breathe. The stonework beneath is first pointed and voids are filled. Pebble-dash is a twentieth-century development, in which the pebble aggregate is thrown onto the wet cement surface.

A Photo of stucco delamination in the Old Town, Nicosia, Cyprus.

B Newly limewashed harling in a courtyard in Edinburgh, Scotland.

C Weathered harling, Edinburgh, Scotland.

D A 1920s pebble-dash wall. Part of the wall has been painted (right).

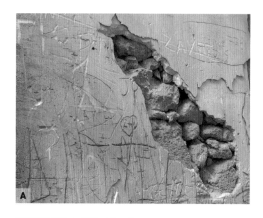

Brick

"I shall first treat of bricks, and the earth of which they ought to be made. Gravelly, pebbly, and sandy clay are unfit for that purpose; for if made of either of these sorts of earth, they are not only too ponderous, but walls built of them, when exposed to the rain, molder away, and are soon decomposed … They should be made of earth of a red or white chalky, or a strong sandy nature. These sorts of earth are ductile and cohesive, and not being heavy, bricks made of them are more easily handled in carrying up the work."

Marcus Vitruvius Pollio, *De Architectura,* Book II, Chapter 3

Bricks are an ancient building material, and are most commonly made of clay and water. Originally they were baked by the sun. They are blocks, usually small enough to hold in one hand, which are mortared and laid in a bond pattern. Both the bond and the mortar hold them together.

Mud bricks date from Neolithic times in the Middle East (8,000–10,000 years ago), and the buildings of the first ancient settlements, such as Çatal Hüyük in Anatolia, were built from sun-dried, clay-mud brick. Often straw could be added to the mud. The ziggurats of ancient Mesopotamia were also built of mud bricks, which were much used in ancient Egypt and India. Mud-brick construction is still current in warm-climate areas such as Africa, on the Danube in Europe, and in India where it is said that over half the country's current construction uses mud bricks.[7] In the Americas, mud-brick construction is called "adobe."

The fired brick dates from about the third millennium BC, and was later used by the Romans. The main types of fired brick used in modern construction are:

- clay;
- calcium silicate;
- concrete;
- slag; and
- terracotta and faience.

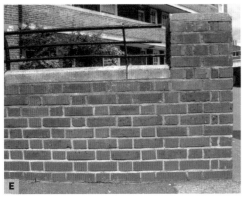

E Flemish-bond brick wall with the lowest two courses in red engineering brick, and precast concrete copings.

F Mud-brick two-story house with stucco removed, Old Town, Nicosia, Cyprus.

G Thin Roman bricks, Pompeii, Italy.

H Adobe wall, Harlemmermeer Floriade, 2002, The Netherlands.

Which material is used, and where, depends in the main on the cost of supply, and this reflects the geology of the area. Calcium-silicate bricks are found in sandy areas, while clay bricks and terracotta depend on clay sources. Until the nineteenth century, it was quite common to dig clay locally for bricks for a major building. Clay bricks tend to be the norm in Britain, The Netherlands and France, where clay is easily found. Calcium-silicate bricks are more commonly found in northern Germany and along the Baltic coastline.

The standard US brick measures 8 x 3⅝ x 2¼ inches. Around the world bricks can vary greatly in size. Before metrication, the standard twentieth-century size in the UK was 9 x 4 x 3 in. The width is the main determinant; bricks are usually the size of a small loaf, something that will fit in one hand.

A Stretcher-bond brickwork with white mortar joints. Because this bond can be built one brick thick it is extensively used for cavity walls. It is also the least interesting bond.

B Flemish bond with alternating stretchers and headers, with a more recessively colored mortar. Note the color variation in the bricks due to temperature changes in the kiln: such color variation emphasizes the individual brick, and from a distance gives the rich pointillistic color and texture of traditional brickwork.

C English bond, comprising alternating courses of stretchers and headers, is a strong structural-wall bond. The example shown here uses handmade brindled or multicolored bricks.

D Dark mortar used in a wall made of old, hard, burnt bricks gives a more recessive appearance to the bond pattern.

E Stretcher bonds can be enlivened by varying the brick colors, whether horizontally, as here, or diagonally.

F The same effect as in the previous image but with a mortar of a more recessive color.

G Struck mortar joints in stretcher bond produce a shadow and throw off water.

H Patterned Flemish bond using different-colored bricks. The perpends—or vertical joints—do not align. Usually this would look sloppy but here, with handmade bricks, the resulting look is vernacular and informal.

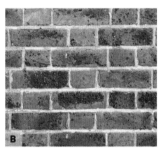

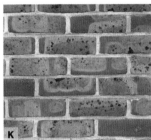

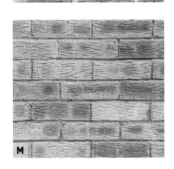

I A struck mortar joint gives some shadows and enlivens a monochrome brick wall.

J A raked mortar joint enlivens this stretcher-bond brickwork by giving a stronger shadow.

K A flush mortar joint in stretcher bond is less attractive and emphasizes the overwide.

L Lightly colored bricks with a raked mortar joint in stretcher bond.

M Freshly laid, flush-pointed, light-colored stretcher-bond brickwork.

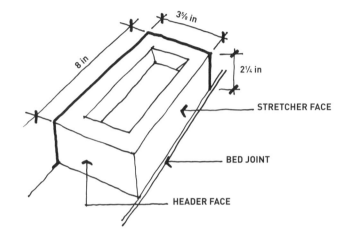

Anatomy of a standard brick

Note that the Dutch had many sizes of bricks, which could vary from small 6 x 2¾ x 1¼ in "Lilliputs" to the rather large 11¼ x 5¼ x 3¼ in *Kloostermop* (monastery stone). In France, the traditional *brique de Bourgogne* was 8¾ x 4¼ x 2¼ in, while the *brique de Paris* was 8½ x 4¼ x 2¼ in. In Germany, the pre-First World War *Reichsformat* brick was 9½ x 4½ x 2½ in.

Roman bricks were long and thin: sometimes 12–16 in long and a mere 2 in thick. By contrast, traditional Russian bricks used in churches are like large bread loaves and very soft so that they can easily be cut with a trowel. In some countries, such as Spain, much larger perforated clay-brick blocks are the norm. (*For tables of US and international brick sizes, see Tables 5 and 6, Appendix, page 228.*)

Above
Traditional Russian bricks are large—more than 12 in long—and soft, so that they can be cut to shape using a trowel. In this photograph a workman makes repairs to the Feodorovsky Monastery, Pereslavl'-Zelessky, north of Moscow.

Materials used in making bricks

The main materials used in the manufacture of bricks are:

Clay An alluvial deposit found in lowland areas. There are three main types:
- strong or pure clays with a natural moisture content which renders them plastic, and therefore suitable for hand molding;
- sandy clays, which contain silica and shrink less; and
- calcareous clays with lime, which make good bricks varying from pink to dark red.

Calcium silicate These bricks are made from a mix of hydrated lime and water and silica sand (or crushed flint), which is pressed into shape and then pressure-steam baked in an autoclave to produce a dull, white, and very regular brick. In 1877, the German chemist Dr Wilhelm Michaëlis first produced "artificial sandstone" and patented this invention in 1880. Pigments can be added in order to color these bricks. The product is a brick of a constant color and an even, or "mechanical," appearance. Popular in north Germany, where clay is not so readily found, they are not suitable in coastal situations because they are vulnerable to salt damage and do tend to chip.

Above
Calcium silicate brickwork with a very pale, even color.

Right
Unglazed terracotta, Old Customs House, Ramsgate, England.

Below left
Glazed faience tiles, The Crown Bar, Great Victoria Street, Belfast, Northern Ireland.

Below right
Glazed terracotta, Russell Square subway station, London.

Bottom right
Horizontally raked brick was characteristic of 1930s Paris, here at the Lycée Gaston Bachelard, near Porte d'Italie.

Concrete Concrete bricks consist of a mix of cement, sand and aggregate, which is pressed and fired in a similar way to calcium-silicate bricks. They are harder than clay bricks, and often used as "building bricks" (non-facing bricks) in areas lacking clay deposits.

Slag bricks These were made in the nineteenth century from molten slag and lime (waste products of iron making), but are no longer produced. They were particularly used for paving.

Terracotta and faience These units are made from fine clays with silica and alumina, and some alkaline material to assist vitrification when fired in a kiln at greater than 1,832°F (normal clay brick is fired at 1,652°F). Terracotta consists of molded hollow blocks, which can be anchored to the front of a building to form a cornice or decorative face. Faience is twice fired: once to vitrify it, and then again to glaze it.

In the US, as in many other countries, the usual brick is made of clay. Bricks were a regional material until the nineteenth century, when canals and then railways made transporting them cheaper. Clay deposits vary in color giving, for example, red or yellow bricks.

Process of manufacture

Traditionally, clay was dug by hand, stockpiled over the winter and then turned, tempered with water and kneaded by foot (and the stones removed). In the seventeenth century, the Dutch invented the pug mill: a tub lined with blades, through which the clay is pressed downwards in a spiral in order to extrude at the bottom. Nowadays, clay is dug by machine, stockpiled and then crushed in a mill. The prepared material can be shaped either by hand or machine:

Hand molding This is done on a bench, either by pressing clay into a mould sprinkled with sand (hence a "sand-faced" brick) or by the older wet process of slop molding, which produces a very wet brick that has to be dried for some days before firing.

Machine pressing In the nineteenth century, slop molding was mechanized by using a press to place high-plasticity clay (or soft mud) into sanded molds, which then released the bricks. The molds are then mechanically washed and resanded. Semi-dry processes involve harder clay, which is ground to a coarse powder and then pressed relying on the naturally occurring moisture content of the clay. This produces a smooth, almost dry, brick, which can pass directly to the kiln.

Wire cutting This later nineteenth-century process is the most efficient form of brick production, and involves cutting extruded lengths of clay with wires attached to a frame. This is now the main industrial method of brick manufacture and produces the typical drag mark of the wire across the brick face. Many wire-cut bricks are perforated in order to reduce the energy cost of firing, but wire-cut facing bricks can be machine pressed to give a smooth, clean-cornered finish.

Drying This is done traditionally by storing bricks in "hacks", or open-sided sheds, where they are stacked and left to dry for three to six weeks prior to firing. In the nineteenth century, heated chamber driers—and then tunnel driers—were introduced, through which bricks pass over three days on rail-mounted trucks.

Firing In ancient Egypt and the Euphrates region, bricks were sun-dried; but the production of rain-resistant bricks requires firing them for some hours at a temperature of 1,652–2,012°F to vitrify them. The temperature and length of firing varies with the clay and type of brick. Hard, water-resistant engineering bricks require several hours of high-temperature firing (and so cost more than softer bricks). The "clamp" is the oldest form of firing, and often took place on the building site. The stack of bricks that formed a clamp usually had firing tunnels filled with wood fuel at its base, and the bricks were spaced to allow heated air to pass through them. This was followed by the "intermittent kiln," which was allowed to cool between firings. The intermittent kiln was the first form of mass production, but today most bricks are fired in tunnel kilns through which the bricks pass on conveyors or rails. Mechanized firing processes give greater control, and therefore less variation in the brick: it is a characteristic of pre-nineteenth-century brickwork that the lack of control during firing gave a greater variety of color.

The tendency when choosing bricks is to look for regularity in shape, size, and color, and for rectangular faces. However, regularity can result in a mechanical and dull appearance. The color variations in traditional brickwork can be part of the beauty of a brick wall. Such a variety of color emphasized the unit construction (which is the essence of brickwork) and, like a pointillistic painting, gave a richness of color.

Certainly, a good brick should be well burned and free of lime, cracks, and stones. Color (except for calcium-silicate and concrete bricks) is determined by the integral chemical composition of the raw clay, and especially the amount of iron. Red bricks contain about 5 per cent iron, blue bricks between 7 and 10 per cent, and iron with some magnesium will produce black bricks. However, the type of firing will also vary the color: oxygen gives reds, while the absence of oxygen will cause the iron to form oxides and produce blue-blacks.

Variations in firing give rise to the variety of color found in London stock bricks which, while basically yellow, include pinks, reds, oranges, purples, and blacks. The color fastness of brick is an important characteristic compared with, say, concrete. Brick is a geological material, like stone, and does not fade. Though weathering may darken its appearance, this is usually the result of carbon deposits.

Types of brick

Building bricks are strong enough to act as internal walls and be faced with other materials, whether plaster, finishes or stucco, tiles, or stone facing—or, indeed, a better brick.

Facing bricks have at least one header and stretcher face that is of good quality and color.

Engineering bricks are dense, strong, impermeable bricks suited to engineering structures, like railway-cutting walls and bridges. They are suitable for underground structures, and are used in garden walls as a foundation and moisture-proof layer. They are typically blue or red.

Moisture-proof course bricks are dense and impermeable, like engineering bricks, but are otherwise similar to facing bricks.

Specials are bricks of a special shape or size: they may have a rounded corner (a "bull-nose"), be saddleback copings or chamfered (canted)—and, of course, specials can be produced to designer's specifications.

Special-purpose bricks range from paving bricks to fireback bricks, and from the glazed bricks used in toilets to bricks used for kiln construction.

Rubbed bricks are soft bricks that can be shaped or rubbed down to form close-fitting, intricate shapes with very fine joints such as archways. They are made with a high-silica clay and, once laid, the bricks harden because of mineral cements which form on wetting.

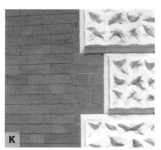

A Dense blue engineering bricks protect walls from groundwater movement and are used to protect corners from impact damage.

B Specials: double bull-nose brick coping, laid on edge.

C Specials: saddleback brick coping with a rebuilt section of light, poorly matched mortar.

D Specials: half-round blue engineering capping bricks with a crease or drip course of header bond on a stone rubble wall.

E Specials: single-chamfered or canted brick coping laid clumsily.

F Specials: double-chamfered or canted stop-end coping brick.

G Specials: chamfered or canted blue engineering-brick cill.

H Stretcher-bond monochromatic brickwork enlivened by recessed joints and a zip corner detail.

I Monochromatic stack-bond brick cladding enlivened by angling the bricks.

J Soldier-course brick capping on a dwarf wall.

K Finely jointed brickwork at the lodges leading to the Old Royal Naval Hospital, Greenwich, London.

L Rubbed-brick arch, London.

The brick-wall bond

The "bond" is the arrangement of bricks in a wall. Stack bond, with continuous vertical joints, is very weak, so bricks are overlapped in structural masonry in order to avoid vertical joints. The minimum overlap is 25 per cent of the length of a brick. Extra strength is provided in walls more than one brick thick by laying bricks transversely across the wall thickness. Indeed, one of the strongest bonds is header bond—built using this method—which results in a surface consisting entirely of headers. This is found on curving walls and on some railroad cuttings. Stretcher bond is very common since the introduction of the cavity wall in building construction, and consists purely of stretchers; it is also the most boring bond. English bond comprises alternate headers and stretchers laid in courses, and is strong; Flemish bond has headers and stretchers laid alternately in each course and is more varied than English bond. For garden-wall construction, consider English garden-wall bond, in which headers are used every fourth or sixth course in between courses of stretcher bond.

Paving bonds

Vertical strength does not apply to paving, and therefore weak bonds can be used, such as stack bond or basket weave. Herringbone bond is suitable if there is to be vehicle movement and heavy point loads, such as those from heavy trucks, because it interlocks and so spreads the load (if laid on flexible foundations). Note that it should be laid at 45 degrees to the curb or edge retention in order to avoid alignment problems. The joint can also be broken in order to avoid cutting small portions of brick at the edge. This is the bond used in railroad yards and dock areas for brick paving, and it was used in the 1950s for Dutch highways.

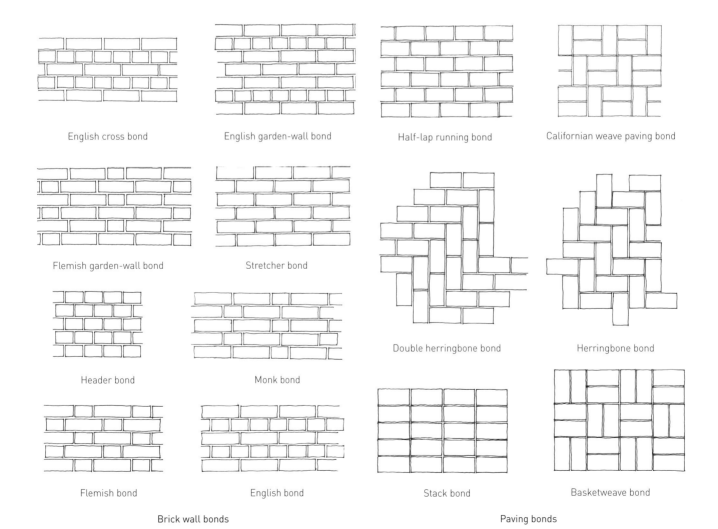

English cross bond

English garden-wall bond

Half-lap running bond

Californian weave paving bond

Flemish garden-wall bond

Stretcher bond

Header bond

Monk bond

Double herringbone bond

Herringbone bond

Flemish bond

English bond

Stack bond

Basketweave bond

Brick wall bonds

Paving bonds

Mortar

Mortar holds brickwork together, and allows for variation in the size of bricks when laying courses. It is a mixture of either sand and cement or sand and lime—both with water. Lime gives workability, while cement gives frost resistance.

Lime mortar is made by burning limestone (calcium carbonate) in a limekiln in order to drive off the carbon (as carbon dioxide) to produce "quicklime" (calcium oxide). The carbon dioxide is given off as a greenhouse gas. The quicklime is then "slaked," i.e. mixed with water, in order to produce lime putty (calcium hydroxide). Alternatively, when mixed with less water this produces dry hydrated lime which can be crushed and bagged for making into lime putty. Lime putty is matured for two to three months before use. To make mortar, the putty is mixed with sand in the proportion 1 part lime putty:3 parts sand by volume.

The lime mortar sets by combining with atmospheric carbon dioxide to produce calcium carbonate. This process can be quite lengthy. Indeed, it is argued that the lime mortar used in the rubble fill in the thick walls of medieval castles did not set at all, but remained in a semi-fluid state: this gave the walls flexibility, which is an advantage when a building is bombarded.

Lime mortar was the traditional mix before the twentieth century, and is the weakest. It is also noteworthy that lime mortar permits easy recycling of brickwork: it can easily be knocked off the bricks, so that they may be cleaned. This is next to impossible with cement mortar. Furthermore, in terms of recycling, lime mortar is simply limestone and sand while disposing of cement mortar is more problematic.

In the US lime mortar is used mainly only for restoration of historic buildings. In landscape construction today, hydrated lime (usually Type S) is used almost exclusively.

Note, however, that chimney stacks, brick barbecues, copings, and retaining structures require stronger mortar —as will below-ground structures.

Non-hydraulic lime mortar is made of calcium hydroxide, produced by heating limestone to 1,749–1,950°F and so driving off the carbon dioxide to form quicklime (calcium oxide) which is slaked with water to produce lime putty (calcium hydroxide). This is stored for two to three months to mature. The putty may be stored dry as hydrated lime which is mixed with sand in a ratio of 1 hydrated lime:3 sand. The lime mortar sets by reacting with atmospheric carbon dioxide, in a process known as "hydration," to form calcium carbonate.

Hydraulic lime mortar is a mortar which can be used to set under water or in waterlogged soils, and can be considered a halfway state to a cement mortar. The limestone used contains elements of clay or silica, which produce a dicalcium silicate (but not any tricalcium silicate, which is a constituent of Portland cement). It is the dicalcium silicate that permits setting under water.

Cement mortar is the strongest mortar, but should only be used with strong bricks. Typically, it consists of 1 part cement to 3 or 4 parts sand by volume, with just enough water to make the mix plastic. A mortar should not be stronger than the brick, as the bricks themselves will crack. Cement mortar is the usual mortar employed with modern brickwork.

Mortar in a stretcher-bond wall, with brickwork that has ⅜ in wide joints, occupies about 17 per cent of the wall surface, so the appearance of the mortar affects the appearance of wall. The mortar's appearance is determined by its color and tone (lightness and darkness) and the finish (or pointing) of the brickwork. The color of mortar is determined by the sand, which can range from golden-yellow to white. Pigments can also be used, but can affect the strength of the mortar; care must be taken in mixing them or the color may vary, which results in a wall with a patchy appearance.

Above and right
When seen close up (above) this recycled brickwork at Insel Hombroich, near Neuss, Germany appears crude, but from a distance it is very attractive (right).

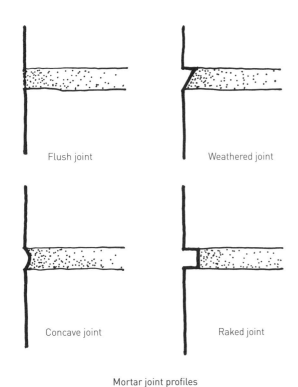

Flush joint

Weathered joint

Concave joint

Raked joint

Mortar joint profiles

Jointing and pointing

Jointing is done when the mortar is still fresh and wet; pointing is done with stiff mortar, which is partially raked out to a depth of about ¾ in and replaced with fresh mortar. Repointing is a similar process. The commonest joints are:

- *flush*, which is flat, does not throw a shadow and tends to be dull;
- *weather-struck*, with a recessed top and flush bottom edge. It throws a sharp shadow and protects the lower brick; trowelling across the mortar to form the joint compresses the mortar into the bricks and forms a more weatherproof joint;
- *weathered and cut*, with a recessed top and projecting bottom edge to horizontal joints. The bottom edge projects some ¹⁄₁₆ in beyond the brick face and so emphasizes the horizontality of an elevation;
- *concave*, which is curved. This also weatherproofs the joint and throws a soft shadow;
- *raked joints*, which are recessed by raking out a layer of mortar. This produces a very strong shadow, but also more rainwater penetration and hence frost damage;
- *thin-joint mortar,* in which the proprietary adhesive mortar is applied mechanically by a hose and applicator rather than with a trowel. This enables the brick to be laid with a very thin joint, about ³⁄₁₆ in wide, recessed by about ³⁄₁₆ in from the face of the brick; the thin-joint technique reduces the mortar to about 9 per cent of the elevation.

TIP CARELESS POINTING

This carelessly pointed brickwork with concave joints has been further disfigured with mortar splashes. Careful craftsmanship is vital for effective and attractive brickwork.

Left
Brickwork showing how the header bond on the curved corner has more mortar joint and so appears whiter than the stretcher bond.

Laying paving

The British tend to lay unit paving with mortar joints on mortar beds on a concrete base; this is often unnecessary, often ugly and usually leads to cracking. The paving acts as a heat sump, thereby contributing to the urban heat-island effect, and produces more global-warming gases. It is also unnecessarily expensive. Flexible construction is the norm in the Netherlands and Germany, with sanded butt joints, a sand bed, and a hard-core base course.

Fundamental to pavement construction is the need to allow for movement of the soil: this can be done by designing a very strong, rigid structure or by designing a flexible one. For most pedestrian paving, the use of a 2 in sand bed and sanded butt joint will produce a flexible paving with clear joints, which will reveal the appearance and unit pattern of the brick or block. A butt joint is one in which the bricks touch or nearly touch; sometimes paving bricks have nibs on their sides to maintain a constant construction width between bricks. In areas of vehicle traffic, a herringbone pattern on a flexible construction will spread the load. However, poor and uneven construction of the base course will lead to problems with flexible construction. Do not use soft facing bricks for paving because they will break up under frosty conditions.

Above left
Clay brick paving in stack bond, rigidly laid on edge. Pallant House Gallery, Chichester, England.

Above center
Flexible Dutch paving, laid on sand with butt joints, Rijksmuseum, Amsterdam. This type of paving is easily relaid.

Above
A typical Dutch street in Wageningen, with a herringbone-pattern brick road and lap-bond pavement, both in flexibly laid materials.

Problems with brickwork

The commonest problems with brickwork are to do with the soluble salts in the brick, which are washed out by water penetration. Hence, correct detailing of joints, copings, and moisture-proof courses is vital in order to minimize water penetration. It is also imperative to ensure that bricks are not soaked on site before being laid (and that overflow pipes are not left dripping). Engineering bricks should be used in the lower courses close to the ground; walls should be detailed to cast off water; and brickwork should not be pointed so that mortar is raised beyond the surface of a wall, which will ensure that water is retained and lead to "spalling"—the faces of the bricks flaking off.

Magnesium and sodium salts leave a white crystalline stain called "efflorescence;" this is unsightly, but over time can be brushed off. Crypto-efflorescence is when soluble salts become trapped below smooth dense bricks; this may expand, causing the faces of the bricks to disintegrate. The only remedy here is to cut out and replace the affected bricks. Soluble lime from mortar can leach from the brickwork if it becomes saturated after laying. The lime "bleed" then reacts with carbon dioxide to produce a white stain; acid-based brickwork-cleaner can sometimes remove this.

Sulphate attack is the most serious form of common damage to brickwork because it can take several years to develop and is the consequence of a reaction between sulphates in the brick and the tricalcium aluminate in ordinary Portland cement. This leads to crystallization and crumbling of the mortar. In damp situations, therefore, use sulphate-resisting cement and bricks with a low sulphur content.

Far left
Eroded soft rubbed-brick arch, West Station, Bexhill-on-Sea, England. Rubbed bricks work well if they are protected.

Bottom left
Raised repointing on crudely sandblasted eighteenth-century brickwork. This type of repair is not advised for fine brickwork as water may become trapped and cause freeze–thaw damage to the bricks.

Left
Efflorescence on brickwork on a railroad viaduct.

STEP BY STEP CONSTRUCTING AN ENGINEERING-BRICK RETAINING WALL

The structural engineer determined the design of this heavily engineered retaining wall, which consists of two brick skins filled with cast-in-place concrete. Although the wall is only 6 ft 6 in high, a strong structure was necessary because of the potential lateral live load of the flowing groundwater underneath. The choice of blue engineering brick reflects local canal and railroad tradition and echoes the use of color in the villa. Engineering bricks also resist frost in wet conditions.

1 The line of the wall is excavated.

2 The engineering bricks are laid to stretcher bond in a double skin. Bull-nose bricks are used on the coping.

3 Wall viewed from the rear with the stretcher bond maintained on the wide-radius curved sections. Note the concrete strip foundation.

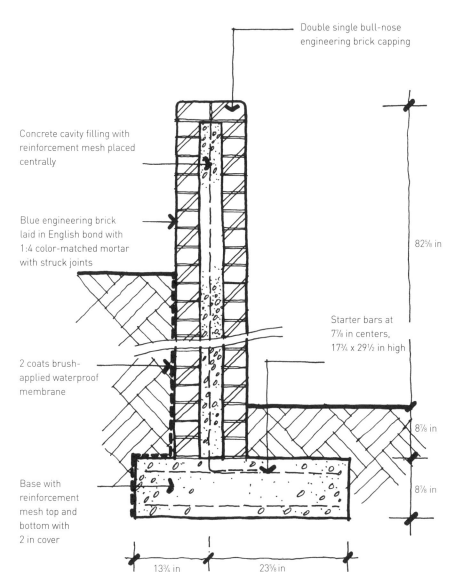

Double single bull-nose engineering brick capping

Concrete cavity filling with reinforcement mesh placed centrally

Blue engineering brick laid in English bond with 1:4 color-matched mortar with struck joints

2 coats brush-applied waterproof membrane

Base with reinforcement mesh top and bottom with 2 in cover

82⅝ in

Starter bars at 7⅞ in centers, 17¾ x 29½ in high

8⅞ in

8⅞ in

13¾ in   23⅝ in

4 The cavity is filled with concrete.

5 Black bitumen paint is used to seal the brick. This ensures that groundwater does not pass through the wall, leach out the cement, and cause efflorescence.

6 The completed wall. The small arch at the base of the wall is a super-sized weep hole intended to relieve the pressure of flowing groundwater.

Metals

The main metals that the landscape designer is likely to meet include both "old" (e.g. bronze, iron, and lead) and "newer" metals (such as stainless steel or aluminum). The decision whether or not to use a particular metal may be based on economics, function, conservation, or context —or, simply, on fashion. A conservation-based design may necessitate the use of lead or cast iron; in the field of contemporary design on the other hand, Corten steel and stainless steel have been particularly fashionable in the past decade. A seaside garden would suggest the use of aluminum or stainless steel. The American landscape architect Garret Eckbo once designed an aluminum show garden in the 1950s, while fellow American Peter Walker is known for his use of stainless steel.

Metal ores have to be heated in order to melt the metal in the rock, to extract it and then discard the slag. Molten metal loses its crystalline structure, and when a heated metal cools that structure re-forms from the points of first cooling. Crystals move most easily where there is a continuous, ordered structure. Metal–crystal structures formed after cooling contain discontinuities that create a "log jam," and thereby strengthen the structure of a metal. The process of annealing, or heating and reheating in order to toughen a metal, is the basis of much metalworking. The amount of energy used in smelting and the manufacture of metals is a sustainability issue in the choice of metals—for instance, aluminum manufacture uses much more energy than steel.

Right
Piazza Metallica: slabs of pig iron at Duisburg Nord Landschaftspark, Duisburg, Germany.

Below right
Polished stainless-steel cladding on expanded galvanized mild-steel mesh, which in turn sits on a galvanized steel frame, Cyprus Olympic Association Building, Nicosia.

Forming and working metals

Some understanding of how metals are formed is necessary to their use. The main methods are shaping from molten metal; from hot, solid metal; from cold metal; and from powdered metal.

Casting This is a molten-metal process, often done in sand molds—but it may also be done by *die casting* (permanent steel or cast-iron dies or molds are used to make castings of zinc, aluminum, or alloys); by *continuous casting* (pouring into a water-cooled mold and withdrawing the billet of cast metal into a tank of water below the mold); or by *centrifugal casting* (in which molten metal is poured into a spinning, cylindrical, mold).

Rolling A method used mainly with steel, which can be hot or cold rolled. Hot rolling involves rolling white-hot ingots through rolling mills, which successively reduce and change the cross-section of the metal, and increase its length in order to produce either flat steel plate or the standard structural beam sections.

Forging This consists of hammering or beating the heated metal. It is the method of the blacksmith's forge, but it can also be industrialized. Indeed, forged metal was much used in large-scale nineteenth-century construction.

Extrusion A method used particularly with aluminum: the heated, solid metal is squirted or pushed through a shaped hole in a heated, semi-liquid form.

Drawing A hot-rolled rod is pulled through a hole in a die at a relatively low, working temperature.

Pressing A method used mainly with hot- or cold-rolled steel. A machine press changes the shape of the metal or bends it, and creates a stronger metal part or object.

Powder technology This has been developed in order to form metals such as tungsten, which are difficult to melt. It allows economical shaping of small parts, and also permits the incorporation of non-metals such as graphite (a lubricant) into a metal.

Iron

The main distinction in construction metals is between ferrous (iron) and non-ferrous types. Iron is of such importance because it is the fourth most common element on Earth. It is strong (in compression and tension), and when heated can be formed and shaped; its melting point is 2,800°F. However, it does not have a high fire resistance and is the heaviest of the common construction materials: three times the weight of concrete and six times the weight of lumber. It conducts heat (and electricity) rather well, which is worth remembering when designing metal structures for climbing plants in hot climates as hot metal can burn them.

Iron is found naturally as an oxide of iron; to make it into pure iron, the ore is smelted by heating with charcoal or coal. In this way, the carbon in the fuel takes up the oxygen and releases the iron. The crude molten metal is cast into ingots of "pig iron," which is between 89 and 95 per cent pure iron—the remainder is carbon (both "free carbon," or graphite, and ferric carbide), manganese, phosphorus, silicon, and sulphur. "Pig iron" is so called because the molten iron used to be run into sand molds, which looked like a set of piglets feeding off a sow.

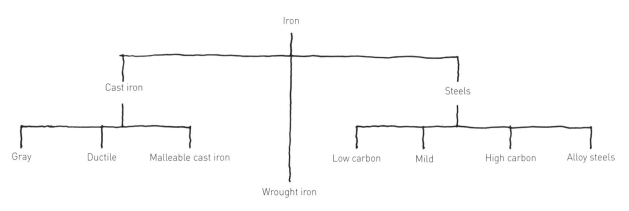

Table of the family of ferrous metals

IRON+ CARBON+ SILICON

COKE

FUEL

ORES

LIMESTONE

FLUX

BLAST FURNACE
at 2,372°F

HOT GASES

HOT GASES

SMELTING PROCESS

SLAG CRUST

HOT GASES

PIG or
CAST IRON

Iron making process

Cast iron

Cast iron is formed by reheating the pig iron in order to reduce the manganese and silicon, to increase the sulphur and to combine the graphite carbon into ferric carbide. The resultant cast iron is of two main types: gray and white. *Gray cast iron* has a high silicon level; it is soft and readily turned or filed. *White cast iron* has a maximum silicon content of 1.3 per cent and no graphite.

Cast iron is brittle unless toughened to make *ductile iron* (also known as spheroidal, or nodular, iron). This is done by heating gray iron with graphite nodules and removing the sulphur, which allows the grains of iron to touch and so strengthens the metal. *Malleable cast iron* is similar to ductile iron but is made by annealing white cast iron; it is particularly used in thin-section castings. There are also cast-iron alloys, but these are not so applicable to external works.

Cast iron was *the* structural metal of the early nineteenth century, and the first cast-iron bridge is that at Coalbrookdale, England, built in 1779. It is easily cast in sand molds when molten; however, as gray iron it is brittle and easily broken under shock. Today, cast iron is used for street and garden furniture, drainage pipes, swale gratings, tree grills, and manhole covers. Cast-iron drainage pipes may be required when repairing historic buildings; pipes running close to tree roots should also be cast iron (and wrapped in concrete). Gray cast-iron drainage pipes have the merit of being stronger and longer lasting, although more expensive, than plastic pipes. Ductile iron is stronger in tension, and so is more suitable for traffic bollards and vandal-prone sites. Both gray cast iron and ductile iron are more rust-resistant than untreated steels, and are therefore often preferable for outdoor purposes. The carbon and the silicon in them produce a stable, oxidized surface that slows corrosion. Their other characteristic is ease of molding—hence their use in decorative metalwork in the nineteenth century.

Right
A typical cast-iron entrance to a Paris métro station, designed by Hector Guimard.

Wrought iron

In popular usage, wrought iron denotes an iron that has been hammered under heat so as to improve its tensile strength. However, it was originally a purified iron, which had been reheated in order to remove the carbon. This was then hammered (a process called "puddling") and rolled in order to produce a fibrous or laminated structure with much greater tensile strength than gray cast iron, and with a better corrosion resistance than steel. Its carbon content is about 0.05 per cent. As such, it is suitable for bending and forging at low temperatures—and hence for wrought-iron fences, gates, balustrades, grills, hinges, and fixings. It is the traditional blacksmith's iron, and indeed has been produced using charcoal since the Iron Age. Landscape designers use wrought iron in gates, fences, and grills. In the latter part of the nineteenth century, it was also used for large-scale engineering: the Eiffel Tower is made of wrought iron.

Wrought-iron foundries in the USA went out of production in the 1960s because of the material's high production costs. However, the Italian company Industria Italiana Arteferro still produces wrought iron.

Steel

Steel is an alloy of iron with other metals. It has between 0.07 and 1.7 per cent carbon—wrought iron is practically free of carbon and cast iron has 4 per cent or more. As a result, steel can be made by adding carbon to wrought iron or removing it from cast iron. Steel is much less brittle than cast iron, and is stronger and easier to work. It is also relatively easily recycled.

The best-known steel-making method is the Bessemer converter process patented by Henry Bessemer in 1856, but steel has been produced for weapons and tools for centuries by the double shear process. Bessemer blast furnaces went out of use in most countries in the 1970s. The Siemens open-hearth furnace largely replaced Bessemer, and Siemens furnaces continue to be used in some countries today—although nowadays steel is mainly produced using electric-arc furnaces or the basic oxygen converter.

Below
Industrial steel-plate paving, Oostelijk Handelskade quayside, Amsterdam.

The main forms of steel for use in landscape and garden design are:

Low-carbon steel This is less than 0.15 per cent carbon, soft and suitable for wire and thin plating: it can be pulled and drawn;

Mild steel Between 0.15 and 0.25 per cent carbon, strong and suitable for rolling and welding but not for casting: the commonest present-day structural steel;

Medium-carbon steel From 0.2 to 0.6 per cent carbon, suitable for structural steel and for casting;

High carbon Between 0.6 and 2 per cent carbon: steel of the highest strength but more brittle than other steels, suitable for machines and tools.

There are a number of metals which, when alloyed to carbon steel, promote a fine crystal-grain structure and also ensure that heat treatments are distributed through the whole of the structure of the metal. The main such alloys are those using chromium, molybdenum, nickel, tungsten, and vanadium; in addition, the non metal, silicon, is also used. The following steel alloys are particularly suited for landscaping:

Stainless steel The addition of 2 per cent chromium to steel adds hardness and strength; 2–4 per cent magnetizes permanently; while 10–20 per cent chromium gives corrosion resistance in the form of stainless steel, first discovered by Harry Brearley in 1913. More recent stainless steels also add a little nickel. The shiny surface of polished stainless steel is a result of the oxidized chromium. Stainless steel is of value in coastal areas, where salts rust mild steel, and for use on structures for which galvanizing and painting is difficult—including handrails, where finger rings tend to scratch the surface. However, the protective chromium oxide film is very thin and if this is not intact stainless steel will rust. Electro-polishing and passivating stainless steel provides the best corrosion resistance.

The three most common grades of stainless steel are:
- *austenitic*, with more than 16 per cent chromium and more than 7 per cent nickel: the highest corrosion resistance;
- *ferritic*, with over 14 per cent chromium; and
- *martensitic*, with a maximum of 14 per cent chromium, but with the lowest corrosion resistance.

Stainless steel is available both polished and unpolished. There are several grades of unpolished finish, such as soft satin; matte; and engine-turned, with its pattern of concentric circles. Unpolished stainless steel has the advantage that weld joints can be more easily blended.

Corten steel Also known as *weathering steel*, this contains 0.25 per cent copper, and sometimes chromium, and has a tenacious iron oxide coating: the rust does not fall off when in contact with air. This is because copper and chromium are smaller elements than iron at a molecular scale, and so they "fix" the iron oxide molecules in a rusty-appearing patina. However, Corten should not be submerged in water or used in maritime locations because it is not resistant to salt attack (the patina does not form in salt-laden air). Similarly, it will suffer if surrounded by dense, damp vegetation; in such situations, it should be protected by painting or with a coal-tar epoxy sealant (or by concrete encasement or cathodic treatment).

During the first few years there will be iron oxide run-off if it is unprotected, and hence there will be staining which has to be designed for. Corten can also be used hot-dip galvanized and painted in order to avoid "undercreepage" by rust. It was used in this painted form when first introduced in the 1930s for US railroad freight cars (COR-TEN® is a trade name and is owned by the US Steel Corporation). In its untreated rusting form it is much used by the artist Richard Serra in his sculpture and was used by Antony Gormley in his public artwork, *The Angel of the North*, in Gateshead, England. Its rusting form is especially popular in contemporary garden design, for instance the new botanic garden in Barcelona, Spain. Note that the intensity of the rusting patina varies with industrial pollution, the degree of exposure and the aspect. Sunnier, west- and south-facing aspects will develop a smoother, more uniform patina than east- and north-facing ones, which dry out at a slower rate.

TIP STEEL FINISHES

Buffing, unlike polishing, does not remove any steel during the finishing process; traditionally, a lubricated felt-based material was used with the buffing wheel. Brushing involves the use of bristles or a nylon fabric. Polishing and grinding, by contrast, use a grit abrasive to polish the metal, and by doing so they remove steel.

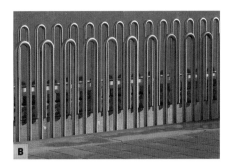

A Stainless-steel and hardwood lumber pergola, Laganside, Belfast, Northern Ireland.

B U-shaped stainless-steel tubular bollard by the Rijksmuseum, Amsterdam.

C Folded stainless-steel plate seats, Barcelona Botanic Garden, Spain.

D Painted welded mild-steel trimtrail sculpture at Aztec West, near Bristol, England.

E Red stove-enameled steel folly at Parc de la Villette, Paris. Since this photograph was taken in the mid-1980s the once bright red has darkened slightly.

F Corten steel-clad cast-in-place concrete walls at the Barcelona Botanic Garden designed by Beth Figueras. The cladding is ⅛ in thick.

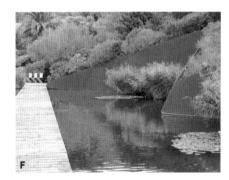

Stainless-steel finishes

Description	ASTM A480
cold rolled, ground	No. 3
dull buffed	
cold rolled, brushed or dull polished	No. 4
cold rolled, satin polished	No. 6
bright buffed	No. 7
cold rolled, bright polished	No. 8

Source: http://www.bssa.org.uk/topics.php?article=90

STRUCTURAL-STEEL SECTIONS

It is important to have some familiarity with the standard rolled-steel sections and tube and pipe sizes because they provide the basic elements the landscape designer can use in fences, bridges, pergolas or other garden structures. (RSA stands for rolled-steel angle.)

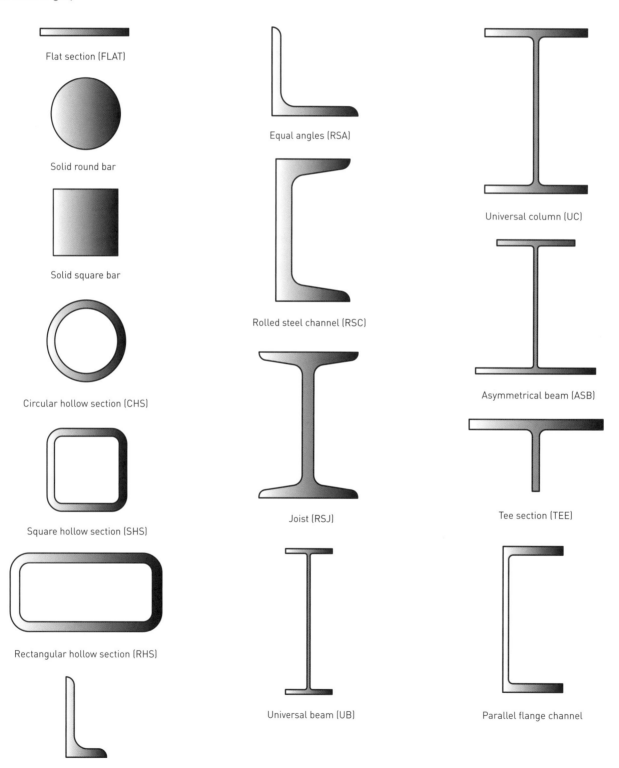

Flat section (FLAT)

Solid round bar

Solid square bar

Circular hollow section (CHS)

Square hollow section (SHS)

Rectangular hollow section (RHS)

Unequal angles (RSA)

Equal angles (RSA)

Rolled steel channel (RSC)

Joist (RSJ)

Universal beam (UB)

Universal column (UC)

Asymmetrical beam (ASB)

Tee section (TEE)

Parallel flange channel

Aluminum

Aluminum is the most widely used non-ferrous metal: it is light, relatively strong, rust-resistant and easily worked. However, aluminum also has one of the most energy-intensive methods of production owing to alumina's high melting point of 2,632°F (aluminum itself has a melting point of 1,220°F). It is extracted from bauxite ore by dissolving the ore in sodium hydroxide to form sodium aluminate. This is treated with carbon dioxide to form aluminum hydroxide and then heated to make alumina (aluminum oxide), which is reduced to aluminum by electrolysis. Aluminum is a product of countries where electricity is available cheaply, for instance from hydro-power sources. It was first isolated in 1825, and therefore has a relatively short history: it is a quintessential twentieth-century metal. The Concorde aircraft was made of heat-hardened (age-hardened) aluminum alloy with copper, manganese, and magnesium.

Used decoratively, aluminum can take a high polish but it is easily scratched; light anodizing gives a harder surface. The natural oxide of aluminum is tenacious, and protects the metal underneath from further corrosion. As with steels, there are standard structural aluminum sections. These section shapes are not produced by rolling; rather they are extruded (the metal is squirted or pushed through a shaped hole in a heated, semi-liquid form). Also like steels, there are alloys of aluminum; however, most are not corrosion-resistant, unlike the pure metal, and therefore their application externally is limited. The main uses of aluminum are in corrosion-resistant fittings such as pool grills, fencing, lightweight structures, and items designed to be moved by hand, such as folding bollards and trash cans. Note, however, that salt-water spray will corrode aluminum. In salt-water environments, the metal should be protected by chemical film coatings such as Alodine, Iridite (both chromate-based)—or by painting. Alternatively, a marine grade aluminum alloy such as a 3 per cent magnesium alloy, which is resistant to salt water, should be used.

Above
Pressed-plate aluminum cladding, La Défense, Paris, France.

Right
The aluminum entrance arch to the People of Britain Pavilion at the Festival of Britain, London, 1951.

Copper

Copper is available in sheet and pipe form, and is known for its green patina (popularly called "verdigris") of copper sulphate and copper carbonate which forms within a few weeks of the metal being exposed to moisture and the weather. Copper is half the weight of lead and is relatively non-toxic (verdigris, however, is harmful). Because of its good electroconductivity, it is used for lightning conductors (including those for trees). It can be cast and welded, may be rolled or drawn, and has a melting point of 1,981.4°F. Copper is good as a roofing and cladding material, for pipes and tubes, for copings on brick walls, as a cover for lumber posts, as a flashing for water features, and also for moisture-proof courses.

Zinc

Zinc is resistant to corrosion and is used for roofing, flashings, channels, and copings and sills—but, most especially, it is used as a coating in galvanizing and sherardizing. A film of dull-gray carbonate forms on the surface of zinc in reaction to the weather and protects it from further erosion; it is a good, but gray, substitute for copper sheeting, and is used in capping (with lumber) and in moisture-proof courses.

Lead

Cast-lead figurines, drainpipes, and cisterns in seventeenth-century gardens come to mind when thinking of lead in the garden, and it still is used for flashings and moisture-proof courses. It is easily melted, at 620.6°F (lead musket balls were often made on the battlefield), but it is toxic. It is corrosion-resistant, because lead exposed to air forms a lead oxide film which stops further corrosion. Like copper, it is used in watertight flashings and cappings, and on roofs. Although dense and heavy, lead is extremely malleable because it has very little tensile strength. It is resistant to attack by most acids, and is not affected by most building materials. The exceptions are new cement mortar and tannin-rich lumbers such as oak and teak.

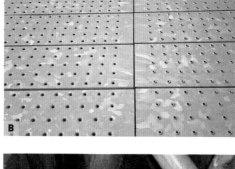

A Copper roof, Pevensey Bay, England.

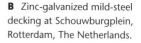
B Zinc-galvanized mild-steel decking at Schouwburgplein, Rotterdam, The Netherlands.

C Handworked lead sheet cascade in the Bosquet des Trois Fontaines, Versailles, France.

D The seventeenth-century lead pipework supplying the fountains of the Bassin de Latone at Versailles is still operational. Cast-iron pipes were used in the straight sections but curved pipes could only be constructed in more malleable lead.

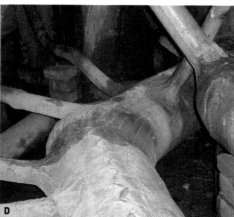

Alloys

Brasses and bronzes are the two main alloys used in garden design—especially for sculpture or sculptural elements such as containers and urns.

Brass is an alloy of copper and zinc, with between 60 and 90 per cent copper to 10–40 per cent zinc: a high copper content forms a reddish brass, while a low copper content gives a silvery-white finish. A zinc proportion higher than 36 per cent yields a much stronger, harder brass; less than 36 per cent zinc and the brass will be ductile, and can be worked into complex shapes. Resistant to corrosion and easily machinable, brass is of use in garden ornaments such as sundials and special fixings.

Bronze is a copper and tin alloy, with the copper content ranging from 75 to 95 per cent copper. *Gun metal* is about 90 per cent, and is the strongest of the bronzes; *bell metal* is about 80 per cent copper. *Phosphor bronze* is a copper–tin alloy to which phosphorus has been added in order to eliminate the copper oxide. This strengthens the bronze and increases corrosion resistance; phosphor bronze is used for cast moving parts such as components in a moving bridge. Bronze is used generally for corrosion-resistant castings, from bells and planters to pieces of sculpture, and is also used for water pumps.

For a list of metal trade organizations and websites, see Table 7, Appendix, page 228.

Left
Bronze nozzle jets in the Bosquet des Trois Fontaines, Versailles, France.

Lumber

"The qualities of trees vary exceedingly, and are very dissimilar, as those of the oak, the elm, the poplar, the cypress, the fir, and others chiefly used in buildings. The oak, for instance, is useful where the fir would be improper; and so with respect to the cypress and the elm. Nor do the others differ less widely, each, from the different nature of its elements, being differently suited to similar applications in building."
Marcus Vitruvius Pollio, *De Architectura*, Book II, Chapter 9

Lumber is wood from trees, and it is used in ways in which the character of the material remains essentially as it was in its natural state. So, rayon and acetate, which are made from wood, are not lumber products but are synthetic fibers, while glulam is a form of laminated, structural lumber. Lumber is a marvellous material for building, providing one understands its properties. It is strong in tension and compression, and correctly detailed lumber structures can last for several hundred years. Lumber that is inadequately seasoned, exposed to regular wetting and drying, and inadequately detailed can twist and crack and fall apart within a year or so.

Types of lumber

There are three main types of lumber in construction use:
- *hardwoods*: angiosperms—mainly deciduous broadleaved species such as ash, oak, and sycamore, which are temperate species, and mahogany, teak, African walnut, ipé, afrormosia, ebony, and balsa are from the tropics;
- *softwoods*: gymnosperms—coniferous and largely evergreen trees with needle leaves, such as pine, fir, spruce, larch, cedar, yew, and the giant redwood;
- *composite woods*: reassembled or man-made lumbers —e.g. plywood, glulam, and pressed wood such as MDF (medium-density fiberboard) etc. They may be softwoods or hardwoods and consist of offcuts and sawdust waste from the milling of lumber which are processed to make usable lumber.

For tables of lumber types and their properties, and lumber grading see Tables 8, 9, and 10 Appendix, pages 229 and 230.

Below
Lumber production process

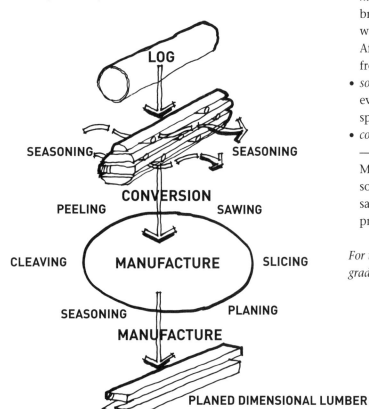

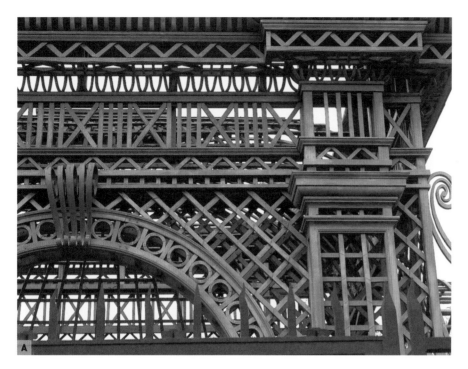

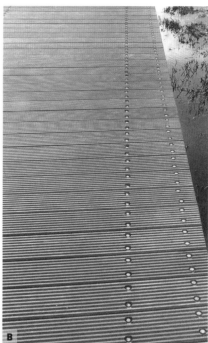

A Oak (hardwood) trellis, Versailles, France.

B Patterned hardwood decking on the boardwalk at Westergasfabriek, Amsterdam.

C The Douglas fir (softwood; *Pseudotsuga menziesii*) brise-soleil on the exterior of the temporary entrance pavilion (2008–11) at the Château de Versailles, France.

D Glulam (glue-laminated composite wood) beams, Kourion Amphitheatre Visitor Centre, Cyprus.

STEP BY STEP CONSTRUCTING HARDWOOD LUMBER DECKING

Iroko was chosen for this swimming pool deck at the Intercontinental Hotel, Aphrodite Hills Resort, Cyprus, because it is a naturally durable hardwood that fades to a light silver-gray in the sun. Lumber decking was used (rather than concrete, for example) because of its thermal comfort in a hot climate—particularly important for barefoot swimmers.

1 Durable hardwood battens and shims are fixed to a concrete base.

2 The finished deck surface just after the countersunk-screw-fixing of the sustainable iroko boards.

3 The deck surface after one year.

4 The deck surface after three years. The color has faded due to exposure to sunlight.

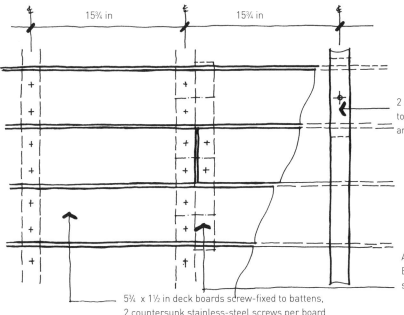

15¾ in   15¾ in

2 x 1½ in durable hardwood battens fixed
to concrete base at 23⅝ in centers using
anchors

Additional braces at board ends.
Braces to be at least 3 board widths
screw-fixed to battens

5¾ x 1½ in deck boards screw-fixed to battens,
2 countersunk stainless-steel screws per board
spaced as shown

Typical decking layout

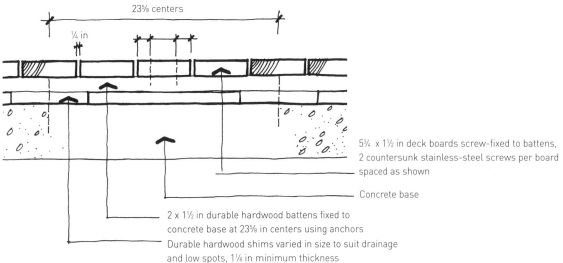

23⅝ centers

¼ in

5¾ x 1½ in deck boards screw-fixed to battens,
2 countersunk stainless-steel screws per board
spaced as shown

Concrete base

2 x 1½ in durable hardwood battens fixed to
concrete base at 23⅝ in centers using anchors

Durable hardwood shims varied in size to suit drainage
and low spots, 1⅛ in minimum thickness

Section through boards

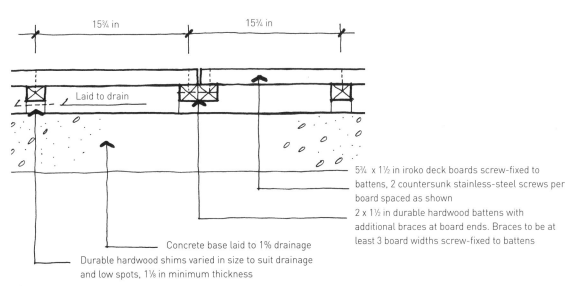

15¾ in   15¾ in

Laid to drain

5¾ x 1½ in iroko deck boards screw-fixed to
battens, 2 countersunk stainless-steel screws per
board spaced as shown

2 x 1½ in durable hardwood battens with
additional braces at board ends. Braces to be at
least 3 board widths screw-fixed to battens

Concrete base laid to 1% drainage

Durable hardwood shims varied in size to suit drainage
and low spots, 1⅛ in minimum thickness

Section through battens

Sustainability of lumber

Lumber can be sustainably sourced, but it is important to be careful. A major concern is the loss of virgin tropical forests, where many hardwoods are found and which are valuable as a carbon sink. The UN Food and Agricultural Organization (FAO) reports that primary forests are being lost or "modified" at the rate of about 15 million acres a year.[8] It should therefore be ensured that the source is a sustainably managed forest.

There are various sustainable lumber certification systems current, including the:

- PEFC, formerly known as the Pan European Forest Certification System;
- American Tree Farm System (ATFS);
- Canadian Standards Association Sustainable Forest Management Program (CSA, endorsed by PEFC in 2005);
- Forestry Stewardship Council (FSC);
- Sustainable Forestry Initiative (SFI, endorsed by PEFC in 2005) in the USA and Canada.

The FSC is a global non-governmental organization (NGO), which operates in 78 countries and certifies about 7 per cent of productive forests worldwide. In 2005–06, roundwood (raw, untreated lumber) from certified forests accounted for about 24 per cent of roundwood used globally, but only a tiny proportion was actually certified. Of all the certification schemes, that administered by the FSC is only marginally the biggest, but it has the most comprehensive worldwide coverage. However, in order to ensure adequate certification sustainable-lumber producers increasingly prefer dual certification.[9]

The lumber specifier should also have regard to CITES, which is the Washington Convention on International Trade in Endangered Species of Wild Fauna and Flora (1973), in order to ensure that the species is not in its appendix. This emphasizes the challenge of ensuring that lumber used in construction is actually as specified and from a sustainable source.

Strength

Hardwoods include some of the strongest, most durable lumbers—but not all hardwoods are necessarily hard. For instance balsa, which is extremely soft, is a hardwood. The essential characteristic of hardwood trees is that they are flowering and broadleaved. Softwoods have the essential characteristic of being conifers, the great majority of which are evergreen; larch is the most notable deciduous (or leaf-shedding) conifer.

The weight of solid wood tissue averages about 94 lbs/ft³, but its density varies according to grain, the proportion of denser heartwood and to less dense sapwood, and moisture content, so many tree species are much lighter than this. They can vary from dense lignum vitae, at 78 lbs/ft³, to balsa, which is a mere 10 lbs/ft³. Hardwoods are predominantly 30 lbs/ft³ and upwards, while softwoods are in the main less than 35 lbs/ft³.

Wood densities as compared to other materials:

Material	Density: lbs/ft³
Metals	162.56–710
Stone	130–200
Plastics	56.19–87.4
Solid wood tissue	c.94
Hardwoods	> 30
Softwoods	< 35

Strength in lumber varies greatly with species; it can also vary between individual trees (depending on how quickly they grew, in what soil, and with how much light), between different parts of the same tree, and with different directions in the grain of the lumber. It is therefore necessary to grade the lumber, and this is done by machine and by visual inspection of the following characteristics:
- knots;
- slope of grain;
- wane (the natural rounded surface of a log, with or without bark, on any face or edge of sawn lumber);
- fissures;
- resin and bark pockets; and
- distortion.

Top
Section through a cut log showing the wane (or rounded edge), fissures due to splitting, and knots at the bottom left and right where there were branches, as well as growth rings.

Above
A trunk which has grown into a twisted shape.

Moisture content and seasoning

Lumber is strong in both tension and compression, and is elastic. However, the moisture content of wood can vary, typically from 5 per cent to more than 20 per cent. The greater the moisture content, the less strong is the lumber. As a result, wood with 28–30 per cent moisture content may be only two-thirds the strength of the same wood at 12 per cent moisture content. When moisture is reduced, the lumber shrinks and in consequence shows fewer tendencies to warp, split or shake, and has greater dimensional stability. Seasoned and dried lumber will be lighter and stronger. The sap in lumber is a food for fungi and parasites, so if it is removed the wood is less attractive to fungus and parasites. For example, reduction to below 20 per cent moisture content reduces dry rot. Dry, well-seasoned lumber is easier to work and therefore safer to machine work. Finally, high-moisture-content lumber is difficult to paint or varnish.

The moisture in wood occurs either in the form of "free" water, used to move nutrients in the vessels of the tree, or cell-wall ("bound") water, which is part of the structure of the individual cells. Removal of the free water reduces the moisture content to about 25 per cent, and this occurs fairly quickly by capillary action. However, removal of the bound water from the cells is more challenging because it changes the size and form of those cells, and so has to be done carefully over time.

Therefore, in order to use lumber as a structural element it is necessary to reduce its moisture content further to about 15 per cent, and this is done by either:
• air seasoning; or
• artificial, kiln drying.

Air seasoning uses natural airflow: the lumber is stacked under cover in order to keep off the rain and sunlight, and this can take from two months for softwoods to 12 months for hardwoods in a temperate climate.

Kiln drying involves heated and forced air circulation at temperatures below 194°F for hardwoods in either a single compartment or in a trolley system in which the trolleys pass through different chambers. This is done for a shorter time than natural air seasoning, usually for 10–14 days. High-temperature kiln drying, with temperatures of 194–239°F, is used for softwoods. Kiln drying cannot be applied to structural lumber in excess of 1¾ in thick, so air seasoning and kiln drying, are often combined. Kiln drying kills fungi and insects in the lumber.

There exist proprietary softwood and hardwood products that have been steam heated to 356–419°F to dry them. This results in a 4–7 per cent moisture content. Such heating changes the chemical and physical structure of the lumber, which renders it more durable but does reduce its

TIP AVOIDING PROBLEMS WITH END GRAIN

One way to avoid problems with end grain is to minimize it: the rails of this post and rail fence have been cleft or split along the grain, which exposes less of the susceptible end grain.

A Green oak fixed with wood dowels at Shakespeare's Globe theatre, London, opened in 1997. Metal dowels and fixings corrode due to the tannin in the oak.

B Detail of green oak construction (note the oak dowels), Centre for Alternative Technology, Machynnlleth, Wales.

C Early sixteenth-century green oak construction, market hall, Pembridge, England.

D Exposed and unprotected end grain tends to rot.

E End grain also splits easily, as is the case with this beam which has been bolted together.

bending strength. It is argued that such heated lumber is more stable than untreated wood, and does not require a preservative.[10]

Note that seasoned lumber can still absorb moisture, and it is necessary to store it carefully. There is no point in ensuring that lumber in the factory or mill is correctly seasoned and then storing it on site in uncontrolled conditions, in a container in which it might be improperly stacked and unprotected for two or three months, resulting in twisting and distortion.

There are a number of chemical treatments for lumber, of which a promising one is acetylation (Accoya is its trade name). This treats the lumber with acetic anhydride, which changes the free hydroxils (molecules of oxygen and hydrogen) in the material into acetyls. The point of this is that it is the free hydroxils that absorb and release water from a lumber. By changing them into acetyls, the material no longer absorbs or releases water and becomes more durable.

Note, too, that it is perfectly possible to use "green" lumber if the relevant processes are understood. Traditional, half-lumbered construction used green, unseasoned oak—as does Shakespeare's Globe theatre in London, which was built using traditional techniques in 1997. Green lumber can be very suitable for landscape and garden structures.

Normal lumber construction uses dried lumber, seasoned by kiln or air drying. However, the drawbacks to the use of seasoned lumber are that it is hard and difficult to cut. Oak dries slowly—and air-dried lumber can anyway take several years to season—and it has a high coefficient of shrinkage on drying. This means that a second cut is required after drying, and seasoned oak tends to split, so making joints difficult to form. Consequently, seasoned-oak lumber frames are expensive and construction takes time.

Newly cut oak is easier to work and does not suffer these disadvantages; there has therefore been a renewal of interest in some countries in its use. Typically, the design will allow for surface splitting and will involve the use of dowels or stainless-steel connectors because of the problems of tannin attack on mild steel. Generally, design follows either the model of traditional methods (like Shakespeare's Globe) or that of modern construction and structural analysis, incorporating the use of metal connectors. Either way, green oak used in this fashion can offer an attractive alternative to glulam (glued, laminated lumber).[11]

For a table of levels of lumber treatability, see Table 11, Appendix, page 230.

Below
End grain rots easily and therefore should be allowed to dry. Here lumber edging has been laid touching, with the result that it has dried slowly and the ends have rotted.

Durability and ease of preservation

The American Lumber Standard Committee (ALSC) oversees accreditation and standards for grading lumber. Several agencies accredited by the ALSC publish gradng rules. The "treatability" of lumber by wood preservatives is determined by the porosity of the lumber: highly porous lumber is more treatable than relatively less porous varieties. Note that sapwood has different characteristics to heartwood, and is discounted—except for certain lumbers, which are predominantly sapwood and therefore not durable.

Lumbers can change and deteriorate for a various reasons, some which can be addressed by lumber selection at felling or in the mill, and some of which need to be addressed in construction:

To protect lumber from these problems it is possible to use preservative treatments, which can be classified as:
- staining;
- painting;
- oiling; or
- impregnation;

and these can be applied thus:
- by brush and spray, as with painting—which typically requires repeating every four to five years—or preservative gels;
- by deluge, dipping or steeping for a short period of minutes—usually using organic solvent treatments;
- by the hot and cold open-tank method used for fence posts, which are submerged in tanks heated to 176–194°F. These are simmered for two to three hours and then absorb the preservatives as the lumber cools;
- by pressure impregnation under a vacuum;
- by diffusion, involving long-term soaking of green lumber in a waterborne preservative or gaseous diffusion of volatile compounds—particularly appropriate for large structural lumber;
- by injection, typically boron-paste injection of large-dimension structural lumbers or joist ends.

Preservatives include:
- oilborne: tar oil and creosote;
- organic solvents, e.g. copper naphthalene; and
- waterborne, e.g. copper, chrome, and arsenic.

As can be gathered from the table of lumber durability (*see Table 11, Appendix, page 231*), some of these materials are not as durable used out of doors as they are indoors, so the best varieties to use are naturally rot-resistant lumbers such as western red cedar (*Thuja plicata*), redwood (*Sequoia sempervirens*) and black locust (*Robinia pseudoacacia*). Their natural polyphenols help protect them from insect attack.

For a table of lumber species resistant to marine borers, see Table 11, Appendix, page 231.

Table of lumber deterioration

Process or agent of deterioration	Effect
Fire	charring
Mechanical, by loading or abrasion	fracture, loss of surface, structural disintegration
Water and freeze–thaw	color fade and splitting
Sunlight	color fade
Chemicals	structural disintegration
Bacteria	discoloration
Fungi, moulds, wet and dry rot	discoloration and structural disintegration
Marine borers	tunneling and loss of strength
Insects	tunneling and exit holes

Glass

"Glass is arguably the most remarkable material ever discovered by man. Made from the melting and cooling of the earth's most abundant material … It has given us the lens, the bottle, the fiber optic cable, fabrics, and the window"
Michael Wigginton, *Glass in Architecture*[12]

The basic ingredients of glass have not changed in some five millennia, since it was first made in the Middle East for decoration and jewelry. Its first use in China dates to about 5000 BC. The basic ingredients of glass are:
- sand (silica: SiO_2);
- soda (sodium bicarbonate: Na_2CO_3); and
- lime (calcium oxide: CaO, from limestone).

The sodium bicarbonate lowers the melting point of silica from 4,172°F to 2,732°F, and the lime, along with magnesium oxide (MgO) and aluminum oxide (AlO), which additionally makes the material more resistant to chemicals, makes the resultant glass insoluble. Glass may also have other elements added to it—such as lead, to make "lead glass," which is more brilliant and sparkling because of its increased refractive index.

Glass is an amorphous solid. Its color depends on the presence of elements; the usual green-colored glass of the classical world owed its distinctive hue to the presence of iron.

Modern manufacture

Typically, glass is made from two-thirds raw materials (15 parts sand:5 parts soda:4 parts lime) mixed with one-third of recycled glass (or cullet): this is batched or mixed in proportion and then heated at 2,732°F in a gas-fired furnace. The consequent molten glass is homogenized and refined by removing bubbles.

Most window, or flat, glass is produced using the float process devised by Sir Alastair Pilkington and Kenneth Bickerstaff in the 1950s, whereby a continuous ribbon of molten glass is floated over a bath of melted tin and then subjected to nitrogen under pressure to make a polished top surface. The glass is then laminated or silvered (to make mirrors), or otherwise treated. Reheating and rapid cooling forms toughened glass. Bottles and jars are formed by blowing and pressing techniques.

Plate glass can be made by rolling semi-molten glass between rollers. This is cheaper than the float process, but does not produce a flat surface. Consequently it is mainly used for greenhouses. (This form of plate glass is easily cut with a glass cutter.)

Left
Glass mulch at the Festival des Jardins at Chaumont-sur-Loire, France.

Below
Glass noise barriers, Musée du Quai Branly, Paris, France.

Applications in external works

Glass can be used to form walls and screens, and can be used as a decorative element: a classic case is bottle-bottom paving, which is just the bottoms of bottles set in mortar or concrete. Noise barriers may be made of glass, though this practice is far commoner in France and The Netherlands than in some other countries. There are four forms of glass we should be especially concerned with:
- toughened glass;
- wired glass;
- laminated glass; and
- glass bricks.

Toughened glass This is also known as "tempered" glass, and is a safety glass which is five to six times stronger than annealed glass. It shatters into small pieces when broken. Safety glass is used in telephone booths and because of its strength it is also used in structural applications such as unframed glass doors. It is manufactured by placing sheet glass on a roller table and passing it through a furnace at 1,112°F and then air cooling it rapidly. During cooling the centre of the glass remains flat, thereby stressing and toughening the structure of the material. Toughened glass cannot be cut after manufacture.

There is an alternative chemical-toughening process where a 0.1 mm thick surface layer of glass is forced into compression by an induced exchange of the sodium ions (which are electrically changed atoms, owing to an electron change). This is done by dipping the whole sheet into a molten potassium nitrate bath. Such chemical-toughened glass is not a safety glass, and has to be laminated to ensure it is safe; however, it is very strong.

Below left
Glass wall at Broadgate Square, London.

Below
A screen of toughened glass at the Muziekgebouw aan't IJ, Amsterdam.

Wired glass This is formed by pressing two plates of semi-molten glass around a stainless-steel mesh to form a sandwich. The result is a cheap glass, but the process weakens the material and the shards when broken are sharp. The wire mesh is usually on a ⅜ in grid. This type of glass has an industrial feel, and is often used for glazed factory roofs. It is available both clear and opaque.

Laminated glass Sandwiched layers of toughened glass may be bonded together, usually using transparent polyvinyl butyral resin (PVB), and the resultant laminations may be duplicate or triplicate. The bonding takes place using both heat and pressure, so the PVB becomes transparent and the sandwich appears clear and acts as one unit (the laminations can be seen at the edges). However, the polymer PVB "interlayers" are ductile and tough, ensuring that cracks do not pass through the sandwich and that, when cracked, the laminated glass holds together.

In practice, the PVB spreads impact loads, thus making the structure stronger as well as binding the lamination so that it does not fall apart. It also increases sound insulation, so glazed noise barriers are best made of laminated glass. The PVB also cuts out most ultraviolet-light penetration.

Glass bricks These are available in various sizes: typical dimensions include 6 x 6 x 4 in, 6 x 8 x 4 in and 8 x 8 x 4 in. They are often square in shape, and laid in a "grid bond" with silicon adhesive or cement mortar. The bricks are available clear, frosted or colored. They were particularly associated with Modernist and industrial architecture of the 1920s and 1930s, and have been recurrently used since then.

Below left
Glass bridge, Victoria Square shopping center, Belfast, Northern Ireland.

Below centre
Screen made of Profilit, a translucent channel section glass, Borneo, Amsterdam.

Below right
Glass wind screen under the Grande Arche, La Défense, Paris.

Left
Corrugated glass wall, Casa da Música, Porto, Portugal.

Above
Glass block wall, Edo-Tokyo Museum, Tokyo, Japan.

Basic types of glass used in construction

Glass type	Uses	Minimum–maximum nominal thicknesses
Clear float	where clear undistorted vision is required	1/16 in
Clear sheet	where some distortion is acceptable; superseded by float glass, except for greenhouses	1/16–1/4 in
Patterned	a decorative glass, acts as a screen; available tinted	1/8–1/4 in
Roughcast	knobbly surface, acts as a screen; used in factories; available tinted	3/16–3/8 in
Polished wired	clear wired glass for fire resistance	1/4 in
Roughcast wired	used for fire resistance and rooflights	1/4 in
Toughened glasses		
Clear float	where impact strength and safety is required, e.g. glazed doors, side panels	1/8–3/4 in
Enameled clad	clear float and enameling, fired and toughened	1/4–3/8 in
Body-tinted float	for safety and solar-gain control	1/8–1/2 in
Surface-modified float	for safety and solar-gain control	1/4–1/2 in
Roughcast	for safety and solar-gain control	1/4–3/8 in
Patterned	for safety and solar-gain control	1/8–1/4 in
Laminated glasses		
Safety	risk areas such as balustrades, screens, and overhead glass, as the broken glass is held together by the lamination interlayer/s	3/16–5/16 in
Vandal-resistant	security	1/4–7/8 in
Bullet-resistant	security	3/4–7 3/4 in

Above
Cullet (waste glass) taken from the site of the 1870s Siemens plate-glass plant at St Helens, England.

Recycled glass In the United States there is increasing use of recycled glass (cullet) in road, footpath, and landscape construction. In particular, mixed-color cullet which consists of unsorted, clear (or "flint"), brown, and green glass is used. For example, Washington State's Department of Transportation specification for roads and bridge construction allows use of 15 per cent recycled glass in asphalt. Glass is also used in grading and ground modeling—as a material, rather like a pea shingle. Glass aggregate has good compaction qualities.

All these applications arise on the basis of cheap waste glass, which has been crushed and screened to 1/16–1/2 in so that it is safe to handle. Bottle glass, the main source of waste glass, contains relatively few shards compared with plate glass, and on crushing it becomes rounded and less sharp. As a result, crushed-glass aggregate is no more dangerous than crushed-rock aggregate, providing it is properly processed.

Design interest in the external use of recycled glass covers applications in which its qualities of sparkle and color are visible. It is used as a "decorative mulch." Glasphalt, a base-course road material marketed by RMC, is 30 per cent crushed glass, mixed with limestone and asphalt. Other uses of cullet include substituting it for sharp paving-bedding sand.

Polymers (plastics and rubber)

Polymers consist of large molecules organized in chains; proteins and DNA are examples. Polymers used in construction include plastics and materials such as rubber, which are classified as elastomers. They are relatively soft at natural temperatures and hence are elastic.

"Plastics" is a general term for a wide range of synthetic or semi-synthetic organic solids. The word derives from the Greek *plastikos* meaning "fit for molding," and the malleability of plastics permits them to be shaped by casting, extruding, or pressing. Because of their organic basis (most synthetic plastics are made from hydrocarbons such as oil or coal), they tend to melt at fairly low temperatures.

Plastics and elastomers are both relatively new materials. Natural rubber from the Brazilian Pará rubber tree (*Hevea brasiliensis*) was first introduced to Europe in the eighteenth century and used for rubberized cloth. In 1839, Charles Goodyear made the first vulcanized rubber by heating the natural material with sulphur.

Plastics have a shorter history of just over 150 years. The first totally new plastics were natural resins, such as a celluloid called Parkesine (1855), made from cellulose and used as a false ivory; and cellulose acetate (1865), made from cotton or tree fiber.

Synthetic plastics are a twentieth-century phenomenon. In 1907, Leo Baekeland invented phenol formaldehyde, or Bakelite, which was the first mass-produced plastic. Produced first as an electrical insulator, Bakelite is the brittle brown material of 1930s radios and 1950s television cases. In the 1920s and 1930s, developments in chemistry technology (stimulated by explosives manufacture in the First World War) led to chemically derived synthetics largely made from coal gas—such as acrylic, polystyrene, nylon, polyethylene, and polyvinyl chloride. Similarly, the Second World War stimulated the production of artificial rubbers, such as neoprene, when the Japanese conquered the major, natural-rubber-producing areas of Southeast Asia.

Glass-reinforced plastic (GRP), or fiberglass, is a composite material consisting of a plastic polymer reinforced with fine glass fibers. Typically thermoset plastics (see overleaf) are used for GRP production —usually polyester (using butanone as a catalyst), but vinylester or epoxy can also be used. Composite materials, such as GRP and carbon-fiber reinforced plastics (CFRP), which combine the properties of two different materials, are increasingly important and tend to be developed for aircraft and spacecraft technology and then spread to other applications.

Above
A 1950s Bakelite television.

Manufacturing and applications

All modern plastics are based on carbon atoms and their abilities to form compounds with:

• hydrogen;
• oxygen;
• nitrogen;
• chlorine; or
• fluorine.

The combinations are arranged in chains of complex molecular compounds called polymers, made of large macromolecules composed of monomers, or chemical-bonded small molecules. Each monomer, therefore, consists of over 10,000 atoms (compare with water, H_2O, which has just three atoms).

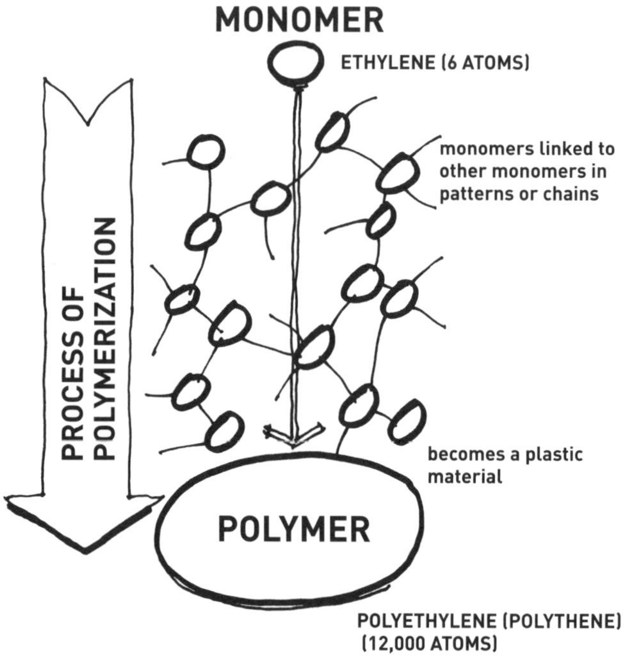

Below
Thermosets can only be heated and cooled once. Thermoplastics, however, can be reheated and reshaped, and therefore can be more easily recycled than thermosets. Forming techniques include compression molding, extrusion, and injection molding.

MONOMER
ETHYLENE (6 ATOMS)

monomers linked to other monomers in patterns or chains

PROCESS OF POLYMERIZATION

becomes a plastic material

POLYMER

POLYETHYLENE (POLYTHENE) (12,000 ATOMS)

Polymerization process

Table of plastics production

Metamorphic change		Plastics		Multi-change
	thermosets		thermoplastics	
	soften	heat	soften	
	shaping		shaping	
	heating/curing		stiff/solid	
	stiff/solid		heat	
	cooling		shaping	

Thermosets are plastics, such as Bakelite and epoxy resin, which once cured (generally by heating at over 392°F) cannot then flex or soften. Thermoplastics such as polypropylene soften in heat and harden when cool, and return to their original shape: they are said to possess a plastic "memory."

Applications of plastics and rubber to landscape construction include the following:
- liners and waterproofing, as in pond liners—e.g. GRP;
- buffers and expansion joints—e.g. epoxy resin or polysulphide expansion joints;
- geotextiles of polypropylene (PP) and polyethylene (PE) —or composites of the two, such as Terram (a permeable, non-woven thermally bonded geotextile made of a composite of polypropylene (PP) and polyethylene (PE));
- drainage pipes and ducts—e.g. polyethylene, polypropylene;
- geogrids (forms of paving): rigid grids of polypropylene or polyethylene, or flexible grids of polyester with a PVC/latex or polyethylene protection;
- paints and coatings—e.g. acrylic paint;
- paving products such as transparent epoxy-resin-bound asphalt;
- adhesives—e.g. epoxy resin; and
- laminated-glass interlayers, such as polyvinyl butyral resin (PVB).

For a table of plastic types and applications, see Table 12, Appendix, page 232.

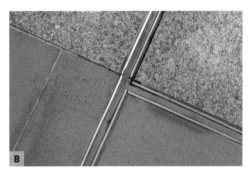

A Butyl liner, wet retention basin, Canon headquarters, Reigate, England.

B Polymer expansion joint in paving.

C Parking lot incorporating an "ecoblock" geogrid laid on a "Terram" filter layer.

D EPDM (ethylene-propylene-diene monomer) safety paving for a play area.

E Conveyor-belt neoprene rubber was used to cover concrete benches at Tate Modern, London.

Above
Rubberized paved play surface,
boulevard Richard Lenoir, Paris.

Elastomers: rubber and synthetic rubber

Rubber is a naturally occuring material found in the latex of plants—particularly the Pará rubber tree (*Hevea brasiliensis*), but also in common plants such as the fig tree and the common dandelion. In the 1840s, rubber from the Malayan gutta-percha tree (*Palaquium gutta*) was used as an insulator and later for golf balls. In 1876, Henry Wickham collected seeds of the Pará rubber tree in Brazil for Kew Gardens, in England, and seedlings were later sent to Southeast Asia. This led to the development of the Malaysian rubber plantations, which are the largest producers of natural rubber in the world. Natural rubber is a polymer of isoprene, and is both a thermoplastic and an elastomer. However, if moderately heated or "vulcanized" (a process invented by Charles Goodyear in the 1830s) it becomes a thermoset, and this improves its durability.

The two main forms of elastomer are those that may be vulcanized—"unsaturated" elastomers, such as natural rubber or butyl rubber—and "saturated" elastomers, such as silicone rubber. Saturated in this case refers to the material's molecular make-up, and this type of elastomer is a compound with no double or triple molecular bonds; unsaturated elastomers have such double or triple bonds.

The first synthetic rubber polymer (a methyl isoprene) was tested in Germany in 1909, but methyl isoprene degrades quickly in the presence of oxygen so it was not successful commercially. Later, in the 1920s, US and German concerns about British dominance of the world supplies of the natural material led to pressure to invent commercially viable synthetic rubber. Its manufacture grew out of independent studies by the American Wallace Carothers, the Russian scientist Sergey Lebedev and the German chemist Hermann Staudinger. In the 1920s, Lebedev developed an industrial process for manufacturing butadiene, and the first factories began production in 1932. In 1931, the US chemicals firm DuPont had developed "neoprene;" highly resistant to heat and chemicals such as oil, it is used in fuel hoses and as an insulating material in machinery.

In the 1930s, German scientists developed "Buna rubbers." These were "copolymers," meaning that their polymers were made up from not one but two monomers, in alternating sequences. One such Buna rubber, known as "GR-S" (Government Rubber Styrene), which is a copolymer of butadiene and styrene, became the basis for US synthetic rubber production during the Second World War.

Toxicity and health concerns associated with plastics and elastomers

Because they are insoluble in water and relatively chemically inert, pure plastics generally have low toxicity in their finished state and can pass through the digestive system with no ill effects.

However, plastics often contain a variety of toxic additives. For example, plasticizers are often added to brittle plastics like PVC in order to make them pliable enough for use in food packaging, toys, tubing, shower curtains, and other items. Traces of these chemicals can leach out of the plastic when it comes into contact with food. In consequence, for instance, the plasticizer most commonly used worldwide in PVC, di-2-ethylhexyl phthalate (DEHP), has been banned in the European Union.

Moreover, while the finished plastic may be non-toxic, the monomers used in its manufacture may be toxic—and small residues of these chemicals may remain in the material. Some polymers may also decompose into the monomers, or other toxic substances, when heated. Some people are allergic to latex and to natural rubber; so, for example, wearing rubber gloves can cause severe anaphylactic shock.

Environmental concerns

Plastics are durable and degrade slowly; however, burning them can release toxic fumes and the manufacture of plastics often creates large quantities of chemical pollutants.

Plastic recycling is therefore a matter of increasing importance. Thermoplastics can be melted and recycled, and thermoset plastics can be ground and used as fillers. Some plastics can be broken down to form a "feedstock" for new plastic manufacture.

However, recycling plastics has been difficult. One problem is the difficulty of automating the sorting of plastic waste, which, as a result, is labor-intensive. However, mechanical sorting processes are being developed to increase plastic-recycling capacity and efficiency. Unfortunately, some products are made up of several plastics and can be uneconomical to recycle. Other products, such as polystyrene packaging, are rarely recycled because they are currently so cheap; however, this may change in view of oil-industry supplies increasing in cost. Unrecyclable plastic waste is currently placed in landfill sites or incinerated.

Furthermore, the high embodied energy in plastics means they are of concern (*see Table 1, Appendix, page 225*). They are very useful materials, but it is salutary to remember that they were not used at all in construction until the twentieth century. If they can be dispensed with, there are arguments for no longer using them.

Below
Plastics bundled up for recycling at a plant.

Biodegradable plastics Biodegradable plastics can break down with exposure to sunlight (e.g. ultraviolet radiation), water, bacteria, enzymes, or wind abrasion. Obviously, some of these forms of degradation only occur if the plastic is exposed, while other forms will only be effective if certain conditions are found in landfill or composting systems. Other tactics include the use of starch powder mixed with plastic as a filler to allow it to degrade more easily, but this does not result in the complete breakdown of the plastic. Genetically engineered bacteria can synthesize a completely biodegradable plastic, such as "Biopol," but this material is expensive. BASF makes "Ecoflex," a fully biodegradable polyester for food-packaging applications. There are also indications that some naturally occuring bacteria are developing the ability to degrade plastics.[13]

Bioplastics or organic plastics These come from a biomass source rather than a fossil-fuel source. They are therefore biologically degradable, and so are of particular interest to packaging or plastic-bag manufacturers. Cellulose is perhaps the best-known bioplastic, and is produced from wood cellulose. So far, bioplastics have not been used much in construction but they are an area to watch.

Wood–plastic composite materials These composites of plastics and wood waste are becoming increasingly available. Wood–plastic composite is wood and a thermoset (such as resins formed from polyester and epoxy) or wood and a thermoplastic (such as polyethylene and polyvinyl chloride, or PVC). Bakelite, the first thermoset plastic, was made from wood flour and phenol-formaldehyde. Today, the wood constituent in wood–plastic composites is either wood flour or sawdust. The fibers in these materials are small, and therefore their structural characteristics are not strong compared to the glass or carbon fibers found in other composites (such as glass-reinforced plastic). They do, however, provide cheap, low-maintenance lumber substitutes for uses such as decking, fence rails, and handrails. The main point of these materials is that they recycle wood waste. Thermoset plastic resins or fiber-reinforced polymers (FRPs) make wood composites, which can be used for water tanks.

Polymer degradation

Plastics are often subject to cracking, fading, and disintegration owing to the effects of ultraviolet light, heat, or chemicals. These break the long chains of polymers, which are the key to the integrity of the material. For example, ultraviolet light—especially sunlight—can cause the disintegration of pool liners, and so the liners should be shaded from the sun by use of overhang edges or by coverings in another material, which might range from cobbles to tiles. The six main plastics found in daily life are polyethylene; polypropylene; polyvinyl chloride (PVC); polyethylene terephthalate (PET); polystyrene and polycarbonate. Of these, polyethylene and polypropylene are sensitive to oxidation and ultraviolet light, PVC loses color at high temperatures and becomes brittle, PET is sensitive to acids, while alkalis break down polycarbonates. However, it is possible to add ultraviolet-light stabilizers to some plastics as a protective layer.

Left
Eco-block (a cell matrix paver or geogrid) made of recycled, high-density polyethylene.

Above
Recycled polyethylene boards made from plastic bags have been used in benches, decks, and revetments as a lumber substitute for more than 20 years. Plastic boards have a high coefficient of expansion compared with lumber.

Earth, turf, and non-conventional materials

Low-technology techniques are seen in traditional structures using soil and sod. They are not widely used much in many developed countries, largely because they have been forgotten (many rural cottages were built of sod until the nineteenth century, but have since disappeared). However, historic building conservation and the rise of interest in "low-tech" or alternative technology has done much to promote some of these techniques. Such structures are low in their use of embodied energy.

Compressed earth, cob, and pisé

Mud bricks have already been mentioned, and rammed earth ("cob" in southwest England; *pisé* or *pisé de terre* in France) is a similar traditional technique of construction that uses earth compacted in layers, 4–10 in thick, between layers of movable lumber formwork. This usually sits on top of a stone foundation, which rises to about 24 in above ground level. The tamping may be done by hand, pneumatically or, reportedly, by using cattle or oxen. Usually, there is no moisture barrier between the stone foundation and the earth wall above for fear that it would cause moisture to condense below the barrier. The formwork traditionally consisted of panels of tongued-and-grooved boards set between lumber posts and kept apart by lateral props, with rope to hold the tops together. Today, the formwork is usually reinforced plywood or metal sheet, and layers of earth are separately rammed.

Compressed earth walls should be wide—about 24 in—and, typically, should taper inwards.

The face of the earth wall is rendered with a quicklime-putty and sand mix, and limewashed in order to offer further protection. The wall should be sheltered by an overhanging roof or capping of at least 8 in to protect it from rain. The cob or rammed earth shrinks as it dries, and so construction has to allow for shrinkage.

Such techniques tend to be thought of as best used for building construction, but they can equally be used for landscape walls, always providing that the rammed earth is protected by a capping with an overhang.

Cob works best with a clay soil–sometimes mixed with dung and with straw added to help bind it and reduce the cracking caused by drying out. Nineteenth-century French accounts describe the addition of gravel. As with stucco, it is important to allow the surface to "breathe," and impervious vinyl paints or cement mortar and gypsum plaster should therefore not be used with cob.

The site should be dry, and it may be necessary to build diversion swales.

Left
Turf field boundary wall at Hoge Veluwe National Park, near Arnhem, The Netherlands.

Above
With a thatched topping and brick base (here hidden behind vegetation), this rammed-earth wall at Ashwell, Hertfordshire, England is at least 90 years old.

Top
To build the turf retaining wall at Canon headquarters, Reigate, England, the sod was thickly cut on site.

Above
The completed turf retention wall at Canon headquarters. The sod was laid stretcher bond and held together by steel reinforcement bars (the bamboo originally specified was not available).

Above
Chunam steep-slope stabilization, Hong Kong, China.

Turf and peat walls

Turf walls consist of thick grass sod—say, 20 x 24 in long and 6 in thick—placed stretcher bond and held together (until the grass roots grow through) by lumber stakes, or even steel reinforcement bars. The walls are best laid with a tapered base. They are very useful for providing a protective face for steep earth slopes at the angle of repose. The authors have used them in situations where the levels at the side of a road were higher than designed for; in such cases turf walls provide a cheap and attractive "rough" solution that uses on-site materials.

The Romans are said to have initially built part of Hadrian's Wall as a turf wall,[14] and in Scandinavia, Scotland and Ireland a similar technique uses peat walls. In Iceland, it is said that as late as 1900 half the dwellings were built of peat. Peat walls tend to be short-lived, unless they are constantly maintained. Terraced peat walls are used at the Royal Botanic Gardens in Edinburgh and the Logan Botanic Garden (also in Scotland) because they give acid soil conditions which are conducive to growing Himalayan plants. In Iceland, the walls were about 3–6 feet wide at the base and were faced with stone, with a vegetated top and stone foundation; the peat blocks were 6 in x 20 in x 5 ft. Both sod and peat blocks are allowed to dry after cutting, and the walls require periodic rebuilding every 15 to 20 years.[15]

Soil cement This is a mixture of soil and Portland cement, used sometimes in road and pipe bedding, and in steep-slope retention. The soil may be gravel, sand, clay, crushed stone, or quarry waste, but should not be an organic topsoil. The paste (cement–water mix) binds nodules of uncoated soil. Soil cement is strong in compression and shear strength but very weak in tension, and so cracks easily. Soil-cement roads require a protective wearing course, which may be asphalt or tar spray. Roadways require a wearing surface, which may be ⅛ in roadstone, or up to 1½ in for heavier traffic.

Chunam is similar to soil cement, and is known in Hong Kong for steep-slope stabilization—often using quicklime. However, it increases rainwater run-off and is unattractive, and has been superseded hydroseeding.

Top three images

This former gravel works at Hedeland, Denmark, has been redeveloped by I/S Hedeland, led by director Eric Juhl, and includes a golf course, woodland areas, footpaths, cycle tracks, and a 3,500-spectator arena (center row). Access to the arena is controled via a mound at the top of the terraces and visitors enter through gatehouses built of turf and lumber. The grassed terraces are 3 feet high with a 45-degree slope. Correct compaction and drainage during construction is the key to creating such mounded features. Beyond the arena are toilet blocks (top image)—with turf walls and roofs—and on either side are gravel parking areas which are screened by 3-foot high grass mounds.

Left

"Hydroseeding" is the term for a sprayed application of grass seed and a slurry mulch mix containing dye and fertilizers. Mulches can also consist of paper or wood. The process is used for steep-slope retention and for places that are difficult to access. In addition to grass seeding, it can be used for shrub and tree seeding. Note that hydroseeding will not stabilize a structurally unsound slope, but will resist surface erosion.

ELEMENTS

Earthworks and topsoil in relation to structures

Any sort of development that involves change to the surface of the Earth—whether roads, paths, pools, parking lots, or buildings—changes the natural lay of the land. The essence of landscape architecture is to ensure that such grading and earthworks fit in with the land and its ecology. Grading should be in sympathy with a natural setting. This is particularly crucial on sloping and hilly ground, but also applies in flat landscapes. However, this does not necessarily mean that the ground should follow the serpentine curves of the English Picturesque garden; it is also possible for formal features to respect the landscape.

Topsoil

Topsoil is a valuable resource, and should not be damaged unnecessarily. Different professions and trades have differing views on topsoil. Stereotypically, engineers view it as a substrate on which a structure must be placed, and their main interest is in its bearing capacity. If topsoil is insufficiently strong, for most engineers it must be cleared and replaced, rafted over or penetrated in order to reach a more solid ground layer.

The mining engineer views topsoil as the covering layer—a barrier to exploitation of the parent material—and therefore as something to be removed and placed to one side. The farmer views it as the basis of the farm's productive capacity. The gardener views topsoil as a habitat, and not at all as something to be exploited. It is the habitat of the plants that may be a garden's *raison d'être*.

Topsoil is a combination of the mineral and the biological: the main components of a silty, loam topsoil are 20–30 per cent water, 20–30 per cent air, 45 per cent

Below
The Water Gardens at Studley Royal, Yorkshire, England, are formal, with curved and circular shapes, but nevertheless complement the valley of the River Skell very well.

Below right
The Grecian Valley at Stowe, Buckinghamshire, England, is a man-made excavation designed by Lancelot Brown.

TIP SOIL COMPACTION

Topsoil is part of the zone of life on earth known as the biosphere. It should be treated gently and moved with care. Construction should be restricted and hauling routes defined and limited. Sandy soils are the most resilient while clay and peaty soils are the most vulnerable to compaction and disturbance. This photograph shows severe compaction after heavy rain on clay soil.

minerals and 5 per cent organic materials (both plant and animal life).

Of the above, the 40–60 per cent which is air and water lies in the "pore space," and so the whole forms a dynamic system that is easily disrupted if topsoil is compacted or moved. Compaction not only reduces the space for water and air, but causes the organic material which supports the soil structure to break down. The soil literally dies: a fertile soil becomes infertile.

Therefore, the extent and programming of construction works should be organized to minimize such damage or interference. Groundworks should be scheduled to avoid the wetter times of the year, and should not take place when it is raining or the site is wet. Furthermore, the extent of construction, including delivery routes, should be limited by fencing. Clay soils are more easily damaged than sand soils.

The process of forming topsoil consists of both chemical weathering, involving a change to the clay minerals in the soil, and mechanical weathering, which is the breaking up of the parent material owing to freeze–thaw action. No single soil is a product of just one process; however, in colder climates mechanical weathering dominates and the organic layer can be quite thin, while in warmer climates chemical weathering tends to dominate.

Below the topsoil lies the subsoil, which holds less visible life and is less fertile. From the point of view of the engineer, topsoil is likely to be of little structural value and should be stripped if a structure is to be built—while the subsoil may well be more suitable for supporting structures.

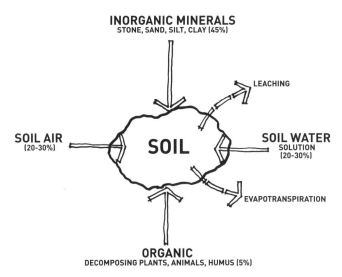

Topsoil composition

The table of soil types at the bottom of this page uses the US Department of Agriculture's categories, but there are other national and international systems. The USDA system has been influential in the Anglo-Saxon world, but in fact soil science has developed equally well in Russia, France and Germany—albeit along different lines. The Food and Agricultural Organization and the International Union of Soil Science have reconciled these different systems in the World Reference Base, but while this permits large-scale comparison and correlation of different national systems it is not applicable at a local scale.[1]

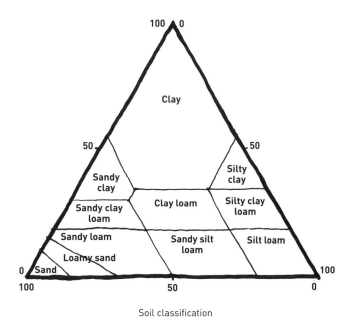

Soil classification

Particle size

Whatever the system, soil classes are affected by the mineral constituents of the soil, which in outline are:
- *sand* (and coarser) particles, which are visible to the naked eye;
- *silt* particles, which are like dust when dry and can be brushed off clothes; and
- *clay* particles, which are sticky when wet and hard when dry, and have to be scraped or washed off hands and boots.

Topsoil storage

If if it is necessary to disturb the topsoil, it should be stripped (only when dry) and stored in loosely dumped mounds no more than 6 ft high, so that the dead weight of the soil does not compact it. One metre high is preferable, if there is space. Compacted topsoil becomes 'dead', and therefore no more fertile than subsoil. Topsoil mounds, if they are to remain during the growing season, should be temporarily seeded with a clover and a deep-rooting plant such as chicory or lupins, which, like clover, are nitrogen-fixing. If storage is to be short-term—e.g. for two or three months—the topsoil should be seeded with a rapid-germinating and growing "green manure," such as a brassica (e.g. ryegrass (*Poa annua*)), which germinates within three weeks in summer and is subsequently dug in when the topsoil is moved. There should be no tracking of machinery or vehicles over the topsoil mounds, and they should be protected while awaiting reuse.

Soil types: US Department of Agriculture Classification

General terms		
Common names	Texture	Basic soil textural class names
Sandy soils	coarse	sandy loamy sand
	moderately coarse	sandy loam
Loamy soils	medium	loam silt loam silt
Loamy soils	medium	loam silt loam silt
	moderatly fine	clay loam sandy clay loam silty clay loam
Clayey soils	fine	sandy clay silty clay clay

Source: Soil Survey Staff, Keys to Soil Taxonomy, 10th edition (Washington, DC: USDA Natural Resources Conservation Service, 2006, http://soils.usda.gov/technical/classification/tax_keys/index.html

Groundwater

Groundwater is the water that lies below the soil surface, including water between soil particles and the water table, where the soil is totally saturated. The level of the groundwater may well vary with the seasons, and so the water table may rise and fall. The soil above the water table will not be dry, but it will not be saturated.

The groundwater may be affected by the laying of new drains and foundations, and this can adversely affect trees and other vegetation which is to be retained. It can also be necessary to drain groundwater locally if works entail cutting into the ground in order to divert the flow away from a new structure. For instance, a parking lot cut into a slope may require a French drain or a ditch laid along the upside of the lot.

Groundwater should not be polluted by disposal of waste liquids—such as sump oil, hydraulic fluid, diesel, paints, chemicals, or solvents—into the ground during construction.

Protection of trees

Existing trees should be surveyed at the beginning of works to ensure that they are healthy. If in doubt, consult an arboriculturist (a consultant tree surgeon), who may need to "core" the tree by boring into its center and extracting a small diameter cross-section to determine if there is significant rot. Generally, it is wiser to aim to keep younger trees rather than mature or old specimens, which are less able to adapt to the changes in groundwater and environment consequent on development happening nearby. Too often, large mature trees become stag-headed (their branches die back) when they are retained in the middle of a parking lot.

Below
How to keep a tree. At the Ecocenter at Hoge Veluwe National Park, The Netherlands, the groundwater was not changed and the light foundations of this single-story building ensured that the extent to which the tree roots were cut was minimized.

Bearing capacity of soil

A geotechnical soil survey is required for sites on which any significant loadbearing structures are to be built. These surveys are based on boreholes and core samples of the ground material. Additionally, check the history of the site to see if there are any quarry workings or underground structures which have been buried and inadequately filled or capped. It is useful to inspect old survey-mapping of the area. Chalk and limestone areas may have sinkholes or natural voids in the chalk. Clay pits may have been loosely filled in. Mining areas have shafts and workings which may not be immediately evident on the ground, so field and core surveys in such areas can be supplemented by other geotechnical techniques, such as geophysical surveys—including electromagnetic surveys and seismic tests if necessary.

Geotechnical surveys should describe the bearing capacity of the soil and its plasticity index, porosity, shear strength, compaction rates, and moisture content as well as the presence of harmful chemicals such as sulphates and salts, and toxic materials such as heavy metals. All this should be available prior to beginning grading design.

- *Bearing capacity* is the ability of soils to support loads imposed by roads, walls, buildings, or other structures. One common measure is the Californian Bearing Ratio (CBR), so called because it was first devised for the design of Californian turnpikes in the 1920s. Typically, this is greater than 5 per cent of the bearing ratio of crushed dolomitic limestone. If it is less than 5 per cent, then you have problems and need further engineering advice. Usually an additional capping layer of 13–23 in may be appropriate (see "Foundations," page 145).
- *Plasticity index* is a measure of the ability of a soil to expand and contract. For instance, shrinkable clay soils have a high plasticity index and expand and contract significantly dependent on water content (whether due to seasonal change or vegetation water demand) while sandy soils have a low plasticity index.
- *Shear strength* is the maximum strength of a soil beyond which collapse (as opposed to compression or consolidation) occurs. Collapse might include slope slippage or a structure sinking into peaty or marshy ground, or wet clay.

The form of the land may be described by contours or by spot elevations. Contours are lines joining levels of the same height, and are marked according to a constant height interval (e.g. 10 in, 20 in, or 40 in), while spot elevations are laid out to a regular grid. Design of the land is best done using contours, because this makes it possible to easily "see" the form of the land. The closer the contours are together the steeper the slope, and verticals —usually in the form of a structure, such as a retaining wall, which would be given spot elevations— are expressed by lines meeting. Both spot elevations and contours may be supplemented by cross-sections. Survey plans are based on either field surveys or on interpretations of aerial photographs, and currently the former are more accurate than the latter.

TIP SHRINKING AND SWELLING

Shrink–swell capacity is of particular concern in shrinkable clays, in which volume changes with water content owing to seasonal change. The ground can rise or fall, and therefore crack, dependent on the groundwater: when wet, the ground heaves or rises; when dry, it shrinks. Both processes can affect inappropriate foundations.[2]

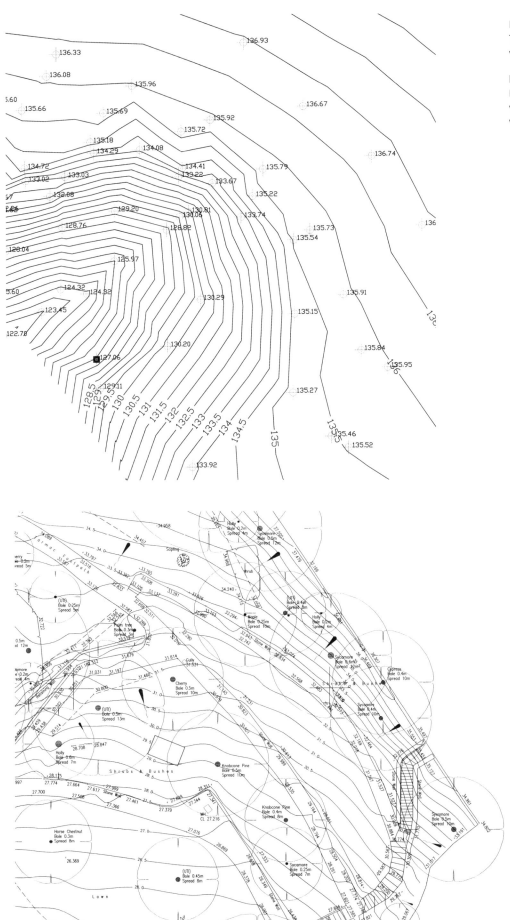

Left
Topographic survey spot elevations with contours superimposed

Below left
Extract from typical land survey with full information about roads, walls, vegetation, and contours.

Below

A grading diagram with analysis of
contours to indicate ridges, cliffs,
ravine, valley, and other slopes.

Rules of thumb for contours

- contours only make sense when read in pairs; a ridge will have a contour of the same height on both sides;
- contours never cross: don't attempt to show overhangs by contouring—use a section instead;
- contours do not merge or split;
- all contours close on themselves at some point: the easiest example to envisage is a small island, where a constant contour height will pass along the shore all the way round the island;
- contours should have a constant vertical interval (i.e. height difference); and
- the steepest slope occurs along a line perpendicular to the contours; this is the direction in which water will drain.

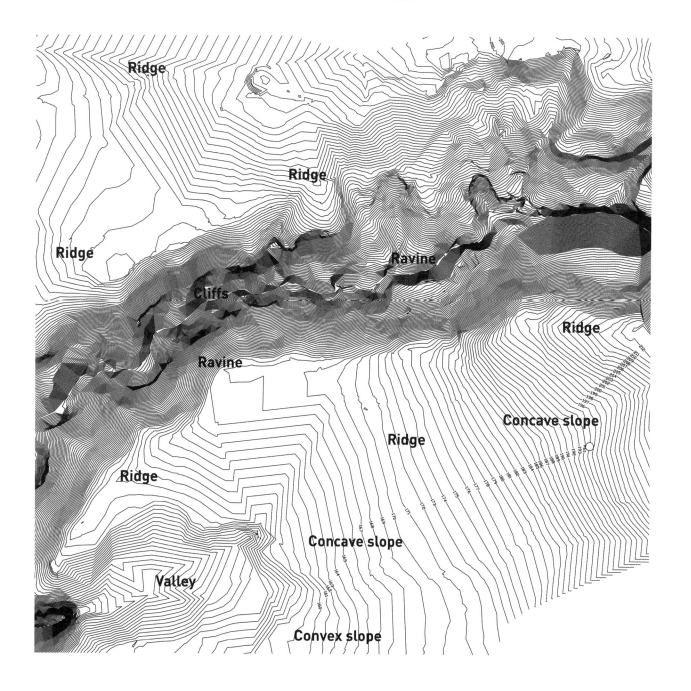

A grading diagram with analysis of contours to indicate ridges, cliffs, ravine, valley, and other slopes.

Cut and fill

It is best to balance the amounts of cut and fill on a site in order to avoid having to import and export material. It is usual to direct surfacewater away from the surface plane, which is the ground-floor slab of a proposed building. Ground levels around a building should be 6 in below the finished floor level. This can be done by:

- placing the floor slab on fill: this will raise the building above a slope and may make it visually prominent;
- raising the floor slab significantly above the finished ground: this may be particularly appropriate on steep slopes and where limited disturbance is desirable—the foundations may take the form of piles—and it can also be suitable in flood-prone areas (additionally, the area underneath the building can be used for storage);
- placing the slab on cut ground, in which case the surrounding earth should also be cut away in order to direct surfacewater around the building slab; earth can be mounded against the side of a building, but this requires sealing against moisture penetration and such seals can break;
- placing the slab on cut and fill, which is the most commonly desirable solution in that it generally involves the least disturbance to the site; the surfacewater drainage around the uphill half of the building should be directed to flow round the building.

Roads and parking lots—and also athletic fields—are essentially large planes, which can be sloped to provide surface drainage. They can be placed on the site as described above. However, in addition the surface itself should be drained—hence, the whole plane may slope, and this can be done by employing:

- *sheet drainage*, consisting of a single slope across the whole area;
- *double-slope sheet drainage*, in which the surface is sloped in two directions, resulting in diagonal contour lines;
- *valley drainage*, in which the drainage water is directed to the center of a road or path; this has the advantage of ensuring that surfacewater does not drain towards the buildings, but can appear strange when applied to large areas;
- *crowned or cambered drainage*, which is the most common technique for roads and streets: usually, the pavements are raised and curbed in order to form an edge channel, to which the road drainage can be directed from the center line of the road.

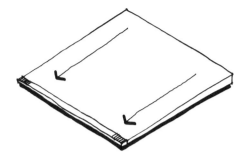

Sheet drainage

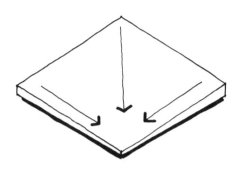

Double-slope sheet drainage

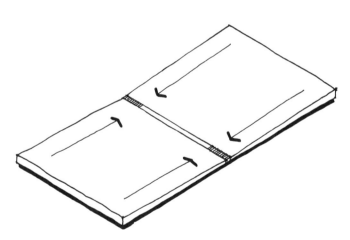

Valley drainage

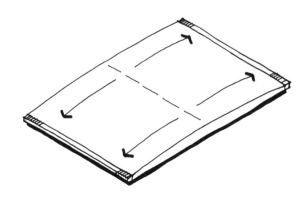

Crowned or cambered drainage

Drainage

Buildings and surfaces—whether roads or parking lots —are usually impermeable, and run-off drainage water has to be accommodated. Ideally, development should be planned in order to maximize the permeability of a site, and the rate of surfacewater run-off should be slowed by ensuring that buildings have a small footprint, by employing green roofs, and by minimizing the use of impermeable roads and footpaths. However, there is usually some decrease in the total permeability and drainage capacity of land when a greenfield site is developed. The consequent surfacewater run-off has to be dealt with either on or off site.

In built-up areas the conventional drainage approach has been to provide a surfacewater or combined drainage system; the latter directs site surfacewater through public sewers. However, one consequence of this can be flooding at times of high rainfall, and also a reduction in the amount of water being directed into the water table. It is better to deal with drainage within a site in part by directing rainfall into the ground by the following means:
- *soakaways*, which are holes filled with stones, into which drainage water is directed;
- *infiltration devices*, which are trenches or basins, rather like infiltration drains or soakaways, designed to direct water into the ground;
- *ditches* (rather than piped drainage), which may be up to 24 in deep and may have a V-shape (or near-vertical

walls in peaty soils) and can permit infiltration and also support wildlife;
- *filter strips*, which are areas of grassed and gently sloped ground designed to accommodate drainage run-off from impermeable hard surfaces, and filter silt and small particles;
- *swales*, which are shallow grassed ditches designed to flow slowly, so that the water is largely absorbed by permeable soils;
- *filter drains or French drains*, which are gravel-filled trenches with a permeable-pipe drain at the base, and permit surfacewater to enter the soil until it is saturated;
- *retention basins*, which may be dry or wet and store surfacewater run-off until streams or drains can cope with storm demand; or
- *bio-retention areas*, which are usually reed-filled basins designed to filter water prior to discharge via a piped or surface system.

Pools and ponds can also increase the total water capacity of a development site, and will additionally foster wildlife.

These approaches are all elements of Sustainable Urban Drainage Systems (SUDS). They work most efficiently in porous soils such as sand, gravels, and limestone, but are also usable in clay-soils areas.[3]

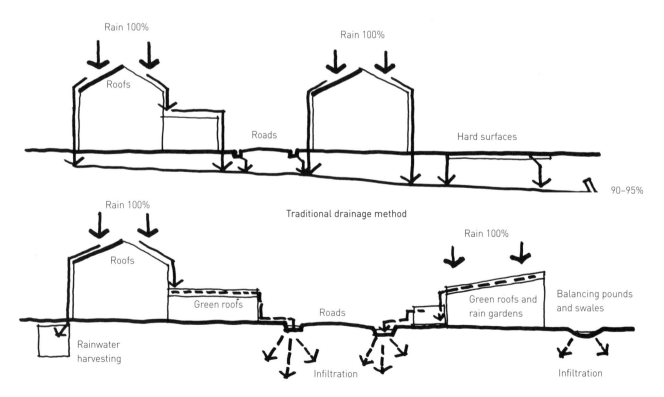

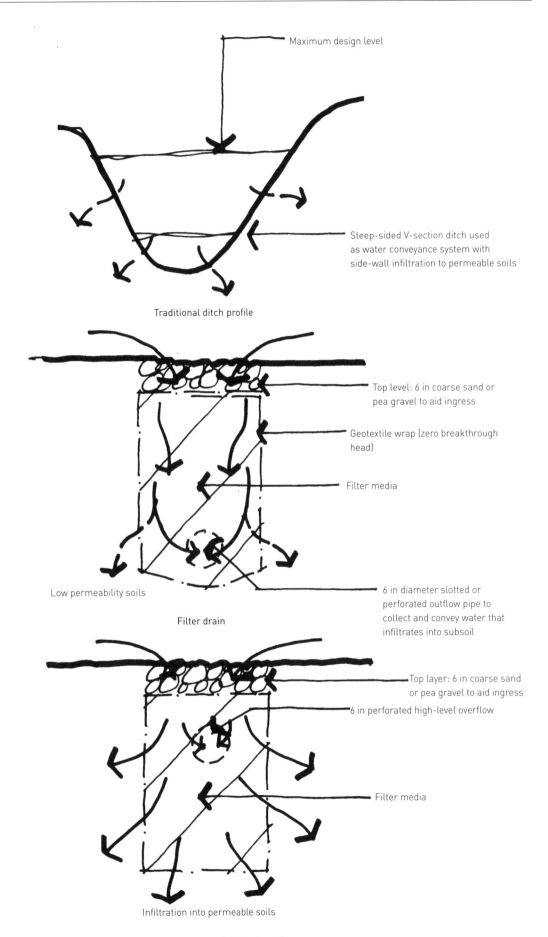

Maximum design level

Steep-sided V-section ditch used
as water conveyance system with
side-wall infiltration to permeable soils

Traditional ditch profile

Top level: 6 in coarse sand or
pea gravel to aid ingress

Geotextile wrap (zero breakthrough
head)

Filter media

Low permeability soils

6 in diameter slotted or
perforated outflow pipe to
collect and convey water that
infiltrates into subsoil

Filter drain

Top layer: 6 in coarse sand
or pea gravel to aid ingress

6 in perforated high-level overflow

Filter media

Infiltration into permeable soils

Infiltration trench with high-level overflow

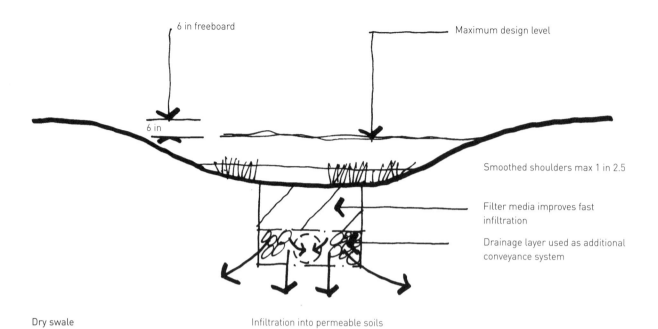

6 in freeboard

Maximum design level

6 in

Smoothed shoulders max 1 in 2.5

Filter media improves fast infiltration

Drainage layer used as additional conveyance system

Dry swale

Infiltration into permeable soils

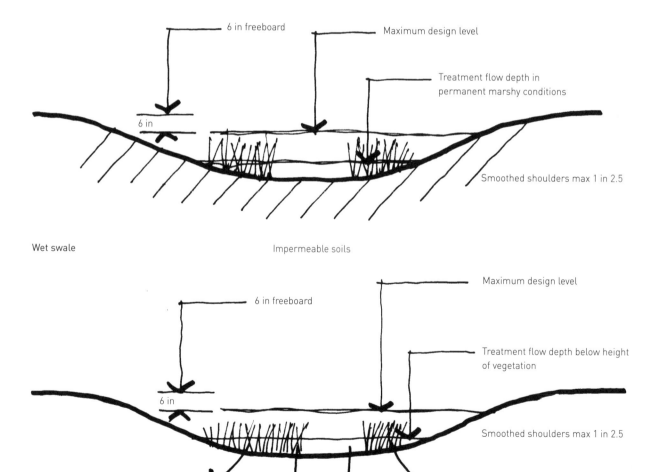

6 in freeboard

Maximum design level

Treatment flow depth in permanent marshy conditions

6 in

Smoothed shoulders max 1 in 2.5

Wet swale

Impermeable soils

Maximum design level

6 in freeboard

Treatment flow depth below height of vegetation

6 in

Smoothed shoulders max 1 in 2.5

Standard conveyance swale

Infiltration into permeable soils

Mounds and landfill

Mounds should be formed in layers, typically 16 in thick, which should be consolidated using site machinery (for example earth-moving vehicles) in order to avoid later subsidence. Clay soils tend to be particularly problematic, because the consolidation of solid clay in layers can produce a mound which does not drain at all and it is therefore difficult to grow plants on it. In such cases, the mound should be formed using the sandwich method of alternating clay and gravel layers in a concave section of the clayey ground material (for example 20 in layers of clay topsoil alternating with 12 in layers of gravel). Grading material should be free of lumber or other vegetable matter, which may form voids. It should also be free of builder's waste.

Topsoil grading

Grading should allow for a topsoil layer to be placed in areas which are to be planted (i.e. where topsoil is specified). Finished levels of the subsoil grading should therefore be low of the finished levels by the following amounts:

- shrub and herbaceous areas: 18 in;
- grass-seeded areas: 6 in;
- turfed grass areas: 4 in;
- tree pits: typically 24 in on most soils (35 in may on be used on well-drained sandy or calcareous soils).

The finished level of the topsoil when laid should be 2 inches above the level of adjacent paving and curbs in order to allow for subsequent settlement. This figure is our recommendation after experience with building and engineering contractors who do not understand the problem of topsoil sinkage. More usual practice is to specify that topsoil be elevated 1–1¼ inches above the level. Note that the main contractor or an earthworks contractor should carry out the general grading, but the topsoiling should always be placed by the landscape contractor in order to ensure that it is not compacted and that there is allowance for the subsoil to be free-draining. The landscape contractor has to guarantee the plants, which are dependent on the soil, and therefore should have to guarantee the soil as well. This is in the landscape contractor's own interest.

Below
Overall view of a mound constructed with clay subsoil using the sandwich method at Canon headquarters, Reigate, England, photographed after ten years of tree growth.

Below right
Toe of a mound constructed with clay subsoil using the sandwich method described.

STEP BY STEP FORMING A BERM USING CLAY SUBSOIL

This sequence illustrates the formation of a berm (a raised embankment) using clay subsoil as well as gravel layers at the site of Disneyland Paris, Marne-la-Vallée, France. The berms on the site's perimeter block views of the outside world.

1 The subsoil and gravel are graded using an earthmover.

2 The berm is formed prior to adding topsoil.

3 Placing the topsoil.

4 The topsoil has been placed. The photograph shows the large scale of the project.

5 The end of the berm after it has been seeded to stabilize the slope.

6 Tree planting in progress.

7 The completed, planted berm.

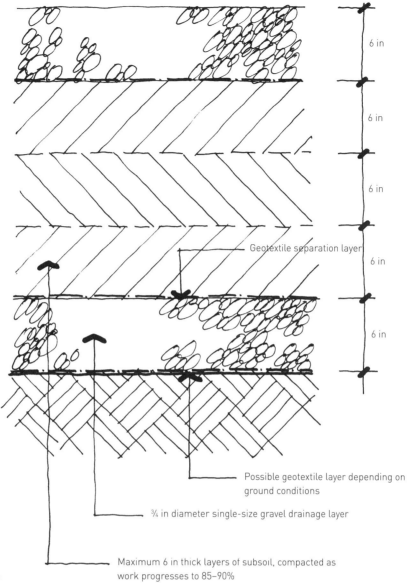

6 in

6 in

6 in

6 in

6 in

6 in

Geotextile separation layer

Possible geotextile layer depending on
ground conditions

¾ in diameter single-size gravel drainage layer

Maximum 6 in thick layers of subsoil, compacted as
work progresses to 85–90%

Mound formation detailed section

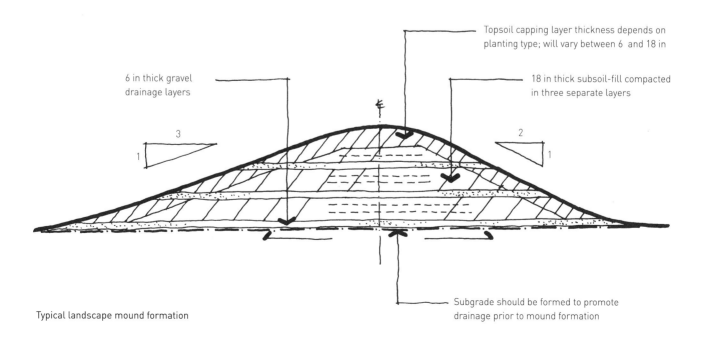

Topsoil capping layer thickness depends on
planting type; will vary between 6 and 18 in

6 in thick gravel
drainage layers

18 in thick subsoil-fill compacted
in three separate layers

3
1

2
1

Subgrade should be formed to promote
drainage prior to mound formation

Typical landscape mound formation

Retaining structures

Where there is a marked change of level and it is necessary to retain the earth there is a choice of structures, as follows:
- steps;
- ramps;
- ramped steps;
- retaining walls;
- the ha-ha; and
- soil reinforcement.

The criteria governing the choice of retaining structure depends on the sort of access proposed, the materials, and the steepness of the level change. Construction methods can vary depending on cost and materials available. Steps, ramped steps and ramps permit access, and steps can also be used for sitting on. Ramps are necessary in order to permit disabled access. Long steps are an alternative to retaining walls. They do not divide a space and can have uses beyond the provision of direct paths or circulation routes.

Sloping and vertical retaining walls enable changes of level, while soil reinforcement is necessary as slopes approach their angle of repose and to counteract slippage and surface erosion. Retaining walls are necessary where sloping sites are developed, and can be very attractive. However, they tend to be expensive and, if possible, it may be desirable to use the elements of the building itself to make major changes of level rather than constructing separate retaining walls.

Steps

Steps are either open or solid. Their horizontal surface is known as a "tread," and the vertical as a "riser." External steps generally have a low riser of 4 or 5 in compared with 6 in for steps indoors, and the tread should be determined by the following equation:

2R + T = 22–30 in
(where R is riser and T is tread).

For example, a riser of 4 in gives a permissible tread of between 14 and 22 in (8 + 14 = 22 in; 8 + 22 = 30 in). High risers, of 6 in or higher, are exhausting to walk up if there are many of them, but serve well as sitting steps.

Another key to good design is to always group steps in a minimum of three risers. An isolated single riser may not be noticed (road curbs are the exception). Long runs of steps should be broken by landings every 12 steps. One observation is that mis-steps tend to happen more frequently on the descent. This is an argument, therefore, for higher risers, which reduce the overall number of steps. Higher steps (5 in or greater) also make for good sitting surfaces.

A Watergate on the Thames Embankment, London. This type of watergate is dangerous to use because of tidal mud, which makes it slippery.

B Steps at St Paul's Cathedral, London.

C Duke of York steps, London.

D British Museum steps, London.

Table of historic steps (in ascending order of height)

	riser	tread	General description
St Paul's Cathedral, London	5 in	14¾ in	Good sitting steps; recent reconstruction of Sir Christopher Wren's design of 1677–1708
Duke of York steps, London	5 in	12 in	Steps in three flights of 9, 10 and 1 0 with risers and two wide landings; designed by John Nash (1827–32) and renewed in the 1980s
British Museum, London	5⅛ in	17 in	Main entrance, in two flights of 6 and 7 risers with 1 in overhangs, designed by Sir Robert Smirke and built 1825–50
St Martin-in-the-Fields, London	5⅛ in	13¾ in	In two flights of 6 and 7 risers with an 8 ft 2 in landing; designed by James Gibbs (1726)
Versailles	5½ in	14½ in	Steps above the Bassin de Latone, in two flights of 11 and 15 risers with a 13 ft landing; designed by André Le Nôtre
Steps to southeast of Palazzo dei Conservatori, Rome *	5¾ in	14½ in	Designed by Michelangelo (begun 1563)
Spanish steps, Rome *	6 in	15¾ in	Designed by Francesco de Sanctis (1717)
The Propylaea, Acropolis, Athens *	6⅞ in	19½ in	The entrance steps to the Acropolis
Steps, London Bridge	7½ in	11¾ in	Functional step, from the remaining arch of the 1831 bridge (on the south bank of the Thames); designed by John Rennie
Steps to Palazzo Senatorio, Rome *	8⅞ in	15¾ in	Designed by Michelangelo and built as part of the remodeling of Piazza del Campidoglio (1536–46)

All steps were measured by the authors except for *, for which measurements were taken from
A. and A. Pinder, *Beazley's Design and Details of the Space between Buildings*, E. & F. N. Spon Ltd, London, 1990, p.261

E Steps to the Propylaea, Acropolis, Athens.

F Steps above the Bassin de Latone, Versailles.

G Steps at Liverpool One shopping centre, Liverpool.

H Sitting steps on the right, walking steps on the left, at the Schlossplatz, Stuttgart, Germany.

A Diagonal steps at London Bridge, London.

B Drainage at the top of steps, Canary Wharf, London.

C A "corduroy"-textured warning surface at top of these steps acts as a safety measure.

D Elegant, simple steps in oolitic limestone at The Economist Building, London.

E Steps with a cycle runway, Stuttgart, Germany.

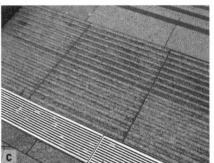

Steps should be non-slip. They should therefore never be made of smooth materials, such as ceramic tiles, terrazzo, polished stone, or smooth-finished concrete. A large, chamfered-edge profile is dangerous, but the outside edge can be slightly rounded in order to avoid chipping and sharp edges which catch shoes. The treads should be free-draining in order to avoid slippery, damp, or mossy surfaces.

The surface of the tread should therefore be laid to drain downwards; this helps to avoid ice layers forming in frosty weather. Where possible, drainage in the area at the top of the steps should be directed away from the steps; if that is unavoidable, a slot drain should be used in order to prevent drainage water flowing down the steps.

It is not good practice to "fade out" steps by merging their treads or by sloping them longitudinally, because this tends to result in them not being noticed. Neither should the height of the risers vary—other than at the bottom step. Therefore, the bottom riser should be designed to take up any slight changes in level across the face of the flight. Often, it is necessary to highlight steps by using studs or a white line at the front of the treads. This should be designed for from the start, otherwise the studs or line may have to be added as an afterthought at the instruction of the health and safety officer. Flights of steps in public areas should have their tops and bottoms identified by "corduroy"-textured warning surfaces to alert the visually impaired. At night, steps will require clear lighting which should not produce glare in either direction. Steps which are diagonal to the direction of movement are unsettling and dangerous.

Steps laid against sloping planted areas require a recessed channel at the side, or should be recessed into the slope and have side walls flush with the tops of the risers. This permits ease of grass mowing, but also ensures that the step foundation is not exposed if the soil on the slope sinks below the foundations of the steps; this edge detail requires care in design. For freestanding steps and wide flights, it is necessary to provide handrails.

Visually, steps should be a solid and strong statement, and traditional stone steps made of simple, solid, stone blocks or well-detailed and constructed cast-in-place concrete are often preferable to thin stone or brick paver-clad cast-in-place concrete structures.

F Cantilevered slate steps, Aberllefenni, Wales.

Ramps and ramped steps

Ramps are intended for older or less mobile people, wheelchair users, and people with strollers and shopping carts. Many people prefer to use steps, so ramps should normally be associated with steps. Generally, ramps have a maximum slope of 1:12 in the UK and 1:15 in Germany; 1:15 is a preferable slope for providing access for wheelchairs. US practice is that ramps should be sloped 8.33% with a 5 x 5 ft landing occurring every 30 ft.

Ramped steps are a way of combining steps and ramps, with goings maybe two or three strides long and sloped. They can be less tiring than steps; however, it is critical that the riser is low—about 4 in—because the total step up from a sloping tread will result in a very tiring riser, which can be difficult to mount. Note that ramped steps are not an alternative to ramps as they do not enable wheelchair access.

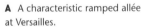
A A characteristic ramped allée at Versailles.

B Railroad tie steps held in place by reinforcement bars.

C Ramped steps in Corsica.

D Ramped steps at the harborside, Penzance, England.

E Cobble-paved ramped steps and a central path of bricks give secure foothold on a slope in Genoa, Italy.

F Long stretcher-bond bricks laid across this slope in Genoa provide a secure foothold while ramped steps at the side aid people climbing the slope.

G Contemporary ramped steps at Channel 4 headquarters, London, designed by Richard Rogers Partnership, 1991. The steps are built of stainless steel and Portland stone slab in stack bond. Note the perforated steel drain-cover at the foot of the steps.

Introduction to retaining walls

Retaining walls are vertical structures that hold back soil or rock: they prevent soil slippage and erosion. In the case of most low walls (less than 6 ft high), gravity or cantilever-wall construction is sufficient, as described below; however, piled walls and diaphragm walls, with or without anchors, are typically used for deep excavations. Many of these retaining structures are faced with stone or brick. However, it can also be attractive to reveal their construction.

Retaining walls may fail by overturning, failure of the foundation or by sliding. There is both a vertical force and a lateral force operating on them, and the combination tends towards overturning. The vertical force is the weight of the retaining-wall structure; the lateral force is that of the soil and backfill material retained by the wall, together with moisture in the soil and any "surcharge" force that may be resting on the wall. Surcharge may range from vehicles to buildings. There may also be an element of water uplift.

The lateral force will be less at the top of the wall, and greater lower down. The lateral force of the soil is the weight of the mass of soil above the angle of repose. Typically the angle of repose will be 1:3 (33 degrees) for most dry, unsaturated soils, from sandy loam to clays, but shallower for fine silts or sand—or for saturated soils and unstable slopes subject to landslip. Therefore, excess soil water should be removed by the use of weep holes, located along the base of the wall, together with cut-off drains above the wall. Note that variations in the water table should be taken into account: a seasonal rise in the water table can double the lateral pressure. Groundwater can also rise owing to a sudden downpour or to a burst water main. Freely draining structures, such as gabions, are particularly useful where there are regular changes in groundwater, and for this reason they are often used in river banks and river works.

There are four main types of retaining wall, classed by their cross-section:
- gravity walls;
- cantilever walls with or without "counterfort;"
- piled walls; and
- anchored walls;

although any individual wall may use a combination of the above.

Above
Gravity wall at Aberdyfi harbor, Wales.

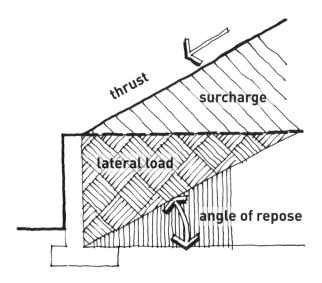

Lateral load on retaining walls

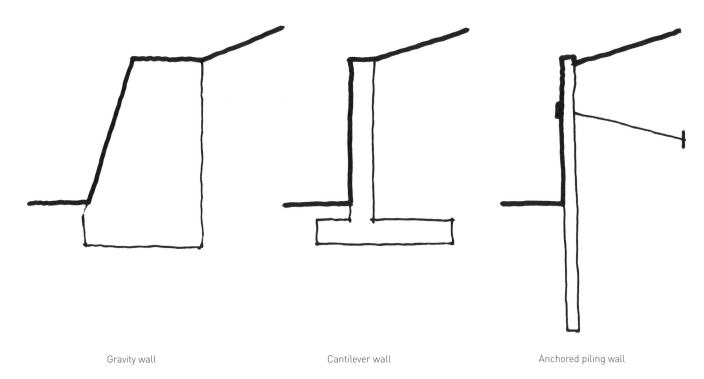

Gravity wall   Cantilever wall   Anchored piling wall

Retaining-wall typology

Comparative table of gravity-wall construction types

Wall type	Durability	Ease of construction	Features
Reinforced-concrete walls	Standard concrete requirements	Built by site workers; access for concrete trucks required	Sometimes more expensive than simpler wall types; permits required
Precast concrete modular walls	Standard reinforced-concrete requirements	Panels delivered by truck; crane access	Often quick to build; factory manufacture can enable special finishes
Brick walls	Standard requirements with concrete foundation	Standard manual technique; built by site workers	Buttresses or piers to brick walls in order to assist stability
Precast masonry (precast concrete or stone) block walls	Standard masonry requirements with concrete foundation	Precast blocks often allow hand-placing	Buttresses or piers to precast masonry walls
Crib walls	Standard concrete or lumber requirements	All components can be hand-placed	Permeable, easily vegetated
Gabion walls	Corrosion protection to wire, durable stone	Pre-assembled and craned into position or hand-placed	Permeable, permits use of recycled materials (e.g. brick, stone); easily vegetated
Reinforced soil	Durability of, and damage to, reinforcement	Hand-placed; access needed for compaction plant	Facing panels and their connection to reinforcement

Source: Adapted with additions from table in T. Chapman and A. Pitchford, "Holding Back the Earth" in *Architects' Journal*, 22 October 1998, p.70.

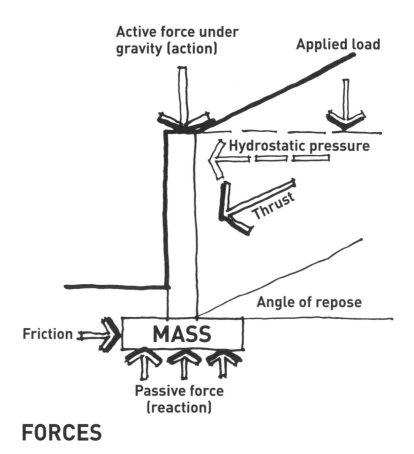

Active force under
gravity (action)

Applied load

Hydrostatic pressure

Thrust

Angle of repose

Friction

MASS

Passive force
(reaction)

FORCES

Section of a gravity wall with an illustration of the forces acting on it

A Cast-in-place reinforced concrete
walls with rock-patterned formwork,
Parc de Cornailles, Ivry, near Paris.

B Curved cast-in-place concrete
wall, Zabeel Park, Dubai.

C Precast concrete key-block wall at Parc de la Villette, Paris.

D Precast concrete modular retaining wall, Friedensplatz, Stuttgart, Germany.

E Gabion wall at Duisburg-Nord Landschaftspark, Duisburg, Germany.

F Lumber crib wall before the mound in front is built up.

G Lumber crib wall under construction.

H Completed lumber crib wall, Cambridge Science Park, England.

Reinforced soil-retaining structures

Reinforced soil-retaining walls are cost-effective and more flexible than conventional earth-retaining walls, such as reinforced concrete cantilever (see right) or solid-structure gravity walls. Reinforced soil-retaining structures are suitable for sites with poor foundations, and for earthquake zones. They have the advantage that they can be planted. They also enable the reuse of site materials, such as broken concrete or brickwork, and use relatively little embodied energy. Structurally, they are gravity walls.

Reinforced-earth technology was developed in France by Henri Vidal, who patented the *terre armée* (earth-reinforced) wall in 1963. This consisted of galvanized-steel strips that were arranged horizontally in order to minimize lateral earth pressure against the face of the wall, and fronted with precast concrete panels or gabion-type cages.

Other systems that have been developed since the 1960s include gabions, which are wire cages, and concrete or lumber crib walls. In the 1970s, geosynthetics (aka "geotextiles") began to be used because of concern about the lifespan of steelwork, which is, of course, liable to rust. Currently, geosynthetic walls have been built up to 65 ft in height, while steel-reinforced retaining walls can go up to 130 ft high.

Cantilever walls

A cantilever wall uses an upturned L- or T-shaped section and the additional weight of the soil resting on the footing in order to resist lateral load. It uses the cantilever cross-section to convert this lateral pressure to a vertical load. Usually, cantilever walls are made of reinforced cast-in-place concrete or of masonry, though in the latter case the foundations would still be made of concrete. These walls use less material than gravity walls.

A counterfort wall is a form of cantilever wall with the addition of vertical supports along its face in order to buttress the lateral load. These buttresses may be buried or exposed on the outer side of the wall. They convert the lateral load of the soil to a vertical load.

Above
Geotextile-reinforced wall at Thames Barrier Park, London.

Right
Detail of the green dock wall at Thames Barrier Park, London.

Far right
Temporary retaining wall of precast concrete panel, Amsterdam.

Left
Sheet piling being driven.

Piled walls

These are often used in soft soils and tight spaces, and are a common choice for river or dockside walls. They may be constructed with spaced steel or lumber piles—or may consist of continuous sheet piling, typically made of interlocking mild-steel plates. The piles are driven into the soil, typically leaving two-thirds of their length underground and one-third above the surface. The process of driving them into the ground compacts the surrounding soil, which in turn increases the strength of the pile. The piles are often anchored with a dead weight and chain, cable or rod, which must be located outside the angle of repose (in other words, beyond the potential failure plane of the soil).

Contiguous bored pile walls

These are cast-in-place concrete piles, constructed by driving a temporary, circular casing into the ground then removing the soil via an auger within the casing. Steel reinforcement is then lowered into the hole, which is filled with concrete, and, while still the concrete is still wet, the casing is withdrawn. The process is then repeated until a wall of contiguous columns of concrete has been constructed, and once the concrete has sufficiently dried, the ground on the lower side of the wall is then excavated to the required depth. This type of pile wall is particularly suited to deep road and railroad excavation, up to 50 ft below the surface. Pile diameters may vary from 14 in to 47 in. These walls are not watertight, but this can be an advantage as it reduces the lateral loading; however, drainage measures will then be necessary.

A variation of contiguous pile walls has universal-section steel columns, acting as reinforcement, being lowered into a hole. Often these do not touch, and may be spaced at 6–10 ft centers with lumber sleepers or precast concrete planks in between.

Secant-bored pile walls

These consist of spaced, unreinforced, weak-mix, cast-in-place concrete "female" piles, in between which reinforced, "male" piles (similar to the contiguous piles described left) are bored two or three days after the placement of the "female" piles, with an overlap of 3–4 in. This forms an intersecting construction which permits less water penetration. This type of pile is so called because a "secant" is a cord or straight line that cuts two points on a circle—which is what the piles do on plan.

Soldier-pile walls ("Berlin" walls or "king-pile" walls)

H-shaped universal-section steel columns are driven into the ground at 6–13 ft centers, and are connected with lumber sleepers, baulks (roughly squared timber beams), or precast concrete planks. This assembly is then backfilled, forming a wall. This is a long-established technique, first employed in Berlin and London in the eighteenth century using timber posts.

Sheet-pile walls

These are made by driving interlocking sections of prefabricated sheet steel into the ground—either by hammer-driving or vibrating. It is not a process suitable for use in stony ground. Although it is often considered an unsightly technique, it can look good—for example, when used with a lumber or precast concrete coping—and it is often used for new canal banks. Sheet piles displace relatively little soil and can be used in loose ground. Sheet-pile walls can be up to 100 ft deep.

Right
Temporary ground anchors used in a diaphragm wall, Canary Wharf, London.

Slurry walls

A slurry wall is formed by making a trench supported by bentonite (see page 170) or polymer-based slurries so that the wall does not collapse. The reinforcement is lowered into the slurry-filled trench, and the slurry is displaced by concrete which is "tremied" into the body of the trench; a tremie pipe is a long pipe used for lowering liquid concrete into excavations. Diaphragm walls were first tested in the late 1940s, and the first one was built by the Italian construction company Icos in 1950. Diaphragm walls are used for excavations up to 330 ft deep.

Anchored walls ("tieback" walls)

These are vertical retaining walls supported by an "anchor," or dead weight, fixed in the ground on the uphill side and tied by a cable, chain or rod, which may be inserted into the ground by boring. The ground anchor is expanded mechanically or may be fixed by the pressure injection of quick-setting concrete, which creates a block set in the soil or rock. Ground anchors must be located beyond the angle of repose of the soil, which is the wall's potential failure plane.

The ha-ha

This is a park feature that consists of a vertical retaining wall on the inner side and a sloping-sided trench on the outer side. Together, these form a barrier which is livestock proof and aims to provide a clear view from a house to its "park" setting with no obstruction.

A form of reverse ha-ha, often with a fence on top of the wall, has frequently been adopted in contemporary Parisian parks. The retaining wall is placed on the outer side and the ditch on the park side, thus giving a clear view into the park.

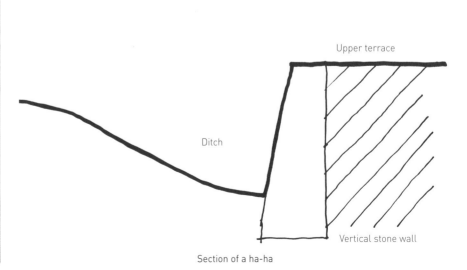

Upper terrace

Ditch

Vertical stone wall

Section of a ha-ha

Soil reinforcement

This is a system of reinforcing the soil strength artificially, so that it can bear a greater load or resist slope erosion.

Typical methods include the following:
- The addition of lime to clay or sticky, silt soils in order to make them more stable. Quicklime is hygroscopic —it absorbs moisture from the air—and therefore dries the soil so that construction vehicles can traffic over a construction site, and it can form a sub-base for road foundations. Note, however, that quicklime-treated soil can be very alkaline (with a pH of 12) and phytotoxic—so it should not be used in areas where it is intended to grow vegetation, and great care should be taken to ensure that dry lime dust does not blow around. Following the application of quicklime, a layer of cement and pulverized fly ash (PFA) or blast-furnace slag is usually added. Note that the use of quicklime is environmentally very undesirable.

- Non-cohesive soils, such as loams, can be reinforced with cement alone, or with a combination of cement, PFA and slag. This is less damaging than the use of lime described above, but it is still not particularly environmentally favorable. However, there is a balance between the use of lime (which is energy-intensive) and the importation of off-site materials. It can be far better to improve the bearing capacity of on-site materials and permit their reuse than to import off-site ones.

- Plastic or composite webbing layers ("geogrids"), sandwiched with compacted soil, produce a strengthened soil structure. They are applicable to steep embankments or cuttings in order to improve strength and stability, and resist surface erosion. Such measures should be combined with cut-off drains to remove the load of water ingress. This material improves the tensile strength and stability of the soil.

Left
The green dock at Thames Barrier Park, London.

Geotextiles as soil reinforcement

Geotextiles are permeable geosynthetics made of textile materials. A geosynthetic is a polymer (plastic) sheet material used with soil, rock, or earth.

- *Geogrids* are used in reinforcement, and are made of a network of tensile elements with gaps of sufficient size to interlock with surrounding fill material;
- *Geomembranes* are impermeable geosynthetics used as fluid barriers;
- *Geocomposites* are combinations of geotextiles and related products, such as nets and grids, and can be used along with geomembranes and other synthetics in order to combine the advantages of each component.

Geosynthetics are made from synthetic polymers—such as polypropylene, polyester, polyethylene, polyamide, or PVC—and are resistant to biological and chemical change. It is possible to use natural fibers such as hemp, cotton, jute, bamboo, and other forms of wood fiber as geotextiles and geogrids, especially for temporary applications, but they have not been promoted as widely as polymer geosynthetics.

There are precedents for the use of natural geogrids and ground structures in traditional Dutch dyke construction, in which bundles of sticks are used; in marshland road construction, where "cord roads" (log roads) have been used since Neolithic times; and in nineteenth-century railroad construction, in which

Above
Terram permeable geotextile used in a cut-off drain, Canon headquarters, Reigate, England.

Right
The steep 45-degree grass slopes of the Palais Omnisports in Paris were achieved by growing the grass through a steel mesh, which holds the soil.

weighted wood-and-heather bundles were used to create a raft foundation across peat bogs. The use of natural fibers in geotextiles needs more investigation, and is very appealing because it uses far less embodied energy and the products are therefore much more sustainable.

Geotextiles are made of fibers or yarns fashioned into sheet textiles. The fibers are either continuous filaments of long, thin polymer strands, or are staple fibers, which are shorter filaments (typically ¾ in to 4 in long). Fibers can also be made by slitting extruded plastic sheet or film in order to make thin, flat tapes. The extrusion or drawing process in both filaments and slit films elongates the polymers in the direction of the extrusion, which increases the strength of the fiber.

R.D. Holtz, professor of civil engineering at the University of Washington, defines six primary functions of geosynthetics:
- filtration;
- drainage;
- separation;
- reinforcement;
- fluid barrier; and
- protection.[4]

Filtration and drainage Permeable geotextiles are used in trench drains in order to prevent fine soil moving downwards into drainage aggregate or pipes and so blocking them. They are also used as filters below "riprap" protective materials in coast and river-bank protection; and in road-edge drains such as French drains, steep-slope interceptor drains, and abutment or retaining-wall drains. One example is the proprietary product Terram, a "nonwoven thermally bonded geotextile." It is made of polypropylene yarn, which is fully encased in a protective polyethylene sheath (polypropylene is more subject to oxidation than polyethylene).

Separation Permeable geotextiles are often used as separators in order to stop fine-grained subgrade soils being pumped into permeable, granular road bases, and to prevent road-base materials sinking into an underlying soft subgrade. Separators, including Terram, maintain the design thickness and integrity of roads and footpaths.

Reinforcement Geogrid and geotextile reinforcement can allow embankments to be constructed over very soft foundations (the modern equivalent of the peat-bog road bundle). It is also used to construct stable slopes at much steeper angles than would otherwise be possible.

Fluid barrier Geomembranes, thin-film geotextile composites, geosynthetic-clay liners, and geotextiles coated with, for instance, PVC coating or polyurea elastomer spray are used as fluid barriers in order to impede the flow of a liquid or gas from one location to another. This geosynthetic function has applications in asphalt-pavement overlays, the encapsulation of swelling soils and waste containment.

Protection layers Geosynthetics can act as a protective, stress- or point load-relief layer. A protective cushion of non-woven geotextile is often used to prevent the puncture of pool-liner geomembranes by sharp stones in the adjacent soil or drainage aggregate, both during construction and subsequently. An example is Bidim (for illustration, see page 178), which is a "continuous filament nonwoven needle-punched polyester geotextile," to quote the manufacturer's description.

Walls

Walls and fences provide enclosure and security; they delimit property boundaries, can control crowds and creatures, and can also provide wind shelter and, if solid, create a noise barrier. In country-house kitchen gardens walls provide space for plants to grow, screened from the wind and within a suntrap. Walls are also a wildlife habitat, whether for bees or bats.

However, they are also a way of creating spaces and can provide the spatial framework for a garden. Therefore, they are a way of making outdoor "rooms"—something that can also be done by using hedges. Walls higher than eye level (say, more than 6–6½ ft high) give a complete physical and visual barrier; walls below eye level provide both a visual and physical separation, and act as a partial enclosure, while low walls provide a physical barrier and can form plinths for seating.

Left
Kitchen garden walls, such as this example in the Potager du Roi, Versailles, France, provide a protected microclimate.

Above
Low wall, Canon headquarters, Reigate, England.

MATERIALS USED IN WALL CONSTRUCTION

Materials used in wall construction include brick, stone, concrete, and clay blocks, cast-in-place concrete, rammed earth, sods, lumber sleepers, steel sheets, gabions, and earth-filled structures.

1 Monochromatic brick wall at the Parc de Bercy, Paris, with recessed sections of stretcher bond and stone coping.

2 Freestanding, limestone wall in the White Garden at Parc Citroën-Cévennes, Paris.

3 Hollow clay block wall, Cour du Maroc, Paris.

4 Cast-in-place oncrete wall with raised stone pattern, Parc de Bercy, Paris.

5 Lumber-sleeper retaining wall, Hadlow College, Kent, England.

6 Sod wall, Hoge Veluwe National Park, The Netherlands.

7 Steel sheet facing on a gabion wall near Amsterdam Centraal station.

8 Gabion wall at Westergasfabriek Park, Amsterdam.

The most common wall materials are masonry units and cast-in-place concrete. Masonry here refers to brick and stone, or to precast concrete blocks. These can be surprisingly flexible in application, but cast-in-place concrete is the most versatile wall material because it can be moulded to virtually any desired form and can be easily curved.

The structural wall material can be revealed or can be covered by a facing material such as:
• brick;
• precast concrete;
• lumber;
• glass and acrylic;
• finishes and stucco; or
• paint.

Key to the choice of wall material is knowing what is on the market and what construction skills are available. Our advice is to first study the context and understand what and why local materials are used—for instance, bricks vary widely in size and shape, and brick construction skills also differ from area to area. Rammed-earth skills are common in some regions, and cast-in-place concrete construction can vary widely: the Japanese, for example, build beautifully constructed and finished cast-in-place concrete work.

Below
The use of flush brick as an edge capping has resulted in staining on this brick wall.

Bottom right
Reinforced-concrete wall with vertical recessed detailing, Kyoto, Japan.

Bottom left
A cast-in-place concrete wall from which the mortar dot-fixed stone cladding is falling off, Parc Citroën-Cevennes, Paris. Steel fixings are more effective.

Above left
Splash-back from the paving
has stained this harling wall in
Edinburgh.

Above
Upwash staining on a limestone
dwarf wall at St Paul's churchyard,
London.

Design issues

Common factors in the design of all types of wall include
live loads from high winds, which produce a lateral
force; and water penetration, from above and below.
From above the concern is rainwater penetration, so
wall tops should be tilted or canted. Additionally, water
should be thrown off the face of a wall: it is usual with
unit construction to have a water barrier—such as a layer
of impermeable tile or slate, or even engineering brick
—below the wall capping or coping. Groundwater from
below can move up a wall by capillary action, and there
should be a similar water barrier in masonry walls in the
form of a moisture-proof course. Driving rain, especially
in maritime areas, is addressed by careful selection of
materials.

Light-colored walls—such as those with a render
finish or that are made from pale-colored brick, stone
or concrete—are subject to dirt and dust discoloration,
especially from rain hitting the ground where fine gravel,
earth or planting beds abut the wall. It is therefore good
practice to detail a window-cleaning strip or narrow path
at the foot of the wall (such as a line of bricks on edge)
in order to avoid this, and light-colored walls often have
their lower section painted black.

Above left
Splash-back from the paving
has stained this harling wall in
Edinburgh.

Above
Upwash staining on a limestone
dwarf wall at St Paul's churchyard,
London.

A summary of the structural considerations relating to wall design would include:

- the dead weight of the wall mass;
- the ground bearing pressure;
- live loads: wind loading and snow;
- context and exposure; and
- surcharge (loads placed on the wall, such as structures leaning against it).

Walls should be stable, durable and aesthetically pleasing.

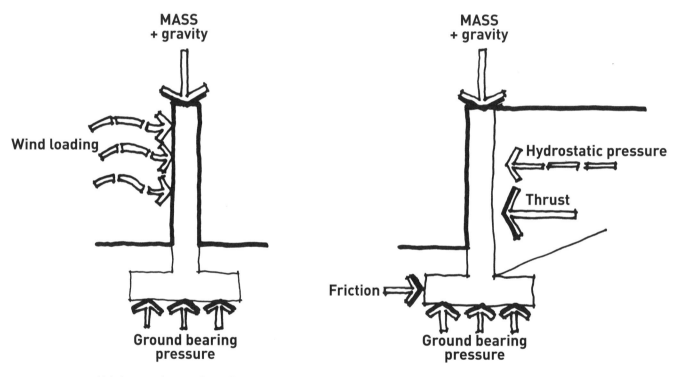

Main forces on freestanding walls

Main forces on retaining walls

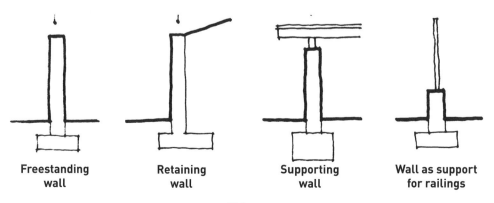

Wall types

Unit walls

A wall consists of the vertical structure, or "stem," and a horizontal support, which is the foundation—usually built of concrete. There may also be a separate top, either a cap or a coping, which has the function of casting off water. It may be more impermeable than the stem of the wall, and may also be an aesthetic choice. A coping should project beyond the face of the wall, while a capping is flush with the wall surface.

A cheap, cast-in-place concrete wall can be stone-capped, and the use of this relatively expensive capping material can give the wall a pleasing visual "trim."

It is also possible to use a metal-sheet capping of zinc or stainless steel—or one made of bricks on edge, whether in the same brick as the rest of the wall or in an engineering type.

Single-brick-thick construction should only be used for low walls no more than 18 in high. Most external brick walls are two bricks wide, but high walls usually require piers or buttresses.

Right
Churchyard wall with coping and a string-course to throw off water, and a buttress to provide lateral support, St Mary's Church, Ashwell, Hertfordshire, England.

Far right top
Stone coping on a concrete wall, Aphrodite Hills Village Center, Cyprus.

Far right bottom
Stone capping on a cast-in-place concrete wall, Parc Diderot, La Défense, Paris.

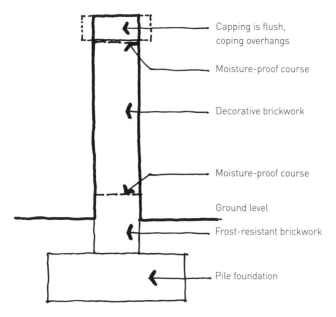

Capping is flush, coping overhangs

Moisture-proof course

Decorative brickwork

Moisture-proof course

Ground level

Frost-resistant brickwork

Pile foundation

Anatomy of a freestanding wall

Foundations and structure

There are two main types of wall foundation: the pile foundation and the post-and-beam construction. Pile foundations are the cheapest and easiest type to build. They consist of a simple slab of concrete, usually buried underground below the frost line, and are commonly a minimum of 18 in deep in temperate areas but greater than 72 in deep in climates with severe winters. The minimum recommended depth on shrinkable clay soils is 30 in to 5 ft depending on the soil's plasticity index.[5]

Freeze–thaw can cause a concrete foundation to move if it is not adequately protected from ground frost by being buried sufficiently deeply. Usually, the concrete strip is reinforced with steel mesh. Conventionally, a pile foundation is twice the width of the wall.

Post-and-beam foundations consist of a concrete beam supported by underground concrete posts. Post foundations are used in weak and unstable ground such as shrinkable clays or peat, or on filled or reclaimed sites.

Walls may be solid, mass structures or may be reinforced by piers at regular intervals. A cavity construction may be used with piers in order to give the impression of a thick, solid wall.

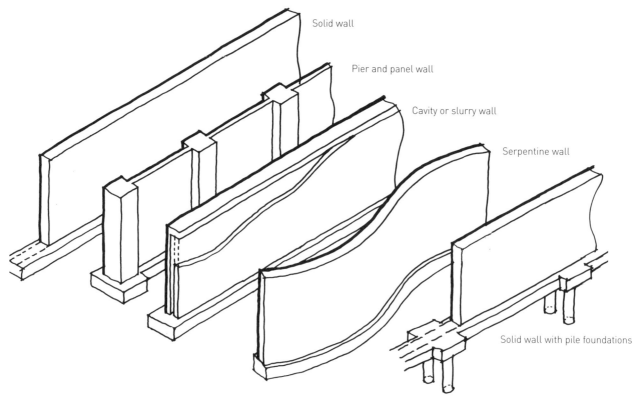

Solid wall

Pier and panel wall

Cavity or slurry wall

Serpentine wall

Solid wall with pile foundations

Masonry wall types

Left
Copper moisture-proof course
on a wall in a private garden in
Denmark.

Moisture-proof courses

A moisture-proof course is a layer of impermeable material intended to stop the upward movement of groundwater owing to capillary action. It is placed at least 6 in above the ground level to protect against rainwater splash-back above the moisture-proof course or localized wet conditions, such as blocked drains. The moisture-proof course usually consists of a polymer membrane (such as polyethelene), an asphalt composite sheet, an asphalt/sheet-metal composite material or mastic aphalt. An alternative approach is to use impermeable engineering bricks in the walls up to 6 in above ground level, or use a slate layer (the latter is characteristic of older structures). Note, of course, that on sloping ground the moisture-proof course may be stepped in order to cope with the slope. In addition, paving should always be sloped to drain away from walls. If the general site conditions do not permit the external levels to be below the moisture-proof course, a channel is usually constructed alongside the wall in order to "divorce" the wall and the relatively high paving. This is typical for ramped approaches to buildings, where an access point level with the internal finished floor is required.

Moisture-proof courses may also be placed under the coping or capping of a garden wall in order to stop rain penetration into the body of the wall. A tile layer projecting from the wall face forms a "string-course," which constitutes another means of throwing water away from the face of a wall. String-courses are also much used in stone masonry.

Expansion joints

Masonry walls (whether brick, blockwork, or stone) constructed using cement mortar must allow for horizontal expansion and contraction of the wall— hence the incorporation of vertical expansion joints, which are generally seen as lines running up the wall surface. Lime mortar is more flexible than the cement variety and consequently it permits a greater degree of movement within a masonry structure; except in earthquake zones— most "old" (i.e. pre-twentieth-century) walls do not have expansion joints. The structure of lime-mortar walls is more "forgiving" than that of their modern counterparts.

Expansion and contraction in masonry walls occurs owing to:
• temperature change;
• clay-brick expansion, caused by moisture uptake (clay brickwork can expand between $\frac{3}{16}$ and $\frac{7}{8}$ in per linear yard, dependent on the type); and
• calcium silicate and concrete-brick contraction, caused by water loss (remember that water is a component of concrete).
(Each of the above movement types occurs in all directions.)
• differential lateral movement, or "creep," between a reinforced-concrete foundation and the brickwork above;
• lateral and vertical movement, consequent on movement of the ground, transmitted through the foundation.

Expansion joints should be designed for, and should be placed at regular intervals in rigidly constructed walls. Typically, they are spaced at 18 ft intervals in freestanding walls. It is also quite usual to have additional intermediate expansion joints for copings and cappings, extending down to the moisture-proof course level. Expansion joints can be incorporated into pier construction, by creating double piers with the expansion joint in the middle rather than placing the joint midway between piers. Usually the joint is a simple gap, with the different panels of the wall being structurally independent. Filler materials in expansion joints should be compressible and they should flex, so that they resume their original width upon the wall contracting. Typical joint fillers are cellular polyethelene and cellular polyurethene. Fiberboard should not be used because it does not resume its original shape. The filler should be sealed with a polysulphide or silicone sealant.

Drystone walls

These are typical of upland, stone country and were often made using the materials of field clearance—though occasionally quarried stone was used. They are usually very attractive and reflect the geology of the area. They can be very old: some examples on St Kilda in Scotland date back three millennia. Drystone is thus an ancient technology which is still in current use. Drystone walls are found worldwide wherever there are traditions of ancient settlement and farming, such as in the pre-Columbian cultures of South America, in Asia, Africa, and the Mediterranean region. They are also found in areas, such as North America and Australia, settled by Europeans. In Europe, they are found in the Alps and in northwestern regions, as well as around the Mediterranean. The drystone wall's use of embodied energy is very low—the stone is typically gathered from an adjacent field—but does require skilled labor.

There are three main types:
• double-stone walls;
• single-stone walls; and
• dykes, with an earth or stone-rubble core, faced by stone walls.

Stone retaining walls are also typical of terraced, agricultural areas on steep slopes, and this is how they most often feature in areas around the Mediterranean.

The typical double-stone construction consists of two main layers with a narrow rubble infill, large "through" or "tie" stones midway up the wall and vertically laid top stones (although there are regional variations with no separate top-stone layer). The "through" stones bond the wall together, and the foundation is a layer of large stones laid on the ground. The face of the walls is canted in order to throw off water.

In the UK, some highway authorities mortar-bed the top-stone coping to drystone walls alongside roads. In the Cotswolds region of the UK, some field walls have short stretches of mortared "jumps," with cement-mortared copings in order to avoid dislodgement by local fox hunters and their horses when they jump the walls.

Because of regional variations in the construction of drystone walls influenced by the nature of the stone and local custom, it is necessary to work with appropriately skilled stonemasons.

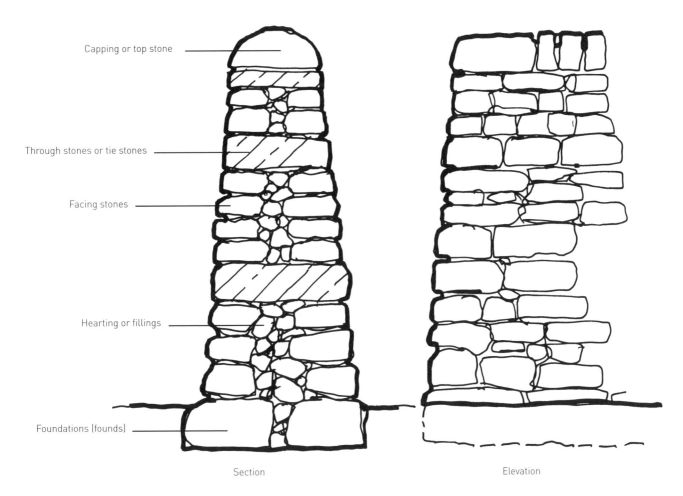

Capping or top stone

Through stones or tie stones

Facing stones

Hearting or fillings

Foundations (founds)

Section

Elevation

Typical drystone wall construction

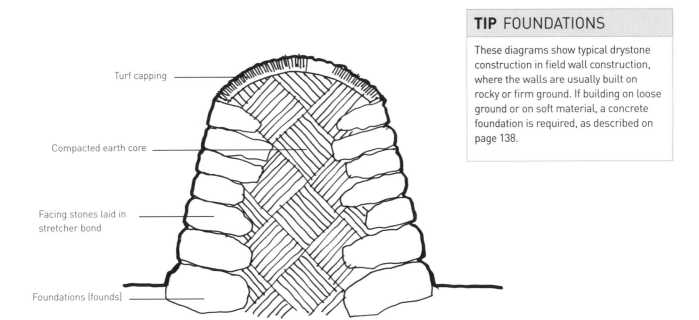

Turf capping

Compacted earth core

Facing stones laid in
stretcher bond

Foundations (founds)

Typical dyke wall construction section

TIP FOUNDATIONS

These diagrams show typical drystone construction in field wall construction, where the walls are usually built on rocky or firm ground. If building on loose ground or on soft material, a concrete foundation is required, as described on page 138.

DRYSTONE WALL TYPES

This sequence of images shows a range of drystone walls in different countries. Common to them all is that the building material was sourced from nearby. Agricultural stone walls are built using stones from the fields they enclose, while more formal walls may be built with stone from local quarries (for example, a quarry would be excavated to build a farmhouse in a nearby field). They are therefore low in embodied energy and sustainable, as well as offering a habitat for flora and fauna.

1 Drystone agricultural terrace wall, Corsica.

2 Drystone wall being constructed, Chipping Norton, England.

3 Slate drystone retaining wall, Aberllefenni, Wales.

4 This traditional Cotswold drystone wall in the Cotswolds region of England acts as a rich habitat for ferns.

5 Ashlar drystone wall, Kyoto, Japan.

6 A wall of dressed-course quarried stone with coping, Aberllefenni, Wales.

7 Rubble wall of field stones, Aberllefenni, Wales.

8 Field wall built from loose stone gathered from the surrounding fields, Cwm Maethlon, Gwynedd, Wales.

Paving

Paving should please the eye and comfort the feet. Paving materials can be a delight, and designers should use them in a way that reveals their qualities. Do not provide beautiful handmade bricks and then spoil them by laying them with a dry mix and covering them with a slurry of mortar. Nor, indeed, should you "overdesign" by providing inflexible, expensive, and unnecessary concrete bases for stone and brick paving. There is a tendency nowadays for paving to be smooth and flat; traditionally it was full of texture (cobbles were river stones) and there is medical evidence that undulating paving promotes good balance—especially in the old. Note, however, that loose or uneven paving may constitute a trip hazard and can be dangerous. Well-designed paving can provide pattern, color and delight; boring paving can lack texture, scale and visual interest.

Below left
Cobble street paving using river stones, Hay-on-Wye, Wales.

Below right
Cobble street paving at Bishops Castle, Shropshire, England. All footpaths in the town were like this until the early twentieth century.

Expect to find utilities, which must be accommodated, underneath any road or pavement.

Foundations

Paving should be designed from the foundation up, and then for the traffic and loads to be applied downwards —and for the drainage of surfacewater. A fundamental criterion is the CBR, or California Bearing Ratio, of the ground (see page 104). Usually, an additional capping layer of 14–24 in may be appropriate.

Most soils move over time: for example, shrinkable clays dry and shrink; peat soils, when drained, may fall in level over time by a yard or more. In recently reclaimed Dutch polders, the removal of the weight of the water resulted in the land rising. Furthermore, tree roots can, of course, lift paving and even walls. Such movement is particularly found in gardens in which natural plant growth is encouraged; design for such movement, and not against it.

Cast-in-place concrete or materials such as bricks, cobbles, or stone slabs, laid in cement on a concrete bed, are examples of rigid pavings; while gravels and asphalt— and bricks, setts, cobbles, or slabs, laid on a sand bed and hard core—are examples of flexible paving. Flexible pavings require an edge restraint, otherwise they will spread like a rolled dough.

The other major classification in paving refers to its surface material: *monolithic pavings* include asphalt, and cast-in-place concrete, which are laid in a liquid or semi-liquid form; while *unit pavings* such as brick, stone, or precast concrete slabs are preformed or cut in a factory, brickworks or quarry, then laid in units on the site.

TIP UNDER-PAVING UTILITIES

This photograph shows how utilities are marked out on a street prior to excavation. When designing paving it is necessary to consider underground utilities.

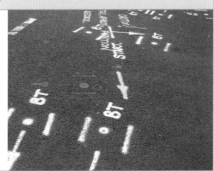

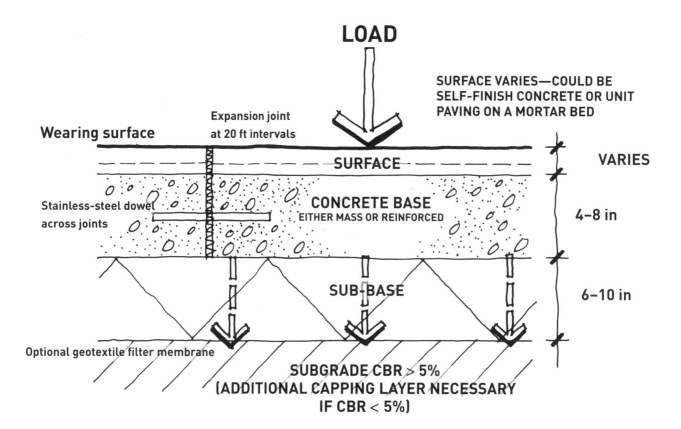

LOAD

SURFACE VARIES—COULD BE SELF-FINISH CONCRETE OR UNIT PAVING ON A MORTAR BED

Expansion joint at 20 ft intervals

Wearing surface

SURFACE — — —

VARIES

CONCRETE BASE
EITHER MASS OR REINFORCED

4–8 in

Stainless-steel dowel across joints

SUB-BASE

6–10 in

Optional geotextile filter membrane

SUBGRADE CBR > 5%
(ADDITIONAL CAPPING LAYER NECESSARY IF CBR < 5%)

Rigid paving profile

Rigid paving

Cast-in-place concrete, terrazzo, and unit paving laid on a concrete bed are examples of rigid paving. This tends to be more expensive than many flexible pavings. It is also difficult to dig it up for utilities trenches, so when using a concrete foundation do allow spare utilities ducts. Rigid construction is recommended for steep slopes (say, greater than 1:10), steps and ramps, places where pollutants should not be allowed to seep into the ground (such as gas-station forecourts) and some areas of high-impact loading. Rigid paving requires design for movement joints consequent on expansion and contraction of the material. Generally, such joints are provided at 20 foot intervals and should be carried through to the wearing surface. Essentially, they are "designed cracks:" they are usually ⅜ in wide and can be filled with a compressible joint filler, such as Flexicell or polyethylene foam. Cast-in-place concrete paving can be attractive, particularly if the aggregate is exposed and the expansion joints expressed.

Imprinted and stamped concrete is especially popular in the United States, under trade names such as Bomanite, but too often it is used simply to imitate forms of unit paving such as brick and stone. It is the main paving used in Disneyland amusement parks, where the paving is washed daily using chemicals to remove chewing gum and stains and to give an "as new" appearance.

There is much scope in developing abstract patterns for use with stamped concrete systems.

Concrete bases for terrazzo and unit paving can be mass concrete or can be reinforced with steel mesh. Mass concrete is used for footpaths and light-traffic residential drives. Typically, concrete slabs are laid 4–6 in thick.

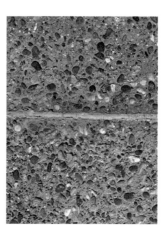

Left
An expansion joint in cast-in-place concrete paving.

Above
Bomanite, or stamped cast-in-place concrete.

Below
Stamped concrete imitating a Roman road at the entrance to the Getty Villa, Malibu, California.

Above
Cast-in-place exposed aggregate concrete path made with local gravel at New Ash Green, England.

STEP BY STEP RIGID PAVING

This sequence of images shows roof-terrace paving adjacent to swimming pools at the Aphrodite Hills Resort in Cyprus. The paving employs a mix of limestone from Cyprus and Indian sandstone and granite. Rigid paving was used to avoid settlement, and the trees were planted in pits sited over the columns of the basement beneath.

1 Aerial view showing the main grid lines for the stone embedded in place.

3 Aerial view of the completed paving, with cut stone infill between the grid lines.

2 Granite setts are laid on a prepared mortar bed using proprietary joint spacers.

4 Detail showing a stainless-steel expansion joint crossing paving patterns.

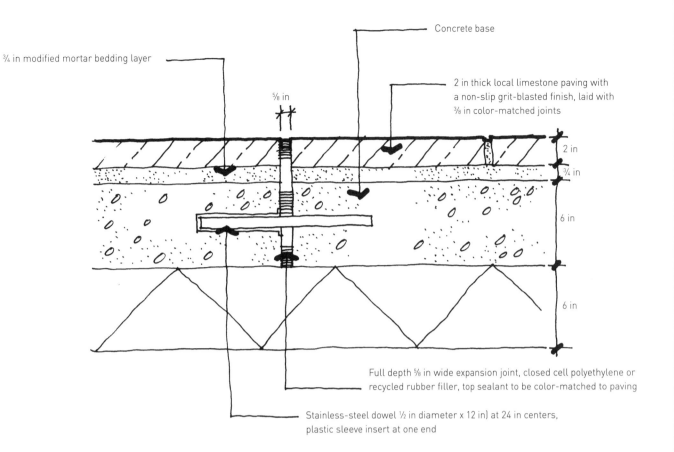

¾ in modified mortar bedding layer

Concrete base

2 in thick local limestone paving with a non-slip grit-blasted finish, laid with ⅜ in color-matched joints

⅝ in

2 in

¾ in

6 in

6 in

Full depth ⅝ in wide expansion joint, closed cell polyethylene or recycled rubber filler, top sealant to be color-matched to paving

Stainless-steel dowel ½ in diameter x 12 in) at 24 in centers, plastic sleeve insert at one end

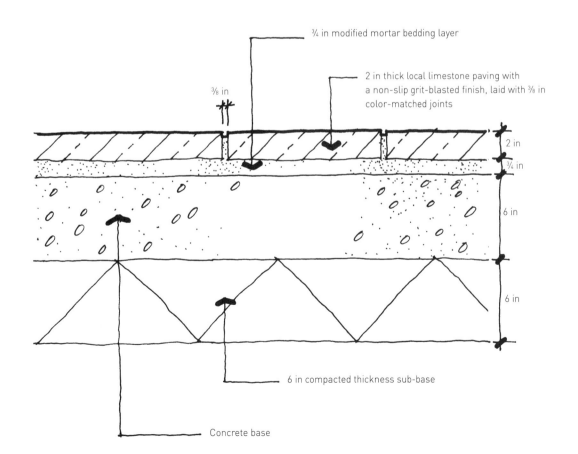

¾ in modified mortar bedding layer

2 in thick local limestone paving with a non-slip grit-blasted finish, laid with ⅜ in color-matched joints

⅜ in

2 in

¾ in

6 in

6 in

6 in compacted thickness sub-base

Concrete base

Unit paving

This includes clay bricks, concrete blocks, ceramic tiles, stone slabs and setts, cobbles and slate pitching, and precast concrete slabs. Points to remember when designing for unit paving include the pattern and its direction. Typically, continuous joints should be laid across a path rather than along it, because irregularities in a continuous joint alignment will show up more readily. Laying the continuous joint across a path or route also allows for the use of stone slabs of differing length and constant width, which is much more economical and less wasteful than attempting absolute uniformity of dimensions. Remember: stone is a finite resource.

A Stones of varying length are laid flexibly with the running joint across the footpath, Merrick Square, London.

B Crazy paving, at the UNESCO garden, Paris, designed by Isamu Noguchi.

C Evenly sized sandstone slabs laid aligned with the footpath. This paving technique results in a bland appearance and wastes stone.

D Characteristic flexibly laid *pavé*, or setts of old Paris, in the rue de la Crimée.

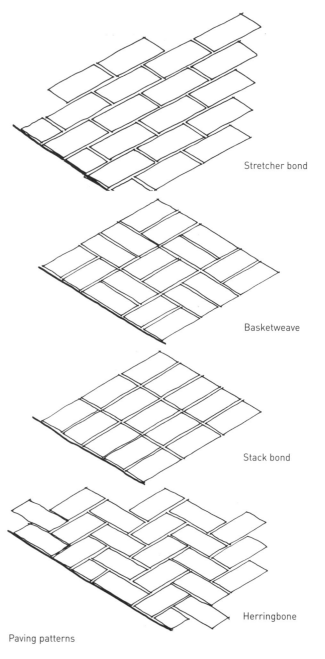

Stretcher bond

Basketweave

Stack bond

Herringbone

Paving patterns

Herringbone paving, laid on sand, interlocks—so has the special characteristic of spreading a vertical load horizontally, which is why it is used in docks and railroad yards and roads, where large point loads are common. It is also particularly suitable for driveways and forecourts where delivery and garbage truck access is required. Other paving patterns are suitable for lighter, pedestrian loadings.

If laying unit paving on a rigid concrete base, there are two main methods of bedding units on a mortar bed:
• wet laying on a ⅝–1 in thick 1:3 cement:sand mortar; or
• semi-dry bedding, consisting of a 1½ in–2¾ in thick semi-dry 1:4 cement:concreting sand bedding layer, onto which a thin (1:1 cement:sand) slurry is spread prior to paving-unit placement in order to increase adhesion. The joints are left open and finished after laying the units—either by troweling in stiff jointing mortar or brushing in a semi-dry mortar.

However, both techniques involve "staining" expensive stone or brick with a slurry of mortar and are not recommended unless the slurry can be totally washed off —as it can with ceramic tiles and non-absorbent bricks.

A third alternative is the use of a synthetic mortar, which can be either epoxy-resin based or polybutadiene based (in both cases, combined with sand). Using these mortars is much more expensive than the first two methods, but they are stronger. The epoxy-resin-based synthetic mortar is also available as a dry, brush-in product (often referred to as a "polymeric mortar"). It cures by absorbing water from the atmosphere. Note that synthetic mortars must be laid in dry weather, because if their surface residue is wetted then it, too, will stain the paving. The residue must be totally swept up.

Thin-unit paving—such as ceramic tiles, old granite setts which have been sawn in two, or thin or soft stone slabs—must be laid on a concrete bed. Most thicker and stronger unit paving should be laid on a sand bed in order to form a flexible construction; this also ensures that the joints remain fully visible. This is usual practice in The Netherlands, Denmark, and Germany, whether for gardens or roads and urban paving. It was also usual practice in the UK until the 1940s. Typically, bricks, setts, or cobbles are laid on a 2 in sand bed on 6 in of material for most footpath construction. The only reason that setts (*pavé*) in Paris have been laid with a mortar joint since the 1968 riots is that they were prised up and used for building barricades or thrown at the police. An effective alternative to sand for unit-paving bedding is granite dust.

It is usually necessary to cut thin-unit paving, and the main choice is between saw cutting (which is noisy, though it can be done off site) and using a chopper, which gives a less crisp cut edge. When cutting slabs or blocks close to a building, ensure that the cut slabs are laid against the building rather than on the side of a path facing away from it: they look far better that way.

Do not use large stone slabs if the paving has to carry heavy vehicles—it is far better to use brick- or sett-sized units: indeed, in Prague and Berlin most footpaths are edged with a yard-wide strip of 2 x 2 x 2 in setts so that vehicles can mount the curbs without cracking larger slabs.

Left
A workman cuts granite with a saw. Saw cutting is noisy (hence the ear protectors) and dusty.

Flexible paving

Flexible paving is cheap, simple and quick to lay—and can be of substantial strength. It allows movement of the sub-base or subgrade, is available for use immediately after construction (cast-in-place concrete takes time to develop its strength) and allows both ease of alteration and for services to be subsequently dug up. Consequently, most public roads are built using forms of flexible construction.

Gravel is a traditional flexible paving and is still used where good, comfortable hoof adhesion is required, as in paddock yards. Gravel needs to be sharp and angular if it is not to be easily kicked around, so do not use round, pea gravel in areas of heavy wear. Usually, gravel paving is permeable; however, there are self-binding varieties with a clay fraction, which, if correctly rolled, become impermeable. CEDEC is a similar proprietary product. Hoggin is a gravel to which clay has been added in order to produce an impermeable surface; however, it tends to be messy until the clay fraction has been washed off the surface.

A recent development has been clear, resin binders such as Clearmac (which uses a polymer-modified thermoplastic) or SureSet (which uses a UV-stable polyurethane resin). These resins are transparent, and so reveal the color and texture of the aggregate. However, they do cost more than standard asphalt, and have a rather false appearance: they look too clean. Asphalt can be imprinted in a way similar to concrete (e.g. the StreetPrint system). Roadstone and gravels traditionally come from local supplies, but increasingly they are carried longer distances by ship or rail and so can be available nationally. The key is to find out what is available at the nearest roadstone depots in order to minimize road-freight costs.

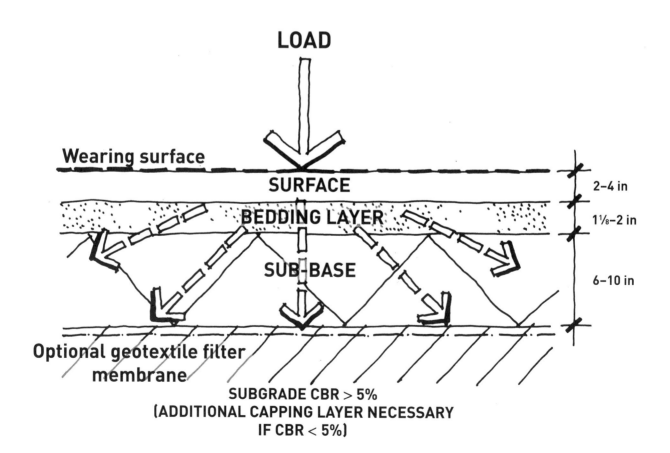

Flexible paving profile

A A traditional nineteenth-century, unbound, unimproved asphalt road, Camberwell Grove, London.

B Hoggin (a clay-bound gravel) paving, The Mall, London.

C Hot-rolled asphalt has, unusually, been used for pedestrian paving at the entrance to Tate Modern, London.

D Hot-rolled asphalt used in road construction.

E Mastic asphalt pavement, granite kerbs and *pavé* or setts, Ile de la Cité, Paris.

F Mastic asphalt with stamped pattern in the foreground, Paris.

G Cold-rolled asphalt.

H Gravel two-track road, West Green, Hampshire, England. Note the absence of edging: the gravel has been placed in a trench cut into the meadow.

I Resin-bound asphalt reveals the color of the stone, Lincoln's Inn Fields, London.

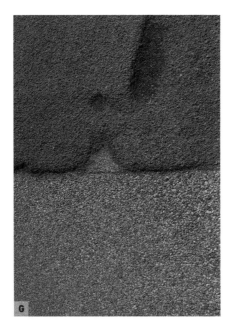

TIP ROAD PAINT

The photograph shows an asphalt road marked with a thermoplastic resin marker line. Road-marking paints include epoxy, water-based paint, and chlorinated rubber. Thermoplastic paint is not suitable on concrete or brick because heat bond involves melting the top layer of the asphalt. Road-line paint can be any color, but yellow, white, and red are the most common.

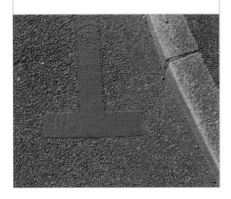

Edge restraint

Flexible roads require edge restraint so that they can be consolidated by rolling. Typically edge restraint can take the form of curbs which are haunched with concrete. Such curbs can take the form of precast concrete curbs, cast-in-place concrete (favoured in North America), bricks laid on edge or in soldier-course fashion, setts, or even steel edging. Private roads can be formed with timber edging, as can informal garden paths where the timber will rot away leaving a "natural" edge. Alternatively, on heavy clay soils newly laid flexible paving can be consolidated by rolling against a cut in the earth: this will produce a wavy edge which may be appropriate on rural sites.

Left
Steel edging to a hoggin (bound gravel) path, Versailles, France.

Below left
Cast-iron curb.

Below right
Stainless-steel curb.

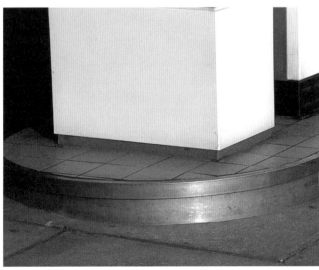

Below left
Gray-and-white precast concrete paving, Jardin Atlantique, Gare Montparnasse, Paris.

Below center
Contrasting black-and-white checkerboard paving of black muddy limestone, known as black marble in the stone trade, and metamorphic white Italian marble, St Paul's Cathedral, London.

Below right
Line of black Diamant schist stones, a metamorphized micaceous rock from the Kalahari Desert, laid in Guildhall Yard, London.

Color in paving

Most stones and concretes are not strongly colored. The strongest-colored concrete is that made using an exposed aggregate, and this is best done in a factory. Strong patterns in paving, however, can be obtained by recessing the joints or by changes of texture—for instance, by using precast concrete channels and asphalt squares in forecourts, or by alternating brick and precast concrete.

The paving materials that do hold color are clay bricks, which are available in a range of yellows, reds, oranges, and blues; and ceramic tiles. Ceramic tiles, which are color-fast, must be laid on a rigid foundation because they are thin. Alternatively, terrazzo, consisting of marble chips set in a cement substrate, can be brightly colored and is much used for street paving in coastal areas of Spain and around the Mediterranean. Terrazzo, however, is slippery in frosty conditions, and therefore should not be used externally in regions where frosts occur. Colored concrete blocks do not hold color very well; the color additives in the cement fade on exposure to ultraviolet light. However, colorful cast-in-place concrete can be made using aggregate made from broken blue or red brick, or black granite.

Marble chippings are available in greens and reds, and can be considered for lightly trafficked areas. Also worth considering are crushed windshield glass and abraded bottle glass (available in green, brown, or blue, and worn down by placing in a cement mixer). However, do not use them in areas where young children might

be tempted to eat the broken glass, and be careful of insurance considerations—above all, do not use broken *plate* glass, because it remains sharp. Stone holds color and is available in reds and grays, whites and blacks. Granite, of course, can produce strong patterns, but much depends on the finish of the stone. Generally, the strongest colors are found in polished or wet stones. Flamed and split stone can produce strong textures, which can be used for patterns in paving.

There is a great deal of scope in using materials developed for road-marking: these are often resins such as epoxy, acrylic, or polyurethane. It is also worth considering materials developed for athletic field surfacing (including plastic grass), and the range of brightly colored rubber-based play surfaces that are available as tiles or that can be poured and then set: these may be laid on an asphalt or concrete base.

Below left
Strongly colored terrazzo, Granada, Spain.

Below
Regular precast concrete slab paving laid stack bond results in a gray, mundane appearance.

Porous paving

Most paving has been designed to cast water off its surface and to avoid water penetration, and the consequent frost–thaw damage to wearing surface, base and sub-base. However, concern about groundwater levels with the fall in the levels of aquifers and the decline of water levels in streams and rivers has led to the development of porous paving—both unit paving and asphalt varieties.

Currently, the following materials are available as porous pavings:

- concrete blocks;
- permeable clay pavers;
- permeable asphalt;
- permeable resin-bound asphalt;
- cell-matrix pavers—e.g. concrete-reinforced grass paving; and
- no-fines concrete.

Unit-paving has developed using no-fines precast concrete blocks and clay pavers with wide, nibbed joints. Resin-bound asphalt is a form of asphalt with a transparent resin binder. Both resin-bound and traditional bitumen-bound open-graded asphalt surfaces are available, and are porous. All these surfaces depend on an open, textured base, and sub-base.

Unit pavers require the construction of a no-fines laying course of $\frac{1}{16}$–$\frac{1}{4}$ in crushed stone on a base course with a 4 in thick topmost level of $\frac{3}{16}$–$\frac{3}{4}$ in crushed-stone, coarse, ground aggregate rather than the traditional (greater) range of $\frac{3}{8}$–$2\frac{1}{2}$ in. The stone aggregate must be strong and hard so that it does not break down, so use granite or basalt. The jointing material (which is brushed in during compaction) between blocks should be the same as the laying-course material, rather than a fine, kiln-dried sand. The use of no-fines in the base course ensures the presence of a higher proportion of voids, which enable the course to act as a sponge.

Note that there are many variations in these sizes in current practice, and the promotion of permeable paving is only about ten years old. Therefore, empirical experiment is tending to lead development and specification. In addition, a geotextile (such as a permeable polypropylene/polyethylene) is often incorporated in order to trap pollutants in cases where the intention is that microbial activity will break down oils and hydrocarbons.

Below
Permeable, gravel-filled precast concrete geogrid parking area, with a herringbone-pattern road to the right. Note how the pattern of the herringbone is broken at the edge to avoid cut bricks.

Above left
Sett paving with grass-filled joints.

Above
Grass-filled joints transform plain cast-in-place concrete in this pocket park at Quai des Célestins, Paris.

Drainage

The late Sir Peter Shepheard had an appropriate anecdote about the opening of the Festival of Britain in London on 2 May 1951: the royal party arrived for their walkabout after it had rained. Fellow landscape architect Peter Youngman had designed the "upstream" half of the South Bank site with paving slopes of 1:100 (see photograph, page 71), while Peter Shepheard had designed the half downstream of Hungerford Bridge at 1:50—the puddles all lay upstream. We would further argue that steeper cross-drainage of 1:50 is appropriate in most landscape or garden areas. Remember to slope pavings away from buildings and away from pools, in order to minimize splash-back staining and to ensure that dirt is not washed into pools. If it is necessary to slope towards a building (as at a garage entrance), then a drainage channel will be required to ensure that water does not penetrate the building.

TIP SITE AND DRAINAGE

Be aware of the geology of a site: on many permeable sand or chalk sites there is little need to provide extensive drainage because paths can be drained onto adjacent beds. On steep slopes and low or clay sites comprehensive drainage is vital.

A Paving in a private garden incorporates precast concrete channels with squares of asphalt, two differently colored wearing courses and a dark brown brick-laid herringbone pattern. The bricks were saw-cut off site and delivered to the garden in plastic-wrapped pallets.

B Anti-slip, diamond-patterned brick paving laid stack bond leads to a chapel's slate steps, Machynlleth, Wales.

C Sandstone of 24 in wide random lengths, 2 in deep, was laid on granite sand with blue bands of engineering brick and 4 in diameter loose granite gravel panels. The granite has some quartz in it, which makes it glisten. Canon headquarters, Reigate, England.

D Gravel in the garden of West Green house, Surrey, England.

E Granite setts laid wide-jointed and edged with brick paving at the Glasgow Garden Festival, Scotland. Wide jointing like this could be equally effectively filled with grass. In the background is Ian Hamilton Finlay's Three Stiles in Three Styles garden.

F Paving (1951–57) by Dimitrios Pikionis at Philopappos Hill, Athens, using remains of classical stones.

Design of paving

Paving design can be a delight, and need not involve expensive materials: simple concrete slabs can be transformed by leaving wide (2–3 in) grass-filled joints, or by filling wide-jointed concrete slab layouts with slates on edge.

It is far better to concentrate expensive effects near entrances, or in special areas and along main axes, and then provide extensive areas of cheaper gravel or asphalt with good edging or drainage channels. Take care with edgings and joints. Boring vehicle forecourts can be transformed by simply dividing them and providing pattern and scale using standard precast concrete channels.

Combine function and pattern, thereby transforming the functional elements of a design. For instance, driveways can be reduced in scale by simply paving the two wheel tracks: many country lanes were so paved until the 1950s. Paving patterns can extend the architecture of a house into the garden. Paths can be abstract compositions in line, texture, form, and color. Paving provides the ground framework of a garden layout, and is therefore fundamental to good landscape and garden design.

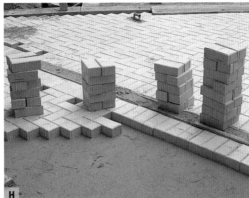

G Sandstone of random lengths laid across a footpath, Trumpington Street, Cambridge. Note the water conduit on the left—drainage need not be underground.

H Herringbone brick pavers being laid on a sand bed, Judge Institute, Cambridge.

I Thin Dutch bricks laid herringbone pattern on a sand bed in the Lange Voorhout, The Hague. The bricks probably date from the late seventeenth or eighteenth century but would be relaid periodically, perhaps every 50 years. The wide color range gives a tweed effect and the paving can flex to accommodate movement due to tree-root growth.

J Slabs of precast exposed aggregate concrete in the Jardin Atlantique above the Gare Montparnasse, Paris.

K West 8's scheme at Sloterdijk station near Amsterdam suggests what can be done with road-marking paint and anti-skid surfaces on asphalt.

L Early nineteenth-century pitching in Llanidloes, Wales.

M Precast concrete slab paving is transformed by the use of white marble and pebble-filled wide joints in Granada, Spain.

N Mixed color metamorphic and igneous setts in Paris.

STEP BY STEP FLEXIBLE HERRINGBONE PAVING

These illustrations from a number of sites show the sequence of preparing and laying flexible paving for roads and parking areas. Flexible paving permits movement, uses less embodied carbon than rigid paving on a concrete foundation, is cheaper, and shows off the unit paving. In addition to these advantages, strong patterns can be achieved with flexible paving.

1 Preparing the levels.

2 Building road curbs to provide edge retention.

3 Compacting the hard-core base using a roller.

4 Laying clay paving bricks on a 2 in thick sand bed.

5 Breaking the herringbone pattern at the edges in order to avoid small-cut bricks.

6 When there is a regular rectangular module the brick can be suppled in pallet panels from the brickmakers, with edge bricks precut to avoid noise on site.

7 A study in paving patterns: herringbone to the left, stretcher bond in the dark-blue brick panels, and fan pattern setts and bricks.

8 After being laid these herringbone bricks were sanded and rolled with a vibrating roller.

9 A multicolored effect is produced in herringbone pattern clay paving bricks using three colors of brick randomly mixed.

10 A similar multicolored effect using dark and light gray concrete blocks.

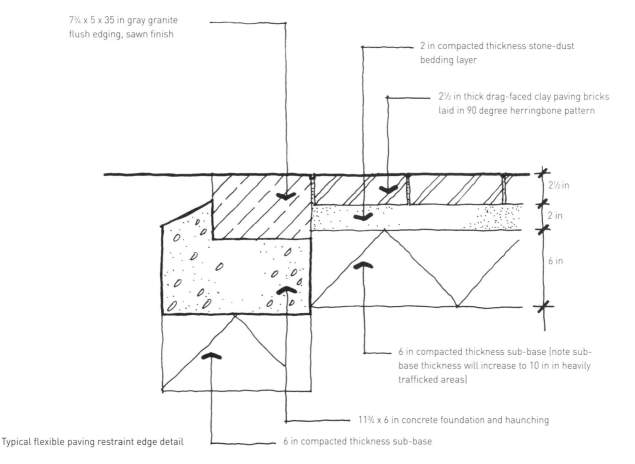

7¾ x 5 x 35 in gray granite flush edging, sawn finish

2 in compacted thickness stone-dust bedding layer

2½ in thick drag-faced clay paving bricks laid in 90 degree herringbone pattern

2½ in

2 in

6 in

6 in compacted thickness sub-base (note sub-base thickness will increase to 10 in in heavily trafficked areas)

11¾ x 6 in concrete foundation and haunching

Typical flexible paving restraint edge detail

6 in compacted thickness sub-base

Dealing with water

Water is one of the elements of life, and revealing it in a landscape scheme can involve far more than its visual delight—vital as that may be. Drainage of development sites may require the provision of retention basins in order to accommodate surface run-off during heavy rainfall, and water can generate power. In the form of ponds and lakes, it can provide a rich wildlife habitat, is a source of fish and plant food, and acts as reservoirs for use in irrigation and firefighting.

Water is predictable and very stable. Its basic characteristics are:
- it usually flows downhill under gravity;[6]
- it freezes, and on freezing expands by 9 per cent;
- it evaporates;
- people are attracted by water, they want to touch it; and
- water can be dangerous: a small child can drown in 24 in water, and anyone can drown in 2 in water if they are unconscious.

Top
The Eleven Acre lake at Stowe, Buckinghamshire, England. This man-made lake was butyl-lined in 1981 and, though artificial, it now has the appearance of a "natural" or Picturesque lake.

Above
The lake at Painshill Park, Surrey, England, where the opposite bank is formed by a dam parallel with the River Mole to create a lake on half the valley.

Introduction to pool construction

Pools can be classed as formal or informal, and as "alive" or "dead." Dead pools are chemically cleaned, while live pools use a balance of artificial and natural systems to maintain aeration and avoid anaerobic conditions (a lack of oxygen), which result in stagnant water.

The main criteria for pool and lake design are:
- climate and microclimate;
- setting;
- scale;
- effect;
- noise level;
- cleanliness;
- water table;
- level of control;
- water supply;
- vandalism;
- budget; and
- maintenance.

Climate and microclimate

In temperate areas, freeze–thaw should be designed for. Many water features are drained in winter in northern France because of frost. If this is to be done, consider the appearance of the pool when empty. In hot weather, water will be lost by evaporation and either "draw down" (the lowering of the water) or topping up should be designed for, as necessary.

Also be aware of microclimate. There is little point in designing high-nozzle fountain displays for a position subject to down draughts from a large high-rise—in which case, the fountains would have to be turned off most of the time.

Setting

A pool is usually designed in accordance with its setting. The top of a hill is not the obvious location for a lake; better to locate it in a valley. The flat landscape of The Netherlands is appropriate for straight, canal-like water features, but a flowing landform can be complemented by a serpentine lake. One of the strangest large lakes is that at Painshill Park (an eighteenth-century park in Surrey), where a long dam was constructed alongside the River Mole and water raised up by a watermill. The dam produces a long, thin, straight-sided lake edge, which appears very odd. By contrast, the formal water pools at Studley Royal in Yorkshire sit in the landscape (a U-shaped valley with a flat bottom) very well.

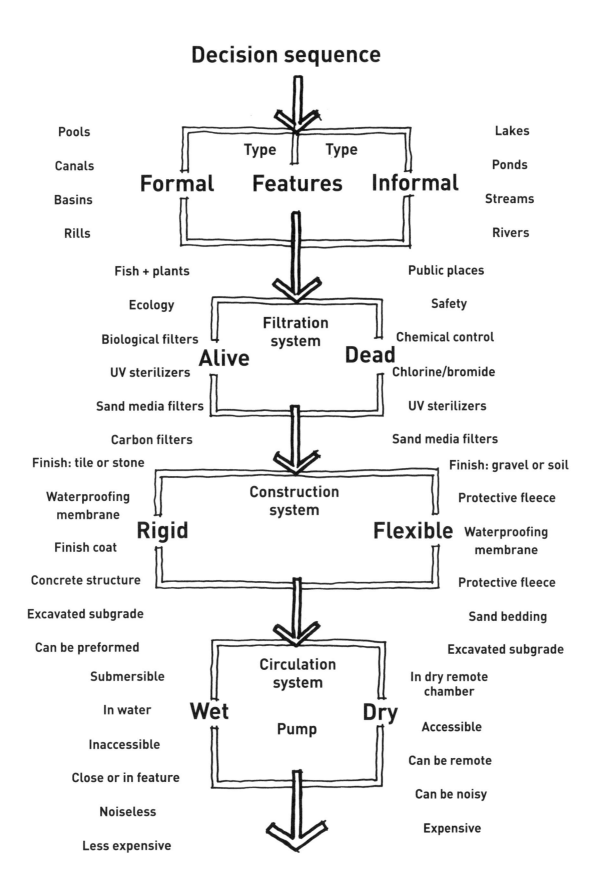

Decision sequence

Formal	Type	Type	Informal
Pools	**Features**		Lakes
Canals			Ponds
Basins			Streams
Rills			Rivers

Fish + plants   Public places

Ecology   Safety

Biological filters   **Filtration**   Chemical control
                            system
UV sterilizers   **Alive**   **Dead**   Chlorine/bromide

Sand media filters   UV sterilizers

Carbon filters   Sand media filters

Finish: tile or stone   Finish: gravel or soil

Waterproofing   **Construction**   Protective fleece
membrane   **system**
                       Rigid   **Flexible**   Waterproofing
Finish coat   membrane

Concrete structure   Protective fleece

Excavated subgrade   Sand bedding

Can be preformed   **Circulation**   Excavated subgrade
                          system
Submersible   In dry remote
                                                 chamber
In water   **Wet**   **Dry**
                          Pump   Accessible
Inaccessible
                                                 Can be remote
Close or in feature
                                                 Can be noisy
Noiseless
                                                 Expensive
Less expensive

Diagram illustrating the choices and considerations when selecting water and construction systems

Benefits of pools and water bodies: scale, effect, and noise

Pools are a way of making a small space appear bigger: they reflect the sky and seasonal change, and introduce movement and life into a space. They can be dark, still and reflective, or full of activity.

Waterfalls and cascades are ways of providing "white noise," which can mask the din of traffic in the center of a city. A small space can be enlivened by a trickle of water into a pool. However, fountains can also be very noisy and dominating.

Cleanliness

Chemical control of water is largely used because of concerns about cleanliness in busy locations, such as shopping centers. The main chemicals used are bromide and chlorine, but both can be dangerous—chlorine, for instance, is a poisonous gas. Ozone gas offers an alternative treatment. Such methods require constant monitoring and maintenance. For most pools, natural methods of management produce a safer and biologically more sound water environment.

All pools require regular clearing of leaves and litter, and this should be programmed into the maintenance schedule. Large pools and lakes liable to silting will require periodic drainage and silt removal.

Water table

Pool construction begins with consideration of the water table and the soil. A high water table makes the creation of a pool or canal easy: dig a hole in such circumstances, and it will simply fill with water. The main factors to decide upon are the depth and edge of the pool. A fundamental question is whether the groundwater is flowing or whether it is still (as in polders). The type of ground will also affect the color of a pool. A clay bottom will tend to give a brown pool, and a peat area will result in a black pool. There is nothing wrong with such effects, but make sure you design for them—don't expect water necessarily to be clear or blue.

Maintenance and water supply

Be aware of the availability and financing of maintenance at the initial stage of a water-feature design. It is appropriate to design a complex water feature for an office development or business park, in which the maintenance costs are met by service charges paid by the tenants and which are costed for at the beginning by the development surveyor. However, the design of similar water features may not be appropriate in public areas unless there is a public commitment to financing the consequent maintenance. For example, finger-nozzle fountains are maintained in Paris parks, but there have been problems with the upkeep of the nozzle fountains

at the Thames Barrier Park in London (maintained by the Greater London Authority).

Vandalism can range from the thoughtless (throwing shopping carts into pools and canals appears to be a British habit) to the criminal (stealing expensive fountain fittings for scrap metal). Design and maintain appropriately—and, where necessary, provide security.

When designing pools, it is important to determine where the water comes from: a large lake can take months to fill with rainfall from a small catchment area. Smaller pools may be filled using a public water supply. Streams can be dammed or diverted to make a pool, and it is worth bearing in mind that marshland and water meadows can be valuable habitats, while the bog garden is worthwhile at the domestic scale. It is also necessary to be aware of the hardness of the water: that from calcareous aquifers has a high pH, which results in calcium deposits in pipework and pumps.

The water barrel fed by rooftop rainwater is the simplest of water features, and every garden should have one for watering during summer droughts. In dry climates, such measures can involve larger tanks. Remember to stock these with fish in order to avoid mosquitoes: a couple of goldfish are the simplest biological control available. A variety of garden pool is simply a barrel or similar container buried in the ground. Alternatively, preformed pools in GRP (glass-reinforced plastic) follow the same principle.

Small pools can be designed without a water supply (and can be filled by hosepipe or bowser). However, most pools should also be drainable so that they may be easily cleaned out—or at least should be designed so that the water can be pumped away.

In larger developments, pools are often designed as part of sustainable urban drainage systems (SUDS), whereby rainwater run-off from roofs and paving is collected, treated by running through reed beds and then directed for use either in pools (as at Potsdamer Platz, see opposite) or as "secondary" water for irrigation.

Lakes and dams

For any significant lake development involving a dam, it is prudent to engage specialist, civil-engineering advice—not least because of the professional-insurance concern.

A fundamental choice is how deep and in what fashion the pool is to be formed and edged. Depth of pool is influenced by ease of public access and concerns about safety. From the point of view of pool ecology, the deeper the better. This is because high summer temperatures can result in a loss of oxygen in the water, and the consequent anaerobic conditions are bad for pond life and result in stagnant water. Ideally, large pools should be greater than three feet deep in the center in order to support fish.

However, the edges of a pool should usually be shallow, so that small children can get out. It is typical in Dutch residential canal and channel construction to have a "shelf," about 24 in or less deep, at the edge. Flexible forms of construction require a sloping edge of a maximum gradient of 1:3. Such slopes also assist pool and marginal vegetation.

Left
Pool at Potsdamer Platz, Berlin, designed by Atelier Dreiseitl.

TIP BUDGET

As with all landscape expenditure, it is necessary to allow for capital expenditure, initial installation, and ongoing revenue-financing for management and maintenance. It is in the nature of all constructions to weather and change, and this process is more marked in water features than in many other elements of the built environment. Water can be very cheap initially—but pools silt up unless drained and cleaned out from time to time, and pumps require regular maintenance.

Below
The beach of a butyl-lined pool in
a private garden.

Bottom left
Vertical-post pool edge, Sydenham
Wells Park, London.

Below right
Post-and-log pool edge at
Thijsse Park, Amstelveen, The
Netherlands.

Informal pools and rigid structures
Unlined pools

Unlined pools use the natural water level, or are made in impermeable ground (such as clay or rock). The main factors determining their design are the pool edge and the required depth.

The edge of the pool may be vertical, or may be shelved and form a beach. From the point of view of habitat diversity, it is good to have either a gently sloping "shelf" edge or a series of terraces because different plants grow at different depths of water. A beach permits ease of contact with the water: one can touch it, or indeed swim in it. A beach can be sandy or covered in cobbles. Vertical edges may be constructed like a retaining wall, and this is usual in canals which have to resist wave action. These edges can be simple timber constructions such as lumber posts driven in side by side and fixed together with galvanized wire, or horizontal-board and lumber-post constructions.

Lined pools

The shape of lined pools may be formal or informal. Both types may be constructed with flexible liners or their construction may be rigid. The latter might use a concrete-slab floor and "walls," which will have a fairly formal shape whether curved or straight—or may be a free-form shape using sprayed concrete (gunnite).

Rigid liners

Cast-in-place concrete slabs and vertical walls of concrete blocks or brickwork (or cast-in-place concrete) are the conventional constituents of a rigid, lined pool. We recommend that a liner be placed over the concrete structure; should there be leaks they are easily repaired by replacing all or part of the liner. The traditional alternative of waterproof concrete is not particularly recommended, but is often used. It tends to be marginally cheaper.

STEP BY STEP BUILDING A RIGID POOL

The channel in the background of this sequence of images is built on site of concrete blockwork with granite coping and a butyl liner, but the contractor suggested an alternative method of construction for the circular infinity pool that sits at the head of the channel. Rather than being built on site, the steel pool was factory built and brought to site as one unit, and therefore only needed levelling to ensure a horizontal, even edge. With this type of pool the edge must be horizontal to achieve the infinity effect.

1 Construction of a rigid pool of galvanized mild steel in a private garden.

2 The steel is painted and cobbles are placed.

3 The filled pool reveals the infinity pool edge.

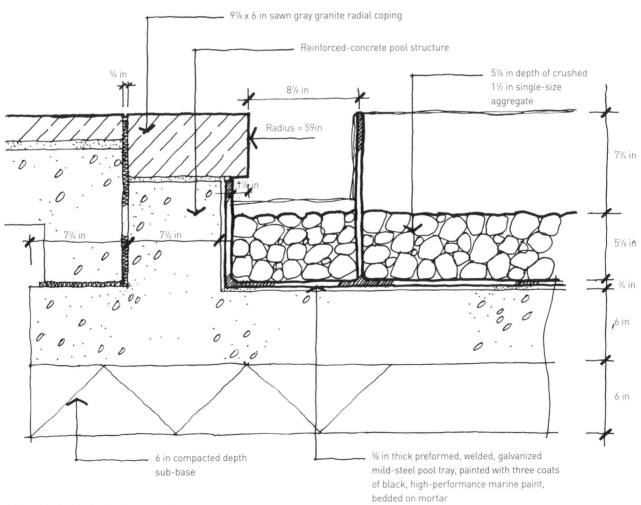

9⅞ x 6 in sawn gray granite radial coping

Reinforced-concrete pool structure

5⅛ in depth of crushed 1½ in single-size aggregate

⅝ in

8⅞ in

Radius = 59in

7¾ in

1¼ in

7¾ in

7¾ in

5⅛ in

¾ in

6 in

6 in

6 in compacted depth sub-base

⅜ in thick preformed, welded, galvanized mild-steel pool tray, painted with three coats of black, high-performance marine paint, bedded on mortar

Detail section of a steel-edged source pool

Informally shaped pools

The traditional liner for an informally shaped pool is puddled clay, but it is also possible to use flexible liners and sprayed concrete.

Puddled clay

This is the liner usually employed in canal building, and in most lake construction until the nineteenth century. The clay may come from the site or be imported, but should be free of stones and vegetable matter such as tree roots. It should be laid in a 12–35 in layer of clay for canals and large lakes, but only a 6 in thick for smaller pools, where there is not likely to be cattle (or other livestock) access which may penetrate the clay. The clay is laid in layers of 3 in or so, and is then "puddled," or pounded together, and trafficked over using feet (cattle and sheep were traditionally used to do this). This makes the clay plastic, closes fissures and forces out air bubbles.

Bentonite clay

Bentonite is a naturally occurring aluminium-silicate clay with a high swelling capacity. It is good for pool design because it can be self-repairing: holes and cracks caused by roots will mend themselves. Bentonite can, in fact, be used to repair puddled-clay pools on site. The clay, when added in powder form, is drawn to the leak and so blocks it. However, this will adversely affect fish (it clogs their gills)—though it is not toxic to plants. Additionally, bentonite is not easily applied to steeply sloping banks.

Shotcrete (sprayed concrete, or gunnite)

In the shotcrete process, concrete is pneumatically sprayed at high pressure onto the surface to be lined, usually over a steel reinforcement mesh. The process was invented by the American Carl Akeley, and he patented its name as "gunite" in 1911. Originally the concrete was applied as a dry mix (as Gunite, which is still its trade name) which was wetted as it was sprayed, but it can also be sprayed using a previously wetted concrete mix. "Shotcrete" is the generic term applied to both methods, and "gunnite" is also used generically with a different spelling to the name Akeley gave his invention to avoid the trade name. As

cast-in-place concrete, it does not require formwork. The concrete mix should be waterproofed and is often painted with a further waterproofing layer, or can be lined with a flexible liner. Like formed concrete, shotcrete is not of itself waterproof. As with formed concrete, there should also be a good cover (minimum 1½ in) of concrete to the reinforcement.

Spray waterproofing for concrete pools

There is a range of spray-applied liners or sealants, which can be used on pools—such as polyurea elastomers, urethanes, epoxies, vinylesters, polyesters, and asphalt.

Flexible liners

Flexible liners can be used to waterproof rigid-constructed pools and informally shaped ones. When used as a "placed" system, without a construction, the liner requires protection above and below. A typical "sandwich" comprises a sand bed, as shown in the diagram opposite.

The main materials in current use as flexible pool liners are:
- *Butyl rubber* in liner thicknesses of fractions of an inch; it is safe for fish and wildlife, is flexible, elastic, and puncture-resistant with a life of up to 30 years;
- *EPDM (ethylene propylene diene monomer)* is not so safe for wildlife, as chemicals used in its production can leach and are harmful to fish and pondlife;
- *Polypropylene (PE)* is chemical-resistant, low cost, and less flexible than butyl and EPDM, and requires specialist site-welding of joints;
- *Polyvinyl chloride (PVC)* is low cost but not easily repaired. It has a short lifespan, especially when exposed to ultraviolet light; however, it performs better when reinforced with nylon.

All the above are subject to deterioration in ultraviolet light where they are exposed above water, but can be protected by the use of overhanging edging, which shades the draw down, or by covering "natural" sloping edges with river cobbles or with sand that rises above the waterline to form a beach.

Puddled clay

Advantages	can be cheap if materials and labor are on site	can be easily repaired	cheap
Disadvantages	labor-intensive	clay liable to crack if the pool dries out	

Bentonite clay

Advantages	more expensive than puddled clay	tends to be self-repairing	can be dried out
Disadvantages	Not suitable (unless isolated) on chalky soils	may require a protection layer of 4 in gravel	expensive

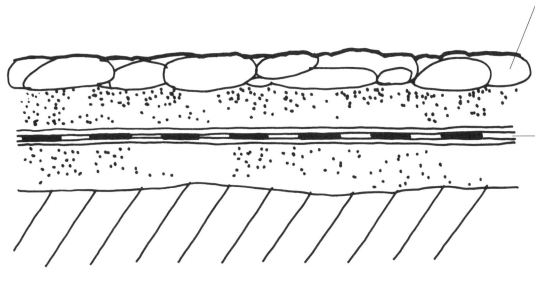

Water level

Layer of rounded cobbles or coarse gravel as protection and substrate for rooting water plants

Coarse sand layer

Protective geotextile fleece
Waterproof liner membrane
Protective geotextile fleece

Coarse sand layer

Prepared and compacted subgrade

Section of flexible liner

A Gunnite-sprayed concrete pool at Las Golondrinas condominium, Don Carlos Hotel, near Marbella, Spain.

B Sprayed concrete water feature, Parc de Bercy, Paris.

C Free-form butyl- and cobble-lined feature pool in a private garden, England.

D Polypropylene lined pool at the Centre for Alternative Technology, Machynlleth, Wales. The pool was constructed in 1990 and photographed in 2009.

STEP BY STEP BUILDING A FLEXIBLY LINED POOL

This sequence shows the construction of a retention basin. The outlet weir controls the normal water level, and the volume above that performs a temporary storage function for surfacewater drainage during storms. The weir regulates the rate of outflow and spreads the outflow over a number of hours so that the drainage system downstream is not overloaded. In short, the pool is designed to flood. It was planned as a simple, flexible butyl-lined pool, but one problem was the fluctuating groundwater table, which lifted the butyl liner. The solution was to install a one-way valve in the bottom of the pool.

1 The area is excavated and leveled to shape.

2 The leveled area: the darker soil is clayey and the lighter soil is a sandy layer.

3 White Terram—a permeable geotextile—is laid in the foreground while in the distance a gray butyl liner is spread in rolls. These will be welded together on site.

4 Checking the edge of the butyl liner once the pool has begun to fill.

5 Because this is a retention basin, only the bottom of the pool is butyl-lined to make a permanent water body. With a weir controlling the outlet level, the upper slopes hold in flood water after heavy rain until the drains can accommodate the flow.

6 The partially filled pool.

7 The pool photographed a year after construction. The concrete outlet weir is on the left.

8 The pool photographed ten years after completion.

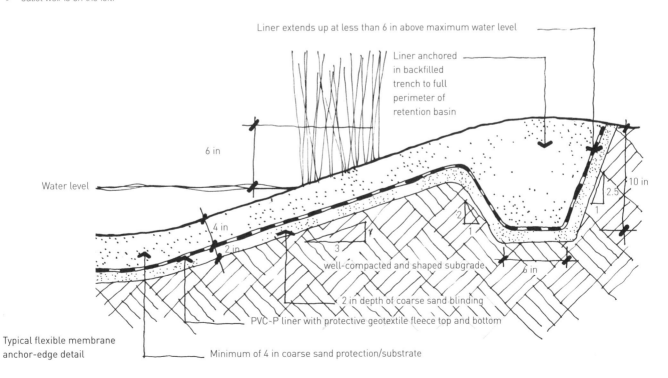

Liner extends up at less than 6 in above maximum water level

Liner anchored in backfilled trench to full perimeter of retention basin

6 in

Water level

10 in

2.5

4 in

2

1

2 in

3

1

well-compacted and shaped subgrade

6 in

2 in depth of coarse sand blinding

PVC-P liner with protective geotextile fleece top and bottom

Typical flexible membrane anchor-edge detail

Minimum of 4 in coarse sand protection/substrate

Rigid construction

This consists of a floor-and-wall construction, and typically the floor or base will be of cast-in-place concrete while walls may be built of cast-in-place concrete, concrete blocks, or brick. The waterproofing is then applied, and may be a flexible lining or a rigid liner such as GRP (glass-reinforced plastic)—or the floor or base can be covered over with a tile or waterproof paint.

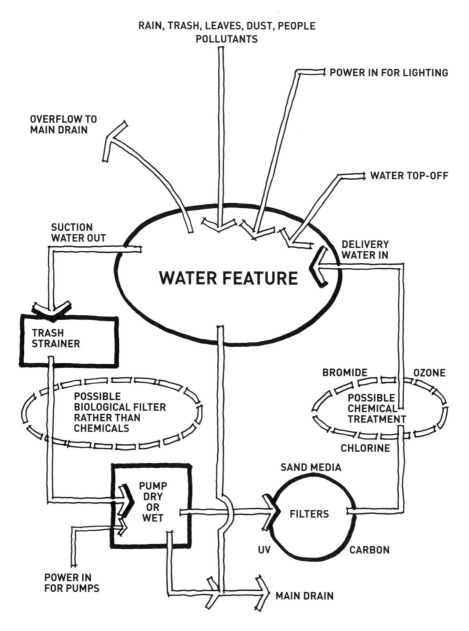

Basic water systems

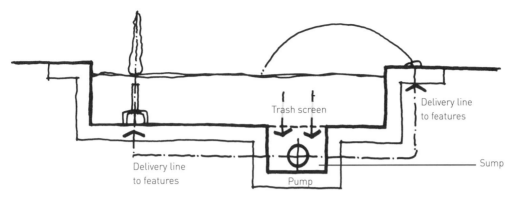

Trash screen

Delivery line
to features

Delivery line
to features

Sump

Pump

Submersible pump in a sump

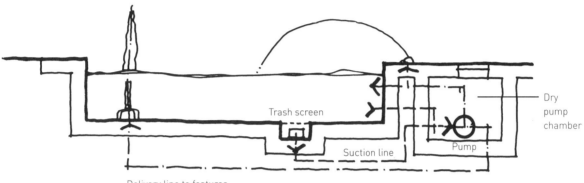

Trash screen

Dry
pump
chamber

Suction line

Pump

Delivery line to features

Dry pump in a remote chamber

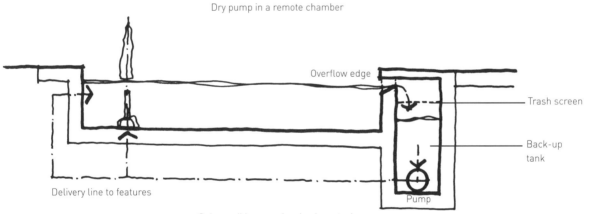

Overflow edge

Trash screen

Back-up
tank

Delivery line to features

Pump

Submersible pump in a back-up tank

Above
Diagrams illustrating three different options for pump location. Dry pumps are problematic in that the chamber has to be kept dry and is noisy. All pumps require regular cleaning and maintenance.

Left
This rigid pool has a freeboard edge and overflow at the far end which runs into a back-up tank with a submersible pump (as illustrated in the right side of the diagram above).

Ponds, pools, lakes, canals, basins, and rills

Ponds are small water bodies—although exactly how small is subjective. Henry David Thoreau's Walden Pond in Massachusetts is 62 acres, and "ponds" tend to be seen as bigger entities in the United States. The Ramsar Convention on Wetlands, however, defines the upper size of a pond as 20 acres. Lakes, by contrast, are larger than ponds. Both are freshwater bodies of water, which may be natural or man-made. A pool, on the other hand, is also seen as a "small body of still water usually of natural formation, a small shallow body of any liquid" according to the *Shorter Oxford English Dictionary*, but there is the suggestion that a pool may be shallow while a pond might be deep. A lake is definitely deep, but depth too is subjective.

Canals and basins are artificial: a "basin" suggests some sort of bowl, and basins in French gardens are often circular, while canals are always linear and often straight. A rill, by contrast, is a small stream that has a "natural" course or shape even when man-made. The serpentine rill at Rousham in Oxfordshire is perhaps the most famous in England.

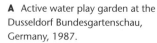

A Active water play garden at the Dusseldorf Bundesgartenschau, Germany, 1987.

B Rills with fountains, Generalife, Granada, Spain.

C Vertical glass waterwall, Haarlemmermeer Floriade, The Netherlands.

D The concrete formal pool with waterproof render sealing and cobble-lined bottom at the Barcelona Pavilion, Spain, a reconstruction of Mies van der Rohe's German Pavilion building for the 1929 International Exposition.

E Front view of a stone-faced cascade water feature, Jardin Atlantique, Paris.

F The rear view of the cascade water feature at the Jardin Atlantique shows weir boxes and delivery pipes.

G Channel at Het Loo, a reconstruction of a seventeenth-century royal palace garden in Apeldoorn, The Netherlands.

H The rill at Rousham, Oxfordshire, England.

I Dancing water jets as part of a formal cascading feature, La Défense, Paris.

J Formal water feature and overflow, place Charles de Gaulle, Lille, France.

STEP BY STEP CONSTRUCTING A RIGID CHANNEL

This sequence shows the stages of constructing a rigid concrete blockwork and butyl-lined channel in a private garden, for a house by the architect John Outram.

1 A cast-in-place concrete foundation is laid and a precast concrete blockwork wall is part built. Note the change of level.

2 The channel walls are built of precast concrete blockwork.

3 A precast concrete road channel is laid out on the walls prior to laying liner (the precast channel is then placed to one side).

4 The architect John Outram inspects the built blockwork wall as Bidim felt is being laid as protection for the butyl liner.

5 The butyl liner is largely laid, but the precast concrete channel is incorrectly placed flush with the walls. The precast road channels were later relaid to overhang the walls.

6 The completed pools system. Note how the overhang shades and protects the butyl liner above the waterline.

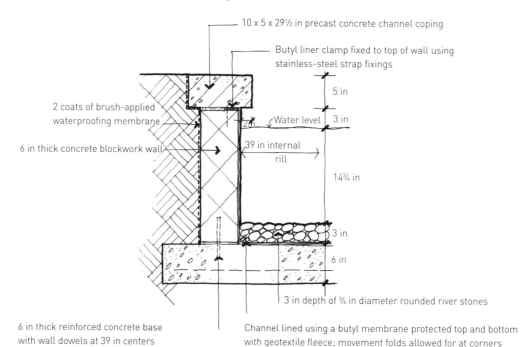

10 x 5 x 29½ in precast concrete channel coping

Butyl liner clamp fixed to top of wall using stainless-steel strap fixings

2 coats of brush-applied waterproofing membrane

6 in thick concrete blockwork wall

Water level

5 in

3 in

39 in internal rill

14¾ in

3 in

6 in

3 in depth of ¾ in diameter rounded river stones

6 in thick reinforced concrete base with wall dowels at 39 in centers

Channel lined using a butyl membrane protected top and bottom with geotextile fleece; movement folds allowed for at corners

Cascades, waterfalls, and weirs

Waterfalls can be delightful: they offer sound (which may form "white noise" in a busy city square), excitement and delight. However, they can demand large quantities of water and this requires a significant pump capacity —so they can be energy- and maintenance-intensive (unless they are gravity fed). A rule of thumb is that ¾ in of water depth has to pass over a spillway for three feet of clear drop. However, aerated falls (as opposed to continuous sheets of water), such as cascades, can work with as little as ⅜ in of water depth.

Smooth sheets of water require a smooth lip to the spillway; this can be made of concrete or sawn stone—or of a metal such as stainless steel or aluminum. A concrete edge can also be leveled by use of a metal or plastic strip. The smoother the spillway the faster and more efficient the water flow, allowing water depth (and pump power) to be minimized. A properly leveled and sloped metal slipway can function with as little as ⅜ in of water depth.

Clearly, though, a metal spillway will appear man-made and artificial. "Natural" stone waterfalls and cascades should be designed to appear as being predominantly water, but the flow rate should allow for irregularities and rivulets between the rocks. The pool at the foot of a waterfall is best in a dark material, which shows off the agitated water to greatest effect.

Waterfalls can be projected or can descend as a sheet of water over the face of the vertical drop, though this "verticality" can vary with the material chosen:
• stone can be 90 degree (i.e. 100 per cent vertical);
• glass should be sloped at 85–88 per cent; and
• acrylic should be sloped at 83–85 per cent.

Inclines, rather than vertical falls, can be very effective and require lesser volumes of water. Such inclines can be smooth, shaped, or have rough surfaces. A classic smooth surface is glass; a rough surface could be exposed-aggregate concrete, or split or flame-finished stone. Exposed-aggregate concrete is best with sharp aggregate (because it gives more water agitation) as opposed to smooth gravel.

Rules of thumb in waterfall and cascade design:
• not under trees;
• not in positions exposed to trees;
• design for water saving: depths should average 16 in;
• allow for a freeboard (at the top of a weir) of 3–4 in;
• always provide an overflow and drainage outlet in order to allow for draw down when a pumped system is switched off;
• provide pump-protection level sensors;
• secure all in-pool fittings;
• should look good empty;
• design for frost protection;
• design with ease of maintenance in mind—e.g. pumps should be accessible;
• design for a 20-year life; and
• design sufficient draw down (distance between the operational water level and the bottom pool-edge level) in a pool system to ensure that the bottom pool can accommodate the water depth above the top of a weir when the pump is shut down.

Far left
Stainless-steel waterchute at Canon headquarters, Reigate, England.

Center left
Boulder cascade at Jumeirah Beach Hotel, Dubai.

Left
Welling pool and rill, Jardin Albert Kahn, Paris.

ASSEMBLY

Fasteners and connections

The various components that make up the elements of a structure—whether a lumber deck, a pergola, railings, or the liner of a pool—require connecting. To do that, you may use flexible or rigid fixings, or you can use hinges. There are two basic types of fastening:

Positional fastenings, which hold components together and comprise:
- *Flexible fasteners*: lumber joints, pegs, and dowels, lashings and ties, and some adhesives;
- *Rigid fasteners*: bolts and nuts, screws, nails, and many adhesives; and
- *Articulation or rotational fastenings:* hinges and springs which permit movement on a plane.

Loadbearing fastenings, such as anchor points or base plates, which transfer a load from, for example, a post to a foundation or from a lumber beam to a wall.

A Rigid connectors for a bamboo structure.

B A loadbearing fastener: the stainless-steel plate and base of the lumber post ensures the lumber does not rot.

C Another example of a loadbearing fastener: a galvanized mild-steel cup footing for lumber pergola poles.

D A galvanized-steel cup support protects the lumber post from moisture.

Lumber fixings

There are four main methods of joining lumber components:
- mechanical (e.g. bolts, nails, screws, and rivets);
- plate fastenings or connectors;
- lumber joints;
- adhesives; and
- lashing.

Sometimes, these are used in combination—for example, a lumber joint can be glued and may be screwed as well. As with all fixings, it is necessary to be aware of the compatibility of the components. Some lumbers— such as oak, chestnut, redwood, and western red cedar—contain tannins, which attack ferrous metals; therefore, use lumber dowels or metal fastenings made of austenitic stainless steel. Tannic acid protects trees from insect and bacterial attack.

Mechanical connections

Nails and tacks: Lumber-construction dating is facilitated by the knowledge that before 1800 the common nail was handmade. Cut nails were used in the nineteenth century; and since 1900 wire nails have been the usual form. Nonetheless, handmade, wrought-iron nails can still be produced by a blacksmith; and cut nails are still made for conservation work. Today, mild steel is the most common material but nails are also available in copper, bronze, and stainless steel as well as wrought iron.

Screws: These were used in ancient times, mainly in jewelry making and other fine processes. Slot-headed screws are said to date back to the sixteenth century, and were used in clock making. By the end of the eighteenth century, blunt-end screws were being manufactured (the hole into which they were inserted had to be predrilled). In the 1840s, George Nettlefield started to make the modern, pointed screw at his factory in Birmingham, England. The early screws were domed-headed, but the countersunk head began to be produced for use in door or gate hinges (where a domed head would have obstructed the hinge). The socket-headed screw was devised by a Canadian, Peter Robertson, in 1907, and in 1936 another North American, Henry F. Phillips, marketed the cross-headed, "Phillips-head" screw, which was easily tightened with a power-operated screwdriver. Wood screws generally have an unthreaded portion of the shaft below the head because they are designed to connect two pieces of wood.

Nuts and bolts: These were first made in medieval times. Jacques Besson, a mathematician and engineer at the court of Charles IX of France, devised the first machinery for making the screw thread in 1568, and around 1740, clockmaker Henry Hindley pioneered a screw-cutting lathe, which mechanized their manufacture.

E A rotational lumber fixing on a lock-gate hinge, Leeds and Liverpool Canal, Leeds, England.

F Metal spike fitting for a lumber beam on a pergola at Parc de Bercy, Paris. Note the splitting in the rafter due to differential expansion.

G Galvanized-steel crown fixing-ring with bolted hidden plate connections, Intercontinental Hotel, Aphrodite Hills Resort, Cyprus.

H Internally plated and bolted lumber bridge with zinc flashing on the top rail, Insel Hombroich, Neuss, Germany.

I Lumber post base-plate with a strap fixing on the top rail, Leeds and Liverpool Canal, Leeds.

J Metal bracket for a lumber pergola, Parc de Bercy, Paris.

K Exposed stainless-steel fixing straps, Aphrodite Hills Resort, Cyprus.

L Laminated softwood post with galvanized-steel base-plate, Kröller-Müller Museum, Hoge Veluwe National Park, The Netherlands.

NAILS

Nowadays, nails are generally made of steel; traditionally, they were wrought iron and made by hand, with a characteristic, square-section shank. From the eighteenth century onwards, they were '"cut"—i.e. punched or cut from a flat sheet of iron —which produced a four-sided cross-section tapering in on two sides. However, from the end of the nineteenth century "wire nails" were produced. Made from coils of thick wire with a characteristic parallel, round, wire-shaped shank, these are weaker than earlier nails but suited to the increasingly thinner-section lumber construction that has become the norm.

Round-wire nails are round-headed nails, mostly used for rough carpentry in which appearance is not important but strength is essential. They tend to split a piece of wood. Lengths from ¾–6 in.

Oval-wire nails are suitable for joinery work in which appearance is important because they can easily be punched below the surface. They are less likely to split the wood if driven in with the longer sides parallel to the grain. Lengths from ½– 6 in.

Round- or lost-head nails are stronger than oval-wire nails, and can easily be punched below the surface of the wood. Lengths from ½– 6 in.

Tacks are short nails with wide, flat heads. They are used for stretching fabric on to lumber or fixing linoleum.

Panel pins are round, lightweight nails used for cabinetmaking and fixing small moldings into place.

Cut-floor brads are rectangular. They have L-shaped heads and are nearly always used for nailing floorboards to joists. Lengths from 1–6 in.

Masonry nails are made of hardened steel. They are used to fix wood to brick, cement block, and most types of masonry.

Square twisted nails twist into the wood. These comparatively expensive nails offer a more permanent, screw-like grip than plain nails.

Annular nails are useful where very strong joints are required. The sharp ridges round the shank become embedded in the wood in order to give a tight grip.

Clout-head nails are made of galvanized steel, with a large, flat retaining head. They are most suitable for soft materials, such as plasterboard and roof felt.

Spring-head roofing nails are used for fixing corrugated sheeting to lumber. The twisted shank and inverted cup head produces a very strong purchase.

Corrugated fasteners are used for reinforcing a weak wood joint or securing mitered or butt joints in rough framing.

Cut clasp nails are rectangular in section, are difficult to remove and provide a very strong fixing in wood and predrilled masonry. Lengths from 1–6 in.

Hardboard nails have diamond-shaped heads, which are virtually hidden when hammered into hardboard. Lengths from ⅜–1½ in.

Upholstery nails are available in chrome, brass, and other metallic finishes; they are used as a secondary fixing with tacks. The domed head gives a decorative finish when nailing chair coverings into place. Various head sizes are available.

Staples are U-shaped round-wire nails with two points in order to hold lengths of wire in position. Some staples have an insulated coating for fixing flex and electrical cable.

SCREWS

Screws are threaded fasteners, often tapered, with a head with a fixture or slot which allows them to be rotated. The helical arrangement of the thread (the corkscrew shape) drives it into the material. The thread is usually right-handed. Screws can usually be withdrawn and reused.

Domed-head wood screw with tapered head

Domed wood screw with parallel thread

Slot-head, countersunk wood screw with tapered thread

Cross-head countersunk wood screw with parallel thread

Deck screw with solid bolthead for driving with a powered screwdriver

Screw eye

Screw hook

Hexagonal-headed coach screw for use with thick lumber

Square-headed coach screw

Countersunk machine screw for use with threaded sockets

Allen-wrench-headed machine screw for secure or theft-proof fixings

Dome-headed machine screw

Right
Durable hardwood treads with countersunk cross-head screw fixings.

Far right
Ribbed durable hardwood decking with recessed stainless-steel coach-screw fixings.

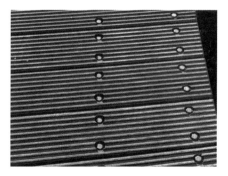

BOLTS, RIVETS, AND PLATE CONNECTORS

Like screws, bolts are threaded but they are designed to fit parts which already have holes, and are tightened with a screw-fixed nut. Bolts are usually used with washers, which are thin circular plates—also with a hole—which spread the load of the nut. When tightened, bolts are in tension, and do not have particularly great lateral, shear strength.

Rivets consist of a smooth cylinder with a curved head. They are placed into preformed holes, and the protruding end is flattened in order to expand it and ensure a permanent fix. Effectively, rivets have "heads" at both ends, so they work well in tension and were typical of iron- and steelwork until the

1950s. There are several varieties of rivet, such as solid rivets (still used in aircraft construction) which require access from both sides for the parts to be joined; and "pop" rivets, which have a tubular shaft and "mandrel" piece that expands the shaft. The latter are the weaker type, but they may be placed from just one side; they are usually used in joinery with metal plates or gate ironwork.

Plate connectors are metal plates, which may be flat or angled and are toothed to "bite" into the wood. They act in a manner similar to bolted washers.

Hexagon bolt fully threaded

Hexagon bolt plain shanked

Coach or carriage bolt

Expansion bolt for permanent fixing into masonry

Domed-headed machine bolt with washer and nut

Toothed lumber connector

Far left
A stainless-steel bolt fixing on a lumber post.

Left
Rivets were used before bolts, as in this seventeenth-century door on the Ile Saint-Louis, Paris.

STEP BY STEP ASSEMBLING A LUMBER PERGOLA

This sequence shows the construction of a pressure-treated, laminated lumber pergola at the Intercontinental Hotel, Aphrodite Hills Resort in Cyprus. To achieve the uninterrupted, approximately 18 ft clear span in the dining area, glue-laminated lumber beams and rafters were prefabricated to facilitate quick assembly. Concrete piers were necessary because of the heavy loads. The woven reed matting shade-screen is periodically replaced.

1 First fix stage of the lumber structure on galvanized mild-steel column head fixings on reinforced concrete columns with unfinished stone-clad plinths.

2 Aerial view showing the completed pergola. The woven reed matting is held in place by screw-fixed battens with semi-tensile canopies at the pool edge.

3 Completed pergola structure with lighting, audio system and climbing plants installed.

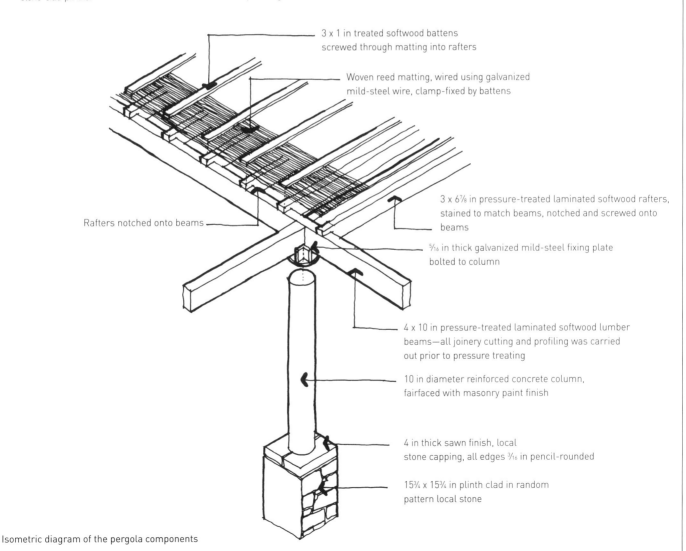

3 x 1 in treated softwood battens screwed through matting into rafters

Woven reed matting, wired using galvanized mild-steel wire, clamp-fixed by battens

Rafters notched onto beams

3 x 6⅞ in pressure-treated laminated softwood rafters, stained to match beams, notched and screwed onto beams

⁵⁄₁₆ in thick galvanized mild-steel fixing plate bolted to column

4 x 10 in pressure-treated laminated softwood lumber beams—all joinery cutting and profiling was carried out prior to pressure treating

10 in diameter reinforced concrete column, fairfaced with masonry paint finish

4 in thick sawn finish, local stone capping, all edges ³⁄₁₆ in pencil-rounded

15¾ x 15¾ in plinth clad in random pattern local stone

Isometric diagram of the pergola components

Joints

The strength of lumber joints depends on:

- the size of the glued area (if adhesives are used);
- the way in which one piece of lumber encases the other; and
- the accuracy of the joinery.

Note that end-grain lumber glues less well than lumber surfaces that run parallel with the wood grain.

The main types of lumber joint are:

- *angle or cross lumber joints*, in which the two pieces of lumber join at an angle—e.g. mortice and tenon, lapped joints, dovetail joints, and comb joints;
- *widening joints*, which widen a lumber board by adding a thin section parallel to it;
- *lengthening joints*, which extend the length of a lumber member; and
- *hinge and "shutting" joints*, which aim to form an air- or watertight seal.

Types of lumber joint and properties

Type of joint	Lumber joint name	Variety of joint	Notes	History
Widening joints	rubbed butt joint		a glued joint; face grain in same direction	
	doweled butt joint		reinforced by dowels; strong	
	rebate joint			
	tongue and grooved joint			
Lengthening joint	miter or scarf joint		an angled joint; either pinned or glued	
Angle or cross lumber joints	halved joints			
	mortice and tenon		a strong joint usually	
			for a 90 degree angle; usually glued, though dowels can also be used	a joint that dates back to ancient Egypt; also used for stone joints
		doweled mortice and tenon	the tenon does not show on the outer side of the joint	a joint that dates back to ancient Egypt and China
		"secret" haunched mortice and tenon		
		edged mortice and tenon	a strong, wedged joint	
	dovetail joint	glued, strong; often used for drawers		
	finger or "comb" joint		glued; often used for box construction	good long-grain to long-grain contact, so easily glued
	shoulder, rebate lapped joint	half-lap	often used for boxes	usually used with a screw or plate fixing
		full-lap	two pieces are overlapped and joined by a mechanical fixing—e.g. a screw or plate	sometimes used for bearing plates that support joists
	lumber joint: 5–shoulder, rebate lapped			
Hinge joint	rebated			

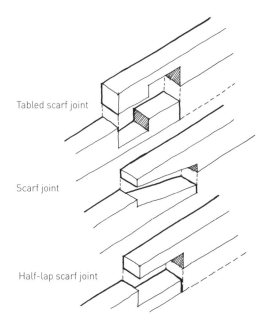

Tabled scarf joint

Scarf joint

Half-lap scarf joint

Scarf joints

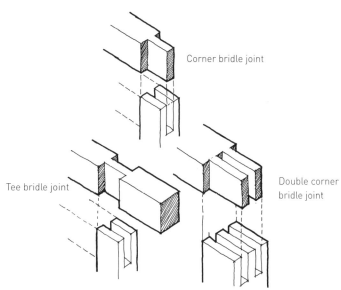

Corner bridle joint

Tee bridle joint

Double corner bridle joint

Mortice and tenon joints

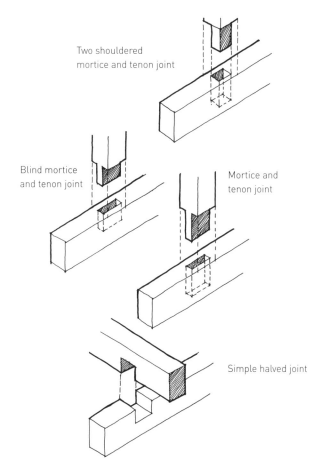

Two shouldered mortice and tenon joint

Blind mortice and tenon joint

Mortice and tenon joint

Simple halved joint

Bridle joints

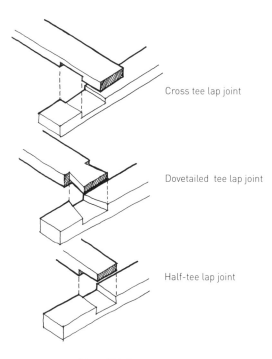

Cross tee lap joint

Dovetailed tee lap joint

Half-tee lap joint

Lapped joints

Lumber joints

Adhesives

Adhesives are used with wood for the following main applications:

- *laminating or surface gluing*: used, for example, for wood veneer or plastic laminate; not so often found in external situations, except for non-slip strips used on steps;
- *frame assembly*: joints with glue lines, which provide close contact between surfaces; conventional, machine-made, glued wood joints are close contact;
- *loose fitting or open joints*: may require gap filling owing to uneven surfaces; and
- *structural joints*: critical to a structure, they need to have good "creep" resistance (i.e. the ability to resist distortion over a period of time).

Adhesives tend to be stronger than many lower-density lumbers, (e.g. below the density of beech, which is 40–50 lbs/ft^3). Note that adhesives do not work effectively on the end grain of wood. The color of the adhesive needs to be taken into account, and colorless or transparent adhesives may be preferred: brown, phenolic glues tend to be a problem unless painted. Moisture content in the lumbers to be joined should be about the same, and should not vary by more than 5–10 per cent. The face of the wood should be smooth, and therefore planed but not necessarily sanded.

There are four main types of wood adhesive:

Thermoset adhesives

Thermosetts are part polymerized on application, with full polymerization resulting from subsequent setting or irreversible solidification. They are mainly amino-plastics, such as UF (urea formaldehyde) or MUF (melamine-urea-formaldehyde); and phenolics (PF, or phenol formaldehyde, RF, or resorcinol-formaldehyde and phenol/resorcinol formaldehyde, PRF, which is used for structural purposes). These are available in stiff, liquid, or powder form, and require a catalyst or hardener. Epoxy adhesives are also thermosets.

Amino-plastic adhesives are the most commonly used, and are based on the acid reaction of a compound such as that of urea with formaldehyde. Melamine is an alternative to urea, but is mainly used to strengthen urea formaldehyde. Usually, these adhesives are applied as a liquid resin—available as a spray-dried powder, or a "one-pack" powder, to which water is added. Urea formaldehyde is colorless, but there can be compatibility problems with some lumber preservatives. For external use melamine and urea resin combined (MF/UF) and mixes fortified with phenol or resorcinol (F-UF or F-MF) last longer.

Phenolic thermosets involve the condensation of a phenol with an aldehyde, and offer good moisture resistance. Phenol formaldehyde is the adhesive used with plywood. Resorcinol formaldehyde and phenol/resorcinol formaldehyde are the main thermosets used for external woodworking—either as a liquid or in powder form. However, resorcinol adhesives may have problems below 40–50°F. Nevertheless, they are neutral and so have the advantage that they can be used with plastics such as PVC and as a wood–metal bond with the use of a suitable primer. However, they are a reddish-brown color, which can be an issue.

Epoxy thermosets are relatively costly, but have been used for metal–wood bonds—especially in boat building.

Thermoplastic adhesives

The main thermoplastics used in lumber work are polyvinyl acetate (PVAc) and hot-melt, special-purpose adhesives. Polyvinyl acetate is a water-based emulsion with additives, and normally air dries and sets at room temperature. However, it is mainly for internal use only. Hot-melt thermoplastics are mainly applied in factory conditions; they are heated and move to a solid state upon cooling.

Elastomer synthetic adhesives

These are solvent- or emulsion-based "contact" adhesives —i.e. they are placed on both surfaces and dry on contact —and are used for fixing veneers, plastic laminates, and some rubber-based mastic adhesives. They include both synthetic and natural rubber-based formulations.

Natural adhesives

These are the traditional forms of adhesive, used before the development of synthetic polymer adhesives, and are animal-, fish- and vegetable-based. Casein, which is a dairy by-product, was possibly the first structural wood adhesive. Natural glues have largely been superseded by synthetic polymers since the 1940s. However, there is an increasing interest in the use of natural glues. This is because of concern about toxicity. For instance, formaldehyde is a carcinogen. New natural wood glues are also being marketed. For instance, Columbia Forest Products, the large US plywood manufacturer, has produced Soyad. This is made from soy, flour, and an amino acid (dihydroxyphenolalamine) found in mussels.

A crucial factor to bear in mind is interaction with the various lumber-preservative requirements.

Adhesives and the preservative treatment of wood

The main problem is likely to be the need to glue lumbers that have already been treated with a preservative. If the preservative is water-borne it will raise the moisture content of the wood. In such a case, it is preferable to reduce the wood to below 18 per cent moisture content before making the joint—or, alternatively, use a PF or RF adhesive. There may also be deposits of salt on the wood, which have to be removed. Organic solvent preservatives generally do not contribute to such problems. *For a table of lumber adhesives, see Table 13, Appendix, page 233.*

Lashing

Lashing is usually associated with temporary structures, such as traditional wood-pole scaffolding, ships and camping—but it should not be discounted in landscape construction. It has some application in permanent lumber constructions, such as bridges (e.g. rope-suspension bridges) and other light structures.

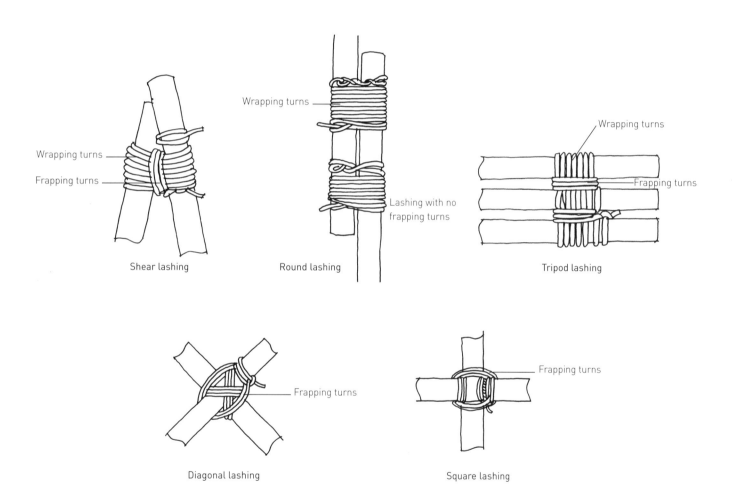

Shear lashing

Round lashing

Tripod lashing

Diagonal lashing

Square lashing

Main types of lashing and their uses

Type	Use	Notes
Square lashing	to bind poles together	strong
Diagonal lashing	to bind poles at 90 degrees or 45 degrees	
Shear lashing	to bind two poles together	can be applied to lumber-post pool edges
Round lashing	to tie two poles together in parallel	
Tripod lashing	to join three poles together to form a tripod	

Metal fixings

Compatibility of metals, welding, and brazing

Joining metal components, whether to make a railing, structure, gate, or seat, requires careful thought. Joining different metals can lead to corrosion. Welding, riveting, and the use of nuts and bolts are classic ways of joining two components and all are subject to problems. Welding can be very clumsy and weak if it is done without skill, while rivets and bolts need to be of compatible metals.

Galvanic and electrolytic activity, rusting, and staining

Galvanic (or electrolytic) corrosion results from dissimilar metals coming into contact, and the consequent flow of electrical current. An electrolytic medium—e.g. water, and especially salt water—speeds up the process. If dissimilar metals are to be used, separate them by means of a neoprene gasket or washer, by fabrics, or by the use of paints. Never place different metals touching without checking their compatibility. Ideally, make all components from the same metal.

Electrolytic corrosion requires consideration when choosing metal fixings: ensure they are compatible. Metal ground fixings may well be preferred for lumber pergolas or decks, so as to protect the lumber from rotting.

Table of dissimilar and similar metals

	Aluminum	Aluminum bronze	Brass	Cast iron	Copper	Phosphor bronze	Lead	Stainless steel	Steel	Tin	Zinc
Aluminum	√	x	x	x	x	x	o	x	x	x	o
Aluminum bronze	x	√	√	x	√	√	√	o	x	x	x
Brass	x	√	√	x	√	√	√	o	x	o	x
Cast iron	x	x	x	√	x	x	o	x	x	o	x
Copper	x	√	√	x	√	√	o	o	x	x	x
Phosphor bronze	x	√	√	x	√	√	o	o	x	o	x
Lead	o	√	√	o	o	o	√	o	o	√	o
Stainless steel	x	o	o	x	o	o	o	√	x	x	o
Steel	x	√	x	x	√	x	o	x	√	o	x
Tin	x	√	o	o	√	o	√	x	o	√	x
Zinc	o	√	x	x	√	√	o	o	x	x	√

+ can be used together in all conditions   X must not be used together unless isolated from each other o can be used together in dry conditions

Connecting metals

There are four main methods of joining metals:

- mechanical—e.g. bolts, nails, screws, and hot and cold rivets;
- soldering;
- welding; and
- adhesives.

Mechanical connections

- *Nails and tacks* are used in thin materials, such as metal-sheet cladding, and involve a rigid fixture. They are generally of steel, but be aware of metal compatibility. A variation is railroad spikes, which are large nails with asymmetrical heads used for fixing railway lines to lumber sleepers.

- *Screws* are threaded fasteners, often tapered, with a head which has a fixture or slot that allows the screw to be rotated. The helical arrangement of the thread drives it into the material. Screws can usually be withdrawn and reused.

The main types of screw used for metal construction are:

- *Sheet metal screws*: These form threads in the metal as they are installed. Pointed panhead screws are coarse-threaded; they are used in light sheet metal, while blunt panhead screws are used for heavier sheet metal. Both types of panhead screw are available with either plain or Phillips-head slots.
- *Roundhead screws*: Partial-tapping roundhead screws have fine threads; they can be used in soft or hard metals. Roundhead screws are available with either plain or Phillips-head slots.
- *Machine screws:* Machine screws are blunt-ended screws used to fasten metal parts together. They are commonly made of steel or brass. Like other fasteners, they are also made with coatings—brass, copper, nickel, zinc, cadmium, or galvanized—for rust protection. There are four basic types of heads: flathead, ovalhead, roundhead, and fillister-head (cylindrical with a convex top), with both plain and Phillips-head slots.
- *Bolts:* These are also threaded, but are designed to connect parts which already have holes, and are tightened by a screw-fixed nut, usually with a circular washer.
- *Rivets:* These consist of a smooth cylinder with a curved head which is placed into a preformed hole. Its protruding end is then flattened in order to expand it and ensure a permanent fix. Effectively, rivets have "heads" at both ends, so they work well in tension.

Soldering and brazing

Soldering involves joining by using a metal or alloy which melts at a temperature lower than the metals to be joined. The most familiar solder metals are tin and lead, which melt at about 392–482°F. Brazing involves the use of a brass solder of zinc and copper, which melts at about 1,560°F.

Welding

Most welding is done either by pressure (as in cold welding) or by fusion (as in hot welding). Cold welding involves hammering (e.g in the case of gold and lead) or using ultrasound (e.g. stainless steel), which actually generates an internal heat in the object. In "plastic welding," the blacksmith fuses metals by hammering them together while they are hot; the hammer method is also used for making chains. Fusion welding is done by:

- *metal arc welding*, which involves an electrode being applied to the joint in order to form an arc that melts the metal, which solidifies to form a solid weld; or
- *using a high-temperature gas flame* such as an oxy-acetylene torch, at a temperature of about 5,400°F. The flame is placed on the metals to be joined and also on a metallic filler rod, which melts.

Thermit welding is a variation that involves placing a mold around the join, into which molten metal is poured in order to join the two pieces: the molten metal is created by chemical means. Given that thermit welding is used for welding steel railroad tracks, it could be employed more generally for similar construction in landscape architecture. Note that steel is a good material to weld, and that cast iron can be welded adequately for some purposes.

Plastic welding is weaker than the parent metal; fusion welding is stronger than the parent metal.

Adhesives

Epoxy adhesives are the type most commonly used in smaller-scale metal construction: they are a thermoset resin. They are mixed with a catalyzing agent, which hardens them.

The advantage of adhesives is that they distribute the joint stress over the entire surfaces that are joined, as opposed to bolt, screws, and rivets, which concentrate the structural forces. They also maintain the integrity of the components—i.e. using them does not involve puncturing or making a hole. Finally, they are particularly suited for joining different materials—e.g. metal and plastics, or metals and glass.

STEP BY STEP STEEL SCREEN DETAILING

These detail drawings and photographs show the development and installation of a steel screen with acrylic panels.

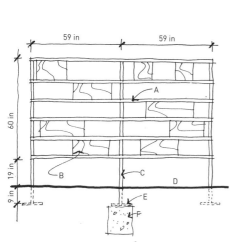

A 2 x 2 x ¼ in "T" horizontal rails
B Colored acrylic infill panels
C 2 x 2 x ¼ in "T" upright
D Ground level
E 10 x 10 x ⅜ in base plate
F Concrete foundation 12 x 12 x 16 in

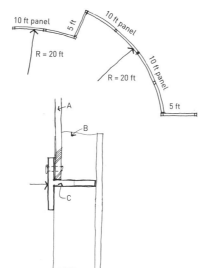

A Allow for ¼ in acrylic panel
B 2 x 2 x ¼ in upright
C 2 x 2 x ¼ in horizontal rail bent to radius

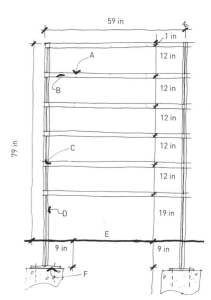

A Rails to have ³⁄₁₆ in drilled holes at 19½ in centers
B Horizontal rails to be 2 x 2 x ¼ in "T" section bent to 20 ft radius
C Horizontal rails to be ½ housed and welded to uprights
D 2 x 2 x ¼ in lightweight "T" section uprights
E Ground level
F 10 x 10 x ⅜ in base plated 4 x bolts to foundation

1 Typical sketch drawing showing the design intention for a coloured panel screen constructed from white-painted steelwork framing and ¼in thick acrylic panels. Note the steel section descriptions and suggestions for welding and panel fixing below the drawing.

3 Plan and section of screen. Note also that the T-sections proposed for the horizontal and vertical rails have been replaced by a slightly thicker flat bar. This was done to improve the quality of the radial form. T-sections can crease during bending.

5 All panels are to be fabricated off site—no on-site welding, drilling, or painting will be allowed. The panels are formed from mild steel bent to radii as shown. All panels are to be galvanized after welding and drilling. The paint finish will be white high-bond epoxy enamel.

2 The design has developed since the initial drawings. The method of fabrication has been simplified to a regular modular form that is bolted together at each upright. This method means that minor modifications to achieve a flowing curve are easier to make on site.

4 The use of steel enables the designer to achieve thin structural sections that when painted white create a minimal visual framework so that the colored areas of acrylic dominate the elevations.

6 Final installation showing the quality of light the designers had in mind at the concept stage.

Plastics

The key to assembling plastics is to be aware that they can suffer in ultraviolet light; this is particularly acute with geotextiles used as pool liners. Long-term exposure to sunlight will affect all plastics, so where possible it is better to shade or protect plastics from direct sunlight or design plastic elements so that exposed surfaces can be replaced.

Solid, rigid plastics, including geogrids and geonets, can be fixed using a combination of mechanical and adhesive fixings. Generally, it is best to have an overlap or seam in order to join geotextiles; this should be a minimum of 13 in wide, and the material can be seamed by sewing. Pool liners also require particular protection from mechanical damage (i.e. sharp objects penetrating the liner), and this usually comes in the form of a sand layer and barrier material. Geomembranes are thermally or chemically bonded or welded—work best done by a specialist.

Sewn geotextiles, geomembranes, and structurally connected geogrids should have a polymer connection (whether thread or fastener) with the same or greater durability than the geosynthetic, whether the seaming is being done on site or in a factory.

Below left
This unprotected stretched high-density polyethylene (HDPE) liner at Parc Citroën-Cévennes, Paris, has been damaged, probably by park users jumping in and tearing it. It is better to use a more flexible butyl liner with a protective Bidim layer above and below it, and to cover the butyl with river stones.

Below right
The edge of the HDPE liner was simply glued to the concrete. It is better to fix liners with a steel edging strip and glue or use a stainless-steel clamp fixing.

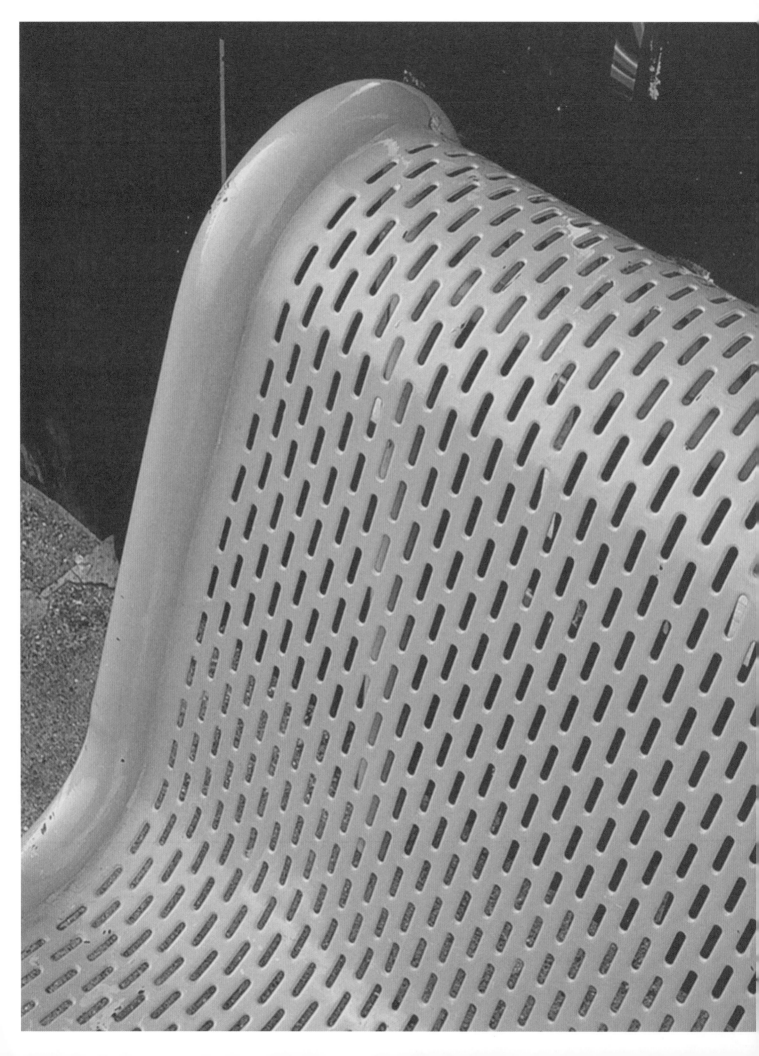

PROTECTION AND FINISHES

The protection and finishing of a component is required in order to preserve it, but also to decorate it—for instance, to add color or pattern. There is a long tradition of painting lumber to give a marble or stone effect. Protection can include coating a metal in order to prevent rust, or painting lumber to protect it from weathering or rot. Paint can also modify the functionality of a material, by changing its light-reflection properties or its heat absorbance. Dark colors will absorb heat and light ones will reflect it; for instance, dark-colored surfaces facing south or southwest can be up to 86°F hotter in the sun than light-colored ones.[1] Greek temples are thought of as being bright, white marble structures, but in ancient times they were painted and full of color.[2] Paints and sealants can also render a matte finish glossy. Thermoplastic paint is used in order to paint red, yellow, or white lines on roads as a graphic instruction.

Paints

Paints consist of
- a pigment;
- a binder, or "vehicle;" and sometimes
- a solvent.

Pigments are usually granular solids or dyes, and may be synthetic or natural, metallic, or pearlescent. Natural pigments include clays, calcium carbonate, mica, white lead, titanium oxide, silica, and talc (magnesium silicate). For example, burnt sienna (a reddish yellow-brown) was originally burned Sienna clay, which contains iron oxide —literally: *terra di Siena* or "Sienna earth." Umber is also a clay, with iron oxide and manganese oxide, from Umbria, and burning it similarly intensifies the color to make burnt umber, a mid brown.

Synthetic pigments include calcined clays and synthetic silica (silicon dioxide). Metallic pigments include zinc and aluminum compounds. Enamel paints contain glass powder or metal flakes as a pigment—and give a hard, glossy finish. Pearlescent pigments are mainly mica-based and often coated with titanium oxide; these give an appreciable "depth" of color owing to the partial reflection and partial transmission of light through the pigment (as with a pearl).

White, or "hiding," pigments are used in order to make a paint opaque; they include titanium oxide. Their effect depends on the refractivity of the pigment: a high refractivity changes the direction of light waves and redirects them so that they are reflected; a low refractivity results in some light penetrating the paint and reaching the material underneath.

Below
Carborundum anti-slip pattern on a boardwalk panel mounted on a demountable steel frame, Bibliothèque Nationale, Paris. Epoxy resin paints with carborundum particles can be applied to lumber, concrete, stone, and metal surfaces.

Binders bind together the pigments and determine glossiness, durability, flexibility, and resistance to impact damage. Like pigments, they may be natural or synthetic. Natural binders include oils and natural resins, while synthetic binders include acrylics, polyurethane, polyester, melamine, and epoxy resins. They are categorized by their means of drying, and five main methods are:

- *solvent evaporation*: a process in which a solid binder is dissolved in a solvent which evaporates, leaving a solid film – e.g. nitrocellulose lacquer;
- *oxidative cross-linking*: this is related to "single-pack" coatings, such as alkyd enamels, which oxidize in order to polymerize the binder;
- *catalyzed polymerization:* this generally involves two coatings which act together chemically to form a polymer, such as the product known as "two-pack" polyurethane;
- *coalescence*: a process that occurs in latex paints, which are water-based polymers: when the water evaporates the binder particles fuse to form chemical networks which redissolve; and
- *cooling of the binder*: this occurs in encaustic or wax paints.

Solvents adjust the curing and viscosity of the paint, and act as a thinner; they are volatile, and disperse, and do not form part of the permanent paint surface. They are not required in all paints. There are, in addition, various additives such as emulsifiers, thickeners, and ultraviolet-light stabilizers—and also biocides, which combat bacteria and moss.

Application of paints
Paint can be applied as a solid powder, an aerosol, or a liquid. Powder-coated paint is largely used in car and industrial applications. The paint powder is "baked" once applied, and this melts and sticks the paint onto the surface. Aerosol application, or "spray painting," involves an atomized gas being suspended under pressure, thus giving an very even application of the paint; the solvent usually binds the pigment and the surface of the substrate or material to be painted. Liquid paints may be applied by paint roller on flat surfaces or by brush. Powder coating and spray painting are the usual methods of factory application, while brush application permits more control on site. Spray painting can be done on site, but it requires the "masking" of adjacent surfaces.

It is usual to clean and then prime many materials. Priming provides better adhesion of the paint, increases durability and so further protects the component. Factory application, because it is in a controled environment, tends to give a better finish. However, all paint has a

finite life and on-site application, using brush or spray methods, will be necessary eventually. The first area to wear tends to be sharp edges or arrises, where the paint is thinnest, or areas exposed to impact damage.

The main types of paint are:
- masonry;
- polyurethane;
- emulsion;
- gloss; and
- varnish.

Varnish, shellac, and stains
Varnish and shellac are transparent protective finishes mainly used on wood. They are available in gloss, satin, or matte finishes. Polyurethane varnish is the most common type of varnish, but it can suffer from exposure to sunlight. Shellac is not used externally.

Stains are used with wood, and aim to color it without covering up its grain or texture. They consist of a pigment suspended in solvent with a binder, and penetrate the wood rather than forming a "skin" on top. The solvent can be an alkyd, linseed oil, acrylic, polyurethane, lacquer, or resin. The wood should not be "green," and it should be remembered that end-grain lumber accepts stain more readily and will tend to darken more.

Paints and environmental concerns
There is concern about the embodied energy of paints and their waste disposal requirements, use of volatile organic compounds (VOCs) and toxicity. Lead is an example of a toxic pigment, and the concern surrounding its use relates to the possibility of it being ingested. In consequence, lead-based paint is nowadays usually not permitted. However, its main substitute, titanium oxide, has a high embodied energy. Synthetic solvents, such as white spirit, emit VOCs. The response has been to promote natural paints and "ecopaints." The former are made from natural materials while ecopaints are synthetic. VOCs may be reduced by the use of solid coatings and by the elimination of organic solvents.

Protection of metals

All coatings or protective layers are best applied after the forming and welding of the metals concerned. The main forms of protection are paints; vitreous enamel; plastic, nylon, or metal coating; and galvanizing and cathodic protection.

A typical steelwork paint specification:
- mild steelwork to be specified as hot-dipped galvanized;
- remove oil and grease by wiping with a T Wash or mordant solution (a weak phosphoric acid solution), and then rinsing in clean water;
- prime with one coat of epoxy zinc phosphate primer;
- two-coat finish: first a high-build epoxy resin, then a final coat of enamel paint.

Plastic and nylon coating In this process, the metal is dipped in or sprayed with nylon (a synthetic polymer), or an electrically charged polyester dust is fixed onto it by electrical attraction. Perforated sheet-steel external seats are a classic example of nylon coating. However, they will shed their dipped coating under penknife or cigarette attack; polyester-dust treatment is tougher and better suited for public areas.

Metal coatings Lead, cadmium, tin, chromium, and zinc can all be employed as metal coatings; however, zinc is the most commonly used metal for external or garden use. Coating is the most common method of protecting

Right
Red folly in stove-enameled steel at Parc de la Villette, Paris. Over two decades it has darkened slightly but held its color very well.

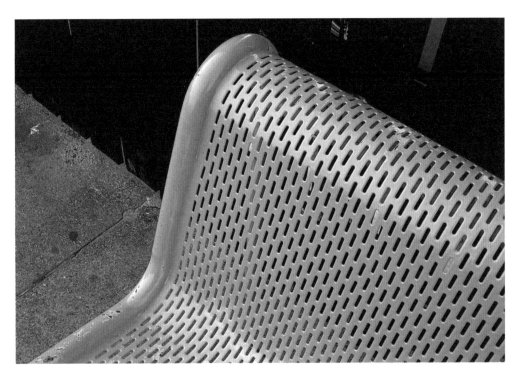

mild steel: it is fine until the metal is scratched or knocked, or until joints or cut pieces fail.

Galvanizing This involves coating steel with molten zinc. A coating of zinc–iron alloy with a pure zinc finish gives a metallurgical bond between the steel and the zinc. Galvanized steel weathers more slowly than unprotected steel, and galvanizing also provides cathodic protection against accidental damage. However, the galvanizing coat of zinc eventually breaks down. There are several methods of zinc coating:
- *hot dipping* is the most common method;
- *sherardizing* involves tumbling steel parts in hot zinc dust;
- *zinc spraying* entails blasting surfaces with droplets of semi-molten zinc; and
- *electroplating* involves bonding the zinc and steel electrolytically in a solution of zinc salts.

Cathodic protection This applies to galvanizing, whereby the zinc corrodes in preference to the steel, and a positive current flows from the steel to the zinc. This ensures that the zinc coating slowly disappears and is sacrificed for the steel. However, there are other methods of cathodic protection: tidal piers can be protected from salt-water corrosion by passing a direct electric current through the sea water to the steel structure through a metal anode of lead or graphite.

TIP FADING

Remember that paints require maintenance, and nearly all paint colors fade upon exposure to ultraviolet light—hence, red-painted metal will change to a light pinkish-gray.

Protection of lumber

When designing with lumber, one of the first things to consider is the durability of the material. Lumber durability is affected by:

- weathering, including freeze–thaw, wet–dry and ultraviolet light;
- insect attack;
- fungal attack;
- marine organisms;
- fire;
- mechanical damage; and
- chemical attack.

Lumberwork liable to chemical attack includes lumber piles used in waste-disposal and landfill sites, industrial areas and in some forms of swamp in which the chemicals in the ground attack the wood. Lumber left unpainted or unprotected will discolor or bleach, crack, and roughen. In order to avoid this, a protective finish can be provided for the lumber, but the designer can also detail using flashings to prevent water penetration—especially in exposed end grain—and provide overhangs to shade the lumber face. Flashing is sheet metal (such as zinc, copper, lead, aluminum, or steel), which is nailed to the lumber in order to protect exposed sections—such as end grains—from rain and frost penetration.

Certain lumber species can be used without treatment if non-durable sapwood is excluded. Therefore, always consider the durability class when choosing the type or lumber.

A Lumber mooring eroded by the tides of the Thames, London.

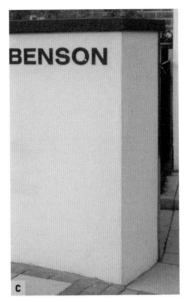

B Copper flashing dating from the 1950s protects the lumber of a porch in a London housing development from water penetration. Copper was relatively cheap in the 1950s, but would be unaffordable for a social housing project today.

C A metal cap on this rendered wall provides protection against water penetration.

D Horizontal lumber slats of untreated European larch (*Larix europaea*, also known as *Larix decidua*) with gaps. Note the stainless-steel screws and the splitting, which is probably because the screws were overtightened. European larch is a durable softwood, like western red cedar, which can be used untreated.

E Metal-cap protection to the top of a lumber post at London Zoo.

Tables of exterior lumber finishes

Finish	Initial treatment	Appearance of wood	Maintenance period
Paint	prime and 2 top coats	grain and natural color hidden	7–10 years
Clear	4 coats	grain and natural color unchanged	7–10 years
Water repelent	2 coats or dip	grain and natural color darkened	2 years
Stain	2 coats	grain visible, color varied	3–6 years
Organic solvent preservative	pressure-treat, dip, or brush apply	grain visible, color varied	2–3 years
Water-borne preservative	pressure-treat	grain visible, greenish stain	none

Source: adapted from National Association of Forest Industries/Australian Government Forest and Wood Products Research and Development Corporation, Timber—Design for durability, Timber Datafile P4, 2003, http://www.timber.org.au/resources/timber%20-%20design%20for%20durability.pdf

Wood preservatives

Wood preservatives protect from biological attack, such as fungal and bacteriological damage.

The two main processes involved are:
- high-pressure vacuum treatment; and
- double-vacuum low-pressure treatment.

The preservative treatments used can be classified as:
- staining;
- painting;
- oiling; or
- impregnation;

and these can be applied thus:

- brush and spray, as with painting, which requires repeating typically every four to five years; or by the use of preservative gels;
- deluge, dip, or steep for a short period of minutes, usually combined with organic solvent treatments;
- hot and cold open-tank method—used for fence posts, which are submerged in tanks, heated to 176–194°F and simmered for two to three hours; the preservatives are absorbed as the lumber cools;
- pressure impregnation under a vacuum;
- diffusion, involving long-term soaking of "green" lumber in a water-borne preservative or gaseous diffusion of volatile compounds—particularly appropriate for large structural lumbers; or
- injection: typically, as with large-dimension structural lumber or joist ends, injected with boron paste.

Preservatives can be classed by the solvent that carries the biocide component (i.e. pesticide/fungicide/herbicide), and the solvents used are:
- water;
- oil; or
- an organic solvent.

Copper, chrome, and arsenic are water-borne; tar oil and creosote are oil-borne. Copper naphthalene is an organic solvent.

As can be gathered from this list, some of these materials are not safe—i.e. they are toxic to plants and animals, including humans. Therefore, it is best to use naturally rot-resistant lumber such as western red cedar (*Thuja plicata*), redwood (*Sequoia sempervirens*) or black locust (*Robinia pseudoacacia*). Their natural polyphenols help protect them from insect attack.

Water-borne preservatives

- *Chromated copper arsenate (CCA)* is now of limited use owing to concern about its arsenic content; it is permitted for use in bridges and on telegraph poles.
- *Alkaline copper quaternary (ACQ)* consists of copper, as a fungicide, and a quaternary-ammonium compound which acts as an insecticide. It has grown in use as a substitute for CCA. Note that the copper content renders it incompatible with mild steel, and so stainless-steel fasteners have to be used.
- *Copper azole preservative* is similar to ACQ, in that it is copper-based, but it uses azole to act as its insecticide element. It, too, has grown in use with the banning of arsenic-based preservatives.
- *Borate preservatives* have the advantage of not including heavy metals like copper, but because they leach out of wood their use is internal only.
- *Sodium silicate-based preservatives* have been used since the nineteenth century, and are produced by fusing or heating sodium with sand. However, they tend to leach out of the lumber.
- *Potassium silicate-based preservatives*.

Oil-borne preservatives

- *Pentachlorophenol and creosote* are toxic.
- *Linseed oil* was recently developed as a preservative in Australia. It acts as a solvent- and water-repellent treatment and is used to treat just the outer wood—up to ³⁄₁₆ in in depth.

Light organic solvent preservatives (LOSP)

These are white-spirit, solvent-based preservatives used to "transport" synthetic pyrethroids as insecticides. However, they produce volatile organic compounds and require treatment in order to drive off the vapor, which therefore makes them expensive.

Below
Laminated softwood beams pressure-treated with a red water-borne preservative.

Varnish

A hard, transparent protective finish used with lumber. Traditionally, varnishes have been made of a drying oil, a resin, and a solvent. Usually they are glossy, but satin and mattE finishes are available. They dry by the evaporation of the solvent, or by oxidation of the oil. Resin varnishes dry immediately; however, acrylic and water-borne varieties take timc to cure. Oil, polyurethane and epoxy varnishes undergo an extended curing process.

The main constituents of traditional varnish are:
- *drying oil*, such as linseed oil, tung oil, or walnut oil; they dry by oxidization of the oil (autoxidation) to form a complex polymer;
- *resins*, which include amber, pine resin (rosin), kaura gum, and balsam of Mecca;
- *turpentine*, which, as organic turpentine, was traditionally used as a solvent; however, there are now several mineral-based turpentine substitutes, such as white spirit.

Modern varnishes include:
- *polyurethane*, which gives a very hard-wearing coat; however, polyurethane varnishes tend to break down under ultraviolet light—therefore, for external applications use polyurethane varnish with UV-absorbers to provide protection;
- *acrylic varnish*, which is water-borne, is resistant to ultraviolet light and does not give off solvent fumes; however, acrylic varnishes tend not to penetrate as well as oil-based alternatives.

Below left
Seating boards on a sleeper retaining wall that have ben treated with polyurethane gloss.

Below center
A coating of white gloss paint—a traditional form of protection for softwood—at London Zoo.

Below right
New oak *treillage* has been given a specialist antiquing paint finish, Versailles, France.

Protection of masonry

Walls are best designed and detailed to cast off water, to deal with splash-back and the capillary flow of water from the ground, to cope with freeze–thaw and to otherwise protect against structural damage. Masonry damage can be the consequence of chemical attack or physical disruption owing to salts crystallizing and the results of freeze–thaw action. Both these types of attack can themselves be affected by biological activity—and they are often the consequence of water ingress caused by failure of a water barrier, such as a moisture-proof course or a capping or flashing. Acid rain can exacerbate such attack.

Biological attacks tend to be bacteriological, and therefore a consequence of dampness. Bird droppings and leaves are sources of nitrogen deposits, which can foster growth of "higher" plants—from lichens and annuals (such as wallflowers) to shrubs, such as buddleia, and even trees. Plant roots can penetrate masonry walls, and crack or lift off finishes or stucco. Such plant life can either be tolerated—or, indeed, fostered—or removed when it threatens the fabric of a wall.

Stucco and rendered walls in a temperate climate should be regularly repainted, every four to five years, with paint that permits the coating to breathe. A well-detailed masonry wall will usually require only very occasional repointing during its lifetime, and should last a minimum of 40 years—and maybe centuries.

There have been traditions of painting or sealing masonry such as the use of stucco, which is usually applied over a brick wall, or coating the bright white marble of Greek temples in order to subdue their glare. Traditionally, stonework has been treated with linseed oil or beeswax to keep moisture out; more recently, silicone-based treatments have been developed which penetrate the stone. However, there is a danger of trapping salts beneath the surface. Water repelents can lead to increased run-off and consequent uneven streaking on a stone surface. Our advice generally is not to seal most stonework or brickwork, but rather to choose stone and brick that will weather well.

A The coping and string-course of this churchyard wall throw off water.

B How not to end a brick capping —in this case with a steel angle-bracket.

C How to end a brick capping —a stop end (or double-width brick) is used to end a capping of engineering brick laid on edge. Note the engineering brick used at the bottom (just visible at the bottom left of the photograph) to resist the upwards movement of groundwater.

D How not to end a brick capping —in this case with an exposed perforated brick.

E Matte stainless-steel capping on a blue engineering-brick wall, Concertgebouw, Amsterdam.

F The tops of these walls built in the 1970s have absorbed water and dirt due to the use of a flush capping made with soft, absorbent brick rather than a projecting coping.

G Garden wall colonized by plants growing from the mortar joints. The efflorescence is due to water penetration from behind, while the cracking is a result of the use of overstrong cement mortar.

H Medieval section of London Wall with plants growing from the mortar. For a plant, a building provides a habitat similar to a cliff or rock face.

I Stone paving is cleaned with a high-pressure scrubber.

J Sandstone sealed with silicone (an organic polymer compound of silicon). Irrigation water from nearby planters has crept under the seal, discoloring the paving.

Endnotes

6–15 INTRODUCTION

1 Corporation of London, Department of Planning and Transportation, *City Street Scene Manual Part Two*, London, 2005, p.7, published on the City of London website, http://www.cityoflondon.gov.uk/NR/rdonlyres/7F3DF93E-176F-4A32-BB1C-F0E6D3E55C2F/0/DP_PL_SS_manual2.pdf (accessed 9 March 2010)

2 Athena Sustainable Materials Institute website, http://ww.athenasmi.ca/about (accessed 9 March 2010)

3 For an introduction to BRE methods refer to http://www.bre.co.uk/page.jsp?id=53 (accessed 9 March 2010)

4 Scottish Timber Trade Association specifiers' guide http://www.stta.org.uk/specinfo.html (accessed 9 March 2010) and Livesey, K., *Replacing other construction materials with wood*, BRE, published on ttp://www.forestry.gov.uk/pdf/nee-climate-conf-livesey.pdf/$FILE/nee-climate-conf-livesey.pdf (accessed 9 March 2010)

5 An international guide to building energy software is produced by the US Department of Energy Building Technologies Program, http://apps1.eere.energy.gov/buildings/tools_directory/tools_new.cfm (accessed 9 March 2010)

6 US Environmental Protection Agency, Heat Island Effect, http://www.epa.gov/heatisland/ (accessed 9 March 2010)

7 Levinson, R. and Akbari, H., "Effects of composition and exposure on the solar reflectance of Portland Cement Concrete," Lawrence Berkeley National Laboratory publication LBNL-48334, Berkeley, California, 2001, http://www-library.lbl.gov/docs/LBNL/483/34/PDF/LBNL-48334.pdf (accessed 9 March 2010)

8 Pomerantz, M., Pon, B., Akbari, H. and S.-C. Chang, "The Effect of Pavements' Temperatures on Air Temperatures in Large Cities," Lawrence Berkeley National Laboratory report LBNL 43442, Berkeley, California, 2002

9 Pomerantz, M., Akbari, H., et al, "Examples of Cooler Reflective Streets for Urban Heat Islands: Cement Concretes and Chip Seals," Lawrence Berkeley National Laboratory, DRAFT

10 M. VanGeem, *Albedo of Concrete and Select Other Materials*, Construction Technology Laboratories, no date, http://www.lehighcement.com/Education/PDFs/Solar%20(Albedo%20from%20M.%20VanGeem)%200910021.pdf (accessed 9 March 2010); see also Akbari, H., Surabi, M. and Rosenfeld, A., "Global cooling: increasing world-wide urban albedos to offset CO_2," in *Climatic Change*, Volume 94, Numbers 3-4 / June, 2009, pp.275–286

28–97 BUILDING MATERIALS

1 Clifton-Taylor, A., *The Pattern of English Building*, Faber & Faber, London, 1987, p.43

2 British Geological Survey, *Mineral Profile, Building and Roofing Stone*, November 2005, available as a pdf on www.bgs.ac.uk/downloads/start.cfm?id=1407 (accessed 9 March 2010)

3 The Pantheon dome is built of rings of concrete, tufa, and brick all held together with lime-pozzolan mortar. See David Moore, *The Pantheon*, 1999, http://www.romanconcrete.com/docs/chapt01/chapt01.htm (accessed 9 March 2010)

4 For a detailed account of the rebirth of concrete construction see Peter Collins, *Concrete: The Vision of a New Architecture* (Montreal: McGill-Queens University Press, 2004), chapter 1

5 John, Vanderley M., Escola Politécnica, University of São Paulo, Brazil, Ed. Engenharia Civil, Cidade Universitária São Paulo, *On the Sustainability of the Concrete*, 2003, p.1, http://vmjohn.pcc.usp.br/Arquivos/On%20the%20Sustainability%20of%20the%20Concrete.pdf (accessed 9 March 2010)

6 Hendriks, C. A., Worrell, E., de Jager, E., Blok, K. and Riemer, P., *Emission Reduction of Greenhouse Gases from the Cement Industry*, International Energy Agency, Greenhouse Gas Program, Greenhouse Gas Control Technologies Conference Paper, 2004, http://www.wbcsd.org/web/projects/cement/tf1/prghgt42.pdf (accessed 9 March 2010)

7 According to the Earth Architecture website: http://www.eartharchitecture.org/index.php?/archives/861-Mud-Brick-Industry-In-India.html (accessed 9 March 2010)

8 FAO, *Global Forest Resources Assessment 2005*, FAO Forestry Paper 147, Rome, 2006, p.11, available on ftp://ftp.fao.org/docrep/fao/008/A0400E/A0400E03.pdf (accessed 9 March 2010) Note the FAO conducts quinquennial assessments and therefore the 2010 assessment was produced in 2010–11

9 For a current overview of certification refer to UNECE/FAO, *Forest Products Annual Market Review, 2008–2009*, Geneva Timber and Forest Study Paper 24, chapter 10, "Forest certification challenged by climate change and illegal logging concerns," pp.111–123, http://timber.un-ece.org/fileadmin/DAM/publications/Final_FPAMR2009.pdf (accessed 9 March 2010)

10 Finnish ThermoWood Association, *ThermoWood Handbook*, 2003, http://www.thermowood.fi/data.php/200312/795460200312311156_tw_handbook.pdf (accessed 9 March 2010)

11 Ross, P., Mettem, C. and Holloway, A., *Green Oak in Construction*, TRADA, High Wycombe, 2007

12 Wigginton, M., *Glass in Architecture*, Phaidon Press, London, 1966, p.6

13 For example, see Colin Barras, "How our green technology may rest on bacterial skills" in *New Scientist* (online version, 25 March 2009), http://www.newscientist.com/article/dn16841-how-our-green-technology-may-rest-on-bacterial-skills.html (accessed 9 March 2010)

14 Simpson, F. Gerald and Richmond, I. A., "The Turf Wall of Hadrian, 1895–1935" in *The Journal of Roman Studies*, vol. 25 (1935), pp.1–18

15 For information on turf structures in Iceland and elsewhere, see http://www.archnetwork.eu/blog/_archives/2005/10/27/1181223.html (accessed 9 March 2010) and http://www.hurstwic.org/history/articles/daily_living/text/Turf_Houses.htm (accessed 9 March 2010) and http://www.skagafjordur.is/displayer.asp?cat_id=1287 (accessed 9 March 2010)

98–179 ELEMENTS

1 FAO, ISRC and International Union of Soil Sciences, *World reference base for soil resources 2006*, World Soil Resources Report no.103, Rome FAO, 2006, http://www.fao.org/ag/agl/agll/wrb/doc/wrb2006final.pdf (accessed 9 March 2010)

2 British Geological Survey on ground shrinkage and subsidence, http://www.bgs.ac.uk/science/landUseAndDevelopment/shallow_geohazards/shrinking_and_swelling_clays.html (accessed 9 March 2010)

3 Wilson, S., Bray, R. and Cooper, P., *Sustainable drainage systems: Hydraulic, structural and water quality advice* (C609B), CIRIA, London, 2004

4 Holtz, R. D., *Geosynthetics For Soil Reinforcement*, Ninth Spencer J. Buchanan Lecture, 9 November 2001, Texas A & M University, College Station, TX, p.4, https://ceprofs.civil.tamu.edu/briaud/Buchanan%20Web/Lectures/Ninth%20Buchanan%20Lecture.pdf (accessed 9 March 2010)

5 National House Building Council, *Standards 2008, Part 4—Foundation*, NHBC, Amersham, 2008

196–207 PROTECTION AND FINISHES

1 Keyworth, B., "Theme Paints, Finishes and Sealants" in *The Architects' Journal*, August 1999, p.47

2 In *Greek Architecture and its Sculpture* (The British Museum Press, London, 2006), pp.34–37, Ian Jenkins describes how all the stone on Greek temples was "washed with a varnish or painted wax" to reduce the glare of the freshly cut marble. He goes on to say that above the capitals there was extensive polychromatic decoration using copper silicate for blue, iron oxide for red, and gold leaf.

Glossary

English language construction vocabulary varies considerably from country to country and even within national regions. Some terminology has Latin roots and comes from the building clerk's table (for example, "vermiculated stone"). Some words come from Old English, such as "weir," and some are foreign borrowings, such as "pisé" (from French), "adobe" (from Spanish), and "stucco" (from Italian). New coinages in the twentieth century are often based on scientific nomenclature. This is especially true in the plastics industry, where many materials begin with the "poly-" prefix. Useful guides include the *Penguin Dictionary of Building* (fourth edition, 2004), and the *Penguin New Dictionary of Civil Engineering* (2005). The ASTM (American Society for Testing and Materials) publishes terminologies in US standards, for example C119 *Standard Terminology Relating to Dimension Stone*.

Italic type indicates a word or term that has its own entry in the glossary.

acetate *Polymer* textile fiber and film made of cellulose *acetate* and produced in part from wood pulp.

acetylation Treatment of lumber with acetic anhydride, which changes the free hydroxyls to acetyls. The free hydroxyls absorb and release water and, by replacing them with acetyls, increase the dimensional stability of wood, and protect it from decay.

acrylic Term covering clear synthetic *thermoplastic* and thermoplastic co-polymers made from *acrylonitrile*. Used to make fabrics, *resins*, paints, adhesives, and a transparent glass substitute (the common trade name is Plexiglas).

acrylonitrile A *monomer* that is a constituent in the manufacture of synthetic polymers, including acrylic fibers, which are precursors for carbon fibers. Acrylonitrile is also a component of synthetic rubber.

admixture An additive to *concrete* or *mortar* that changes its properties, by acting, for example, as a retarder, an accelerator, a pigment, or an air-entraining agent.

adobe A type of *brick* made by mixing clay with chopped straw and water. The mixture is stamped on and then worked with a hoe to form a paste, which is then placed in a wood mold and dried in the sun.

aggregate Granular material used in *concrete* or *mortar*. It is usually gravel or quarried stone, but may be crushed concrete or *brick*.

air seasoning Process in which lumber is dried or seasoned by stacking it in a way that allows air to flow around it.

albedo A measure of the ratio of light and radiant reflectivity. Measured on a scale of 1 to 10, 1 is low reflectivity (black) and 10 is high reflectivity (mirror-like).

alloy A mixture of metals, for example bronze is an *alloy* of *copper* and tin.

ALSC American Lumber Standard Committee.

alumina Common name for aluminum oxide —a metal oxide formed during *aluminum* processing, also a constituent of many clays. Alumina is also used as an abrasive, and in anodizing aluminum.

aluminum A light and rust-resistant metal found in *bauxite*. It requires large amounts of energy to smelt but is easily recycled.

amine Organic compounds derived from ammonia (NH_3) by the substitution of one or more hydrogen atoms with a hydrocarbon.

anchored piling wall A *piled* wall or foundation additionally secured by use of *ground anchors*.

anchored wall A vertical retaining wall supported by an anchor or dead weight, fixed in the ground on the uphill side and tied by a cable, chain, or rod. The ground anchor may be fixed in the ground by expanding it mechanically or by the pressure injection of quick-setting concrete. Ground anchors must be fixed beyond the *angle of repose* to avoid collapse. Also known as a *tieback wall*.

angiosperms A phylum of plants which have a vascular system and bear flowers. The seeds are enclosed in an ovary in the flower. Typically, but not invariably, angiosperms are broadleaved and are deciduous. Examples include oak, ash, beech, and sycamore (which grow in temperate climates) and mahogany, teak, and ipé (which grow in tropical climates). Angiosperms produce *hardwood*.

angle of repose The potential failure plane of earth or a granular material.

annealing The process of heating and reheating a metal to change and thereby strengthen its crystalline structure.

arris An edge at a corner or angle.

ashlar Walls of cut stonework.

asphalt A bituminous paving material, consisting of a mix of pitch or bitumen with stone *aggregate*, which is rolled to make paving and road surfaces in the form of either *mastic asphalt* or *rolled asphalt*.

asphaltic concrete *Asphalt* road paving.

ASTM American Society for Testing and Materials.

ATFS American Tree Farm System. A sustainable lumber certification system run by the American Forest Foundation"s Center for Family Forests, established in 1941. 24 million acres of forest in the USA (2009 figure) are ATFS certified.

augite Calcium magnesium iron silicate, a constituent of many *igneous* rocks such as basalt and gabbro.

austenitic stainless steel Stainless steel with more than 16 per cent chromium and a nickel content of 7 per cent, it has the highest corrosion resistance and is suitable for external features such as fences and furniture in exposed situations such as sea coasts (though it is not totally corrosion resistant).

axed Finishing process in which stone is worked with masonry tools to give a smooth, broad, chisel-marked surface.

base course The foundation layer of a road or paving beneath the wearing surface (road base).

basketweave bond A *brick bond* consisting of squares of *stretchers* in parallel, alternating in direction, so as to form a pattern. Because this bond has little strength it is only used as a paving bond or as a pattern in brick cladding.

batted Finishing process in which a fine, straight, strong, chisel pattern is worked vertically across stone.

batten A thin strip of wood to hold members of a structure together (for example between *beams* or *joists*) or to provide a fixing point. A batten would be placed over the joints in vertical wood plank siding to seal the joints.

baulk A roughly squared lumber *beam*.

bauxite A rock and the ore from which *aluminum* is smelted.

beam A horizontal structural member that supports a load and resists bending stress. Beams include *joists* and girders and may be of metal, reinforced *concrete*, *lumber* or *composite materials*.

bearing capacity The ability of soils to support loads imposed by roads, walls, buildings, and other structures.

bending stress A force that causes the rotation of both ends of the length of an object.

bentonite clay Naturally occurring clay that swells when mixed with water. It is therefore suitable for forming a clay liner through which plant roots can be grown because the holes will self-seal. Bentonite powder is used as a way of repairing leaks in clay-lined pools, but should not be used where there are fish because it will clog their gills.

berm (i) An earth mound or bank alongside a river or for retaining liquid. (ii) A strip of land at the foot of a dike or alongside a road or canal.

Bidim Proprietary name for a continuous-filament, nonwoven, needle-punched

geotextile used as a separator and as a protective layer for pool liners.

biodegrade Chemical and physical breaking down of materials by living organisms.

bio-retention area A reed-filled basin designed to filter water prior to discharge via a piped or surface system.

biosphere The part of the earth"s crust, seas and atmosphere inhabited by living organisms.

bitumen Black or brown viscous liquid or solid obtained naturally or from crude oil as a by-product of distillation, used as a binder in paving construction (see *asphalt*). Chemically, bitumen consists of complex organic compounds with more than 25 carbon atoms in the main compounds.

black soot mold A black powdery mold that grows on the sugar honeydew deposited on masonry by aphids in overhanging trees.

blitzcrete *Concrete* using broken *brick aggregate*, as if from blitzed (bombed) buildings.

block A rectangular *masonry* unit which is larger than a *brick* and must be lifted with both hands. *Precast* blocks are usually made of precast concrete and may be solid, hollow or cavity. Often used for internal walls or as a structural backing that is cheaper than fairfaced brickwork.

board-marked concrete *Cast-in-place* concrete patterned by the impression of the boards used in the *shuttering*.

bollard A short post of metal, stone or *concrete* installed to limit traffic. In the nineteenth century many bollards were made from old cannon filled with *cement* or capped with a cannon ball, hence the shape of traditional cast-iron bollards.

bolt A metal fastener with a square, hexagonal or round head and screw thread, which is secured by a *nut*.

Bomanite A proprietary form of *stamped concrete*.

bond An arrangement of *courses* of *bricks* in a wall or paving.

brad A nail with an L-shaped head used for fixing floorboards or decking.

brass An alloy of *copper* and *zinc*, with a ratio of 60–90 per cent copper to 10–40 per cent zinc. It is resistant to corrosion and easily machinable, and is used externally in ornamentation and fixings.

brazing A process (similar to *soldering*) in which two metal components are joined by melting a filler *alloy*, such as *brass* (*copper* and *zinc*), at a high temperature (above 842°F). Brazing can have advantages over *welding* in that the component metal is not melted so there is less distortion. It also can permit the joining of two dissimilar metals.

brick A rectangular, modular, molded, loaf-sized block, which can normally be held in one hand. They may be made of baked clay, calcium silicate, or *concrete*. Bricks

are held together by mortar joints and are laid in *bonds*, or patterns of courses, which have different structural and decorative characteristics. Brick *joints* differ widely depending their width, profile, and the color of the *mortar*.

brise-soleil A permanent sunshade, usually of horizontal or vertical slats, or a decorative screen wall, used to reduce glare and heat load on a building.

bronze A corrosion-resistant *alloy* of *copper* and tin, which tends to turn green due to copper oxidization. Used in sculpture, garden ornaments, and pump fixtures.

building brick A term for a cheap *brick* that is strong enough to be used for internal walls and to be faced with other materials.

bull-nose brick A *brick* with a rounded *arris*.

Buna rubber A synthetic rubber, first produced in Germany in 1935, consisting of a *co-polymer* of butadiene and styrene.

burr (i) Term for *brickwork* that has been heavily burned or fused, either as a result of kiln temperature or fire damage. (ii) A rough edge, for example on metal after it has been cut.

bush-hammered i) A finely textured stone finish, also known as *fine-picked*. ii) A *concrete* finish in which the surface is removed to reveal the *aggregate* using a bush hammer, which is an air- or electric-powered, hand-operated hammer with a serrated edge. Because bush hammers are hand-operated their use may lead to white knuckle or *HAVS*, and therefore *grit blasting* is a preferable technique.

butt joint (i) A touching or nearly touching *joint* in paving or in lumber joinery. Butt-jointed *pavers* are laid touching, for example *concrete* block pavers laid flexibly and touching without a mortar joint. Sometimes nibs in the sides of paver units act as spacers. After laying, the joints are filled with sand and then rolled to ensure a good key between paving units. ii) A joinery joint of two parallel pieces of lumber.

buttress A support projecting at right angles to a wall, which resists lateral forces or thrust and thereby strengthens the wall.

butyl rubber Synthetic rubber used as a flexible pool liner.

calcareous sandstone A type of *sandstone* that is rich in calcium carbonate.

calcite A calcium carbonate deposit. Calcite crystals are used for *grotto* decoration.

California Bearing Ratio (CBR) The standard penetration test for comparing the strength of soils, expressed as the ratio of resistance of a soil compared with the standard resistance of crushed *limestone* rock, which has a value of 100. The test was devised by the California Department of Public Works in 1929.

camber Term to describe the slight curvature of a surface, such as a road, which is crowned or raised in the centre to permit drainage to the sides.

canted A splayed or sloped surface.

cantilever wall An L-shaped or inverted T-shaped retaining wall.

capping A protective wall topping that is flush with the wall face.

capping material A type of ground material placed on the *sub-grade* to strengthen it or make it suitable for construction (often used as a synonym for *sub-base*).

carbon fiber See *CFRP*.

cast-in-place Term for *concrete* that is placed and formed in its final location.

cast iron Reheated *pig iron* in which the carbon has been converted to ferric carbide and the sulphur content increased. Cast iron is available as gray cast iron (with a high silicon content) and white cast iron (with little silicon and no graphite). Cast iron is brittle, but rust-resistant and used for swale gratings and bollards.

casting Shaping process in which molten metal is poured into a mold.

cavity wall A wall consisting of two skins of *brick*work held together by wall ties of steel.

cell matrix paver A paver with a cell-like or hollow form into which soil or gravel can be placed to permit drainage, and which can support grass growth.

celluloid A cellulose-based natural *resin*, an early form of *plastic*.

cellulose A carbohydrate and the main constituent of plant cell walls including wood. Used in some plastics and in paints.

cement (i) In building construction, a binder, usually *Portland cement*, which holds together the *aggregate* in *concrete* and is used in *brick mortar*. (ii) In geology, the matrix that holds together a rock, for example the *calcite*, *clay*, or *silica cement*, which hold together the sand grains in *sandstone*.

cement mortar *Mortar* made with *cement* (usually Portland), *sand* and water, with a typical ratio of 1 part cement to 3 or 4 parts sand. It sets hard when used for the bedding and jointing of *brick*work, for laying floor tiles, and as a *finish*. The mix can also include *plasticizer*s and *polymer*s.

ceramic A material made by firing dry-pressed *clay* (usually from high-quality refined clay powder) at 1,832–2,192°F. Ceramics are water-resistant and maintain their color.

ceramic tile A type of water-resistant, hard-wearing, fired vitrified clay tile, usually thinner than *quarry tile*, and usually made from pulverized, refined clay powder which has been fired until vitrified, and often glazed. Ceramic tiles hold their color and are frost resistant.

CFRP Carbon fiber-reinforced *polymer* (also known as *carbon fiber*). A strong, light and expensive *composite material* or fiber-reinforced polymer with many applications in structural engineering including the strengthening of existing structures.

chalk A form of soft, white, fine-grained pure *limestone*. It is of use in *concrete* manufacture but of little use as a building stone.

channel i) A shallow U-shaped stone or series of stones or *concrete* units formed to gather water in paving. ii) A stream bed. iii) A long *precast* concrete or stone unit that is rectangular in section.

chert A silica-rich *sedimentary* stone found as a nodule in *limestone*, chalk, and *sandstone*. It is used crushed as a *roadstone*.

Chinese step A flight of steps against a wall, with a recessed drainage channel between the side and the wall.

chromacity A term to describe purity of *hue*, the extent to which a color contains white or gray.

chunam A technique originating in Hong Kong for steep slope retention using *soil cement*.

clay A fine *sedimentary* soil material less than 0.002 mm in diameter. Clay is sticky, plastic when wet and hardens if dried. Clay *topsoil* can be very fertile and holds water well when it has a good soil structure; if it is compacted when wet and then hardens it loses its structure. Clay is used in construction in *rammed earth* walls and as a pool liner as *puddled clay*.

cleft A finish in which stone is split.

cob Mixture of clay soil and straw used to make *rammed earth* walls. The term is associated with southwest England, particularly Devon.

cobble A water-worn, rounded stone from a stream or a beach used in paving. Cobbles are popularly (but incorrectly) used to refer to *setts*.

color saturation Term referring to the brightness or dullness of a color.

color value Term referring to the darkness or lightness of a color.

column A vertical structural member that carries a vertical *compression* load. Columns may be built of reinforced *concrete*, *lumber*, *masonry*, or steel stanchions and may be round, square, or rectangular.

combined drainage system A system in which both blackwater and *surfacewater* are carried through the same drains.

compatible metals Metals that are close in the scale of the galvanic table and which therefore may be used together.

composite material Substance made of different materials with complementary properties, for example, reinforced concrete, which is made of *concrete* (because it is strong in compression) and *steel* (because it is strong in tension). Other examples include *CFRP*, *GRP*, and traditional construction mixtures such as mud and straw.

compression A force that condenses an element, for example the force that tends to shorten a column. The opposite of *tension*.

concave joint A *brick joint*, curved in section, which weatherproofs the joint and throws a soft shadow.

concrete A mixture of water, sand, stone *aggregate*, and *cement* (as well as any *admixtures*) that forms a stone-like mass as the water dries and the concrete cures. Concrete is easily molded, strong in *compression*, and cheap. It is also highly alkaline, which helps prevent the rusting of *steel* reinforcements.

contiguous bored piles *Cast-in-place* concrete *piles* that have been cast touching in order to form a continuous retaining wall.

contour A line on a plan joining points of equal height.

coping A protective top to a wall which projects beyond the wall's face.

co-polymer A *polymer* made from two or more different *monomers*.

copper A rust-resistant metal that is brightly colored when fresh and turns green when weathered. It is used in *alloys* (for example *bronze* and brass), in fittings and flashing, in paint as a *pigment*, and as a fungicide.

cord road A road made of logs laid flat and side by side.

corduroy textured paving Paving with a raised, ridged pattern that acts as a hazard warning (also known as *tactile paving*).

Corten steel Generic name for a type of *steel* (also known as *weathering steel*) that contains 0.25 per cent *copper* and sometimes some chromium. It has a tenacious iron-oxide coating that does not fall off when in contact with air. Because *copper* and chromium are smaller molecular elements than *iron* they fix the iron-oxide molecules in a tenacious rusty patina.

COR-TEN® steel The trade name for what is known as *Corten steel* or *weathering steel*.

course i) A parallel layer of *bricks* or *blocks* usually laid horizontally including any *mortar*. ii) Any layer of material such as a *moisture-proof course*.

creosote A term for oil-containing *phenols* used as a wood preservative, which covers a variety of oils, wood creosote, coal-tar creosote, and naturally occurring resin. Because creosote is carcinogenic it should not be used in certain places, for example those accessible to children.

crib wall A grillage of steel or lumber elements that cross each other and interlock, which is filled with hand-placed crushed or quarried rock.

crown A raised dome-like structure such as a road, pavement, or athletic field.

crushed roadstone A hard rock (such as *granite*) crushed to make a road.

CSA Canadian Standards Association. The CSA operates the Sustainable Forest Management Program, which has certified 195 million acres (2007 figure) of sustainable forest under the CAN/CSA-Z809 SFM Standard.

cullet A piece of waste glass from glass-making.

curb A raised *edge restraint* to separate a roadway and footpath.

curing (of concrete) The process by which *concrete* is hydrated and hardened while water is incorporated into the concrete's molecular structure, for example when calcium oxide becomes calcium hydroxide.

cut and fill A method of construction for *earthworks*, or railroads, roads, or canals, usually executed with the aim that the amount of material from the cut balances the amount of fill needed to make nearby mounds or embankments, thereby minimizing construction and the importation and carting away of material.

dead load An immoveable load, for example paint or other finishes and fixings such as fixed planters on a deck.

deadman A *concrete block* or *beam* used to secure a *ground anchor*, a deadweight (also known as an anchor log).

deck/decking Flooring or a platform made of lumber.

delamination The tendency to separate into layers, for example the peeling away of a *finish* or *stucco* from a *masonry* wall.

deluge A form of wood-preserving treatment in which lumber is passed through a tunnel while preservative is jet-sprayed at it. The process is usually used for applying organic solvent preservative, *tar oils*, and *creosote*.

density The mass of a given unit of volume, usually expressed as weight per unit volume, for example lbs/ft^3.

designed mix concrete A *concrete* for which the specifier states the properties and performance and the producer determines the mix.

diamond-pattern paver A hard-burned *brick paver* to which an incised diamond pattern has been applied to provide a non-slip surface.

die casting Casting molten metal under pressure into reusable steel molds.

dike (or dyke) i) An intrusion of *magma* forming a vertical wall of *igneous* rock (geological). ii) An earth embankment in a polder or alongside a river (engineering construction). iii) A water-filled ditch or channel (topographical).

diorite Coarse-grained *igneous* rock.

dissimilar metal corrosion See *galvanic corrosion*.

ditch A water channel up to 24 in deep with a v-shape (or near vertical walls in peaty soils). Ditches permit infiltration and also support wildlife.

dolerite A medium-grained *igneous* form of basalt rock usually formed in a sill or *dike*.

dowel A short, round wooden peg used to join lumber components, often associated with *green oak* construction.

drafted A type of finish resulting in a flat, smooth margin around the face of stonework, with the area inside the draft being left rough or *rock-faced*.

draw down (i) The lowering of a reservoir or of a pool system in dry weather. (ii) The localized lowering of *groundwater* for construction by pumping.

drawing (of metals) A hot-rolled rod is pulled through a hole in a die (a reusable mold) at a relatively low working temperature.

driving rain Wind-blown rain, which may be horizontal. Surfaces exposed to prevailing winds may be eroded by driving rain.

drystone wall Stone wall made without *mortar*.

ductile iron A form of *cast iron* consisting of gray iron that has been reheated with *graphite* nodules, which strengthen the metal and improve its tensile strength.

dyke See *dike*.

earthworks Work associated with the excavation, backfilling, compaction and grading of earth.

ecoconcrete Process in which *concrete* is made with *cement* using magnesia (magnesium oxide) to allow the reduction of the required kiln temperature to 1,382°F (the kiln temperature for ordinary *Portland cement* is 2,642°F). Ecoconcrete production may also use calcium carbonate (produced using waste flue heat) and carbon dioxide from other processes, or by-products of other processes, such as *fly ash*.

edge restraint The retention edge to flexible paving, designed to resist lateral pressure from rolling and consolidating and to maintain structural integrity.

EDPM Ethylene propylene diene *monomer*, a *polymer* used as a flexible pool liner.

efflorescence The crystallization of calcium and sodium salts resulting in a white stain on *brick*work. The salts may come from the *mortar*, the water used in the mortar, or the clay of the bricks, or it may be due to the passage of water through the structure.

eggshell/honed A stone finish in which abrasives are used to produce a smooth, matte finish.

elastomer An elastic material (for example, *rubber*) that resumes its original shape after being pressed or otherwise deformed.

electrical conductivity The property of a material that permits the passage of an electric current, the reciprocal of electrical resistance.

electro-polishing A process involving the immersion of a metal component in an electrolyte (typically phosphoric and sulphuric acid) and the application of a direct electrical current. Electro-polishing selectively removes microscopic high points and saturates the surface of the component with dissolved metal. The process ensures polish and corrosion-resistance in *stainless steel* and other metals, for example high- and low-carbon *steel*, *aluminum*, and *bronze*. It is often undertaken after *passivation*.

embodied energy The energy required to extract, process, transport, install, maintain, and dispose of a product or component.

engineering brick A dense, strong, impermeable, hard-burned *brick* suited to engineering structures, commonly blue or red.

English bond A strong *brick bond* consisting of alternate courses of *headers* and *stretchers*.

English garden wall bond A *bond* in which *headers* are used every fourth or sixth course in between courses of *stretcher* bond.

entrained air The presence of tiny air bubbles in *concrete*, which can be induced with an *admixture* in order to reduce the weight of the concrete.

epoxy A synthetic *thermoset* resin used in fiber-reinforced plastics such as *CFRP* and adhesives. It is formed from a resin and a hardener which, when brought together, form a *thermoset*.

epoxy resin A synthetic *polymer* that requires a curing agent to convert to a resin. Epoxy resins, which are *thermosets*, are tough and adhesive and therefore suitable for use as a binder, for example in paving and as a resin mortar, in *sealants* and *expansion joints*, and in paints.

expansion joint A joint in a wall or paving or other structure that permits expansion and contraction caused by changes in temperature or moisture levels (also known as an *expansion joint*).

extrusion A method of metal forming used particularly with *aluminum*: the heated solid metal is squirted or pushed in a heated, semi-liquid form through a shaped hole.

extrusive rock A very fine-grained, volcanic *igneous* rock with small crystals, which are the result of quick cooling, for example, lava.

facing brick A *brick* that has at least one *header* and *stretcher* face of good quality and color, used for facing walls.

faience A brightly glazed, fine-grain *ceramic*, of relatively low porosity and water-resistant. A decorative material much used in the early twentieth century for trimming and edging.

fairfaced concrete *Cast-in-place concrete* with a uniform color and finish and free of blemishes.

fair-picked A chiseled stone surface.

FAO United Nations Food and Agriculture Organization.

fat lime A pure lime with a high calcium content, characterized by good workability.

feldspar Aluminosilicate rock with varying amounts of calcium, potassium, or sodium. It is used in the making of *ceramics* and *polymers*.

ferritic stainless steel A type of *stainless steel* with 14–16 per cent chromium, which tends to be used internally.

ferrous A material made of, or containing, *iron* or an *alloy* of iron (for example, *cast iron* and *steel*).

filter drain A gravel-filled trench with a permeable pipe drain at the base, which permits *surfacewater* to enter the soil until it is saturated. Also known as a *French drain*.

filter strip A grassed and gently sloped area of ground designed to accommodate drainage run-off from impermeable hard surfaces and to filter silt and small particles.

fine-picked A finely textured stone surface, a synonym of *bush-hammered*.

fine-rubbed A stone surface that has been mechanically rubbed for a smoother finish.

finish A coating of *mortar* or *stucco* that is applied to *masonry* to weatherproof it and/or make it look like stone.

flag A paving stone or a concrete *slab*.

flame-textured A stone surface that has been heated to give an undulating, non-slip finish.

flashing A strip of metal (for example, *lead* or *copper*) used to seal an exposed junction or window opening against water.

Flemish bond A bond in which *headers* and *stretchers* are laid alternately in each course; it is more varied than *English bond*.

Flexcell The trade name for a common, fiberboard-based *expansion joint* filler, used externally with a waterproof layer.

flexible construction A construction method that permits movement, for example paving that has been laid *butt-jointed* on sand on a *hardcore* bed, or *green oak* construction, or brickwork laid with *lime mortar* joints.

float process A process invented in the 1950s for manufacturing large areas of flat plate glass by which a ribbon of molten glass is "floated" over a bath of liquid tin.

fluorite See *fluorspar*

fluorspar A crystalline mineral of calcium fluoride, used in *steel* production as a flux to lower the melting point.

flush mortar joint A *masonry* mortar joint that does not project and therefore does not throw a shadow.

fly ash A by-product of coal-fired power stations. It contains *silicon* dioxide and calcium oxide and, dependent on the coal type, usually also contains toxic *heavy metals*. It has pozzolanic properties and hence can be used in *concrete*. Usually used in the form of *PFA*.

forest certification Third-party certification of managed forest products began in the 1990s and is a measure of their environmental and social sustainability. Many certification systems are nationally based, including the US *ATFS* and the Canadian *CSA*. The *FSI* is North American, the *FSC* is international, and the *PEFC* is an international umbrella system that endorses national certification schemes. FAO reported that in 2008 there were 790 million acres of forest world-wide, which is 8.3% of the global forest area and 13.4% of the managed forest area. Western European countries have certified more than 50% of their forest area and North America more than one third, but Africa and Asia have certified only 0.1%.

forging The process of hammering or beating a heated metal. This is the method used by blacksmiths, but it can also be industrialized —forged metal was much used in large-scale nineteenth-century construction. There are various forms of forging, including pressed plate and drop hammer.

formwork A mold in which to set fresh, liquid *cast-in-place concrete*, made of plywood, fiberglass, *steel*, or *lumber* boards together with supporting props.

foundation An element, usually made of *concrete*, that transfers and spreads the load of a wall or structure to the ground.

freestanding Term to describe a wall that is unattached, not connected with another structure.

freestone An unstratified, even-textured stone that may be worked in all directions (for example *granite*).

freeze–thaw The process whereby water expands in volume by 9 per cent on freezing and thereby can cause structural damage to materials.

French drain A gravel-filled drainage trench, usually with a perforated pipe at the base to carry away water.

frog A depression in the top and bottom bedding faces of a pressed or molded *brick*.

FSC Forestry Stewardship Council, a sustainable lumber certification system started in 1993. It is recognized in 50 countries and has certified around 314 million acres (2010 figure).

fugitive color Term for a color or pigment that lightens rapidly over time due to the discharge of a volatile pigment. Exposure to ultraviolet light breaks down pigment molecules. Typically, blues and reds tend to be fugitive.

furnace clinker The slag and ash recovered from blast furnaces, which can be used in cement making.

gabion wall A wire cage filled with rocks or broken *bricks*, used for wall construction and the protection or reinforcement of river banks.

galvanic corrosion Galvanic corrosion (also known as bimetallic or *dissimilar metal corrosion*) is the process by which two electrochemically dissimilar metals in contact with each other oxidize or corrode. Dissimilar metals are those that are far apart on the galvanic table. Corrosion occurs where there is an electrically conductive path between the two metals through which metal ions move from the more anodic metal to the more cathodic metal.

galvanizing The process of coating *iron*, *steel*, or *aluminum* with a thin layer of *zinc*, by dipping the metal in a molten bath of zinc at a temperature of around 860°F. The zinc reacts with carbon dioxide in the air to form zinc carbonate, which protects the metal beneath.

gang saw A power saw with several parallel blades.

geogrid A network of elements that are strong in tension with gaps sufficiently wide to interlock with surrounding fill material.

geosynthetic A *polymer* (i.e. plastic) sheet material.

geotechnics Geotechnical engineering, concerned with the stability and strength of soil and rock.

geotextile A *geosynthetic* or natural material such as *cord road* construction.

GGB Ground, granulated blast furnace slag, a by-product of steel manufacturing, which can be used in the manufacture of *concrete*.

girder A *beam* of steel or iron.

glass A translucent or transparent material which solidifies from its molten form on cooling without forming crystals and is usually hard and brittle. Glass is made from silicates fused with sodium carbonate or nitrates and lime; glass is considered a supercooled liquid rather than a true solid.

glass bricks Brick-sized *glass* blocks available as clear, frosted, or colored and laid with a *silicon* adhesive or *cement mortar*.

glass fiber A material made of thin threads of *glass* used as insulation and reinforcement in *composite materials*.

glass fiber-reinforced plastic or polymer A waterproof, *thermoset* plastic composite material consisting of a plastic *polymer* reinforced with fine glass fibers, used in boatbuilding and pool construction to form a rigid pool liner. Also known as *GRP*.

global warming potential The measure of the mass of greenhouse gas released into the atmosphere during the extraction or making of a product or component, including processing, transportation, and installation, maintenance or disposal. It is expressed in terms of the CO_2 equivalent.

globalization The development of an integrated global economy characterized by the free trade and movement of goods, services, and materials worldwide.

glulam Glued, laminated, *softwood lumber* that has parallel-grain veneers (unlike plywood) and that is made with kiln-dried lumber for use in long structural spans.

gneiss A *metamorphic* rock formed from clay that has been intensely heated or compressed by geological forces to form a mineral-rich rock.

grain (of wood) The longitudinal arrangement of fibers in wood.

granite A very hard form of *plutonic igneous* rock with a high crushing strength. It has a large, coarse crystal grain due to slow cooling during its formation. It is a durable building stone and is suitable in crushed form as a *roadstone*.

gravity The force that attracts a smaller body to a larger body, for example gravity pulls an object to the centre of the earth and thereby gives an object weight.

gravity retaining wall A retaining wall where the overturning lateral force is resisted by the self-weight of the wall. Such walls are usually made of rock, stone, *brick*, or *mass concrete*.

GRC Glass fiber-reinforced *concrete*.

green oak Unseasoned lumber that has free

water (i.e. the water outside the lumber's cells) present in a way which permits movement, including splitting, after construction.

greenhouse gas A gas that contributes to the greenhouse effect, whereby gases in the atmosphere absorb much of the longwave infrared radiation radiated by the earth's surface after being warmed by shorter wave sunlight. The absorbed heat is transferred to other gases in the atmosphere and re-radiated upward into space and downward to the earth's surface. Greenhouse gases include carbon dioxide, water vapor, and methane.

gray cast iron *Cast iron* with a high *silicon* content.

grit blasting A finishing method that involves blasting a surface, for example *concrete*, with coarse sand or grit in order to roughen the surface and remove cement from it to expose the *aggregate*.

gritstone A form of *sandstone* composed of coarse sand grains and pebbles.

grotto A picturesque man-made cave.

ground anchor A way of reinforcing a retaining structure and tying it into the ground by using a metal chain or rod, which is buried underground and secured against a *deadman* (i.e. a *concrete* block or *beam*).

groundwater Water in the soil above the *water table*.

groundworks Construction work carried out in the ground in open trenches and excavations, such as foundations, earth movement, and drainage.

GRP *Glass fiber-reinforced plastic* or glass fiber-reinforced polymer. A rigid plastic used for regular-shaped pools, planters, etc.

gunite The US trade name for what is generically termed *gunnite* or *shotcrete*.

gunmetal An *alloy* of 90 per cent *copper* and tin and the strongest of *bronze* alloys, used formerly for cannon barrels, but also for heavy duty garden features such as planters.

gunnite The generic name for sprayed *concrete*, which is applied either as a dry mix and then sprayed with water, or which is sprayed as a liquid *concrete* mix. Also known as *shotcrete*.

gymnosperm A phylum of trees and shrubs with cones, the seeds of which are borne on the surface of the cone scales. Typically, but not invariably, gymnosperms have needle-like leaves and a majority are evergreen. Gymnosperms produce *softwood* lumber, including pine, cedar, and redwood.

gypsum A soft white or gray mineral of hydrated calcium sulphate.

ha-ha A livestock-proof dry *ditch* with a wall on the inner side that permits an outward view without interruption. It is a feature characteristic of parks.

hand arm vibration syndrome (HAVS) A form of Raynaud's syndrome whereby arterial blood distribution is impeded and the fingers and knuckles may turn white due to vibration,

for example from operating power-assisted vibrating tools (also known as *white knuckle syndrome*).

hardcore A coarse, granular material (such as crushed *roadstone* or *concrete*) used as a base course below flexible or rigid road and paving construction.

hardwood Lumber from *angiosperm* broadleaved trees, such as oak, beech, ash, teak, and mahogany. Hardwood lumber structure is characterized by vessels or pores in the xylem (tissue), which are absent in *softwoods*.

harling A lime-based *finish* used in Scotland and Ireland. Harling is usually applied in two layers about ⅜ in thick using a lime cement and a *slurry* of small stone *aggregate*, which is thrown against the wall from a trowel.

hauling route The route on a construction site used for the transport and delivery of materials. It is often made of compacted earth, or reinforced with gravel or by temporary *precast concrete* slabs or metal sheet roadway.

HAVS See *hand arm vibration syndrome*.

haunched *Concrete* that has been applied behind a road *curb* or around a drainage pipe to support and reinforce it.

HDPE High-density *polyethylene*, a *thermoplastic* used in wood composite, *geotextiles* and root barriers and pipes.

header The short face of a *brick*.

header bond A strong *brick bond* formed entirely of *headers* laid overlapping, often used for retaining walls and also for curved walls.

heartwood The darker wood that comes from the inner part of a tree trunk and that has ceased growing. It is stronger and more durable than *sapwood*.

heat island Term for built-up areas that have higher average temperatures than surrounding undeveloped land. Higher temperatures occur because the materials in built-up areas are darker and retain more heat than vegetated countryside, and also because of the waste heat that is produced in developed areas. Heat island effect can be counteracted by planting on roofs and in urban spaces, by using light-reflective surfaces, and by insulating buildings and reduction of heat wastage.

heavy metal A metal with a high atomic mass. Heavy metals (for example *lead*, arsenic, cadmium, chromium, and mercury) are toxic because of their tendency to bind with organic compounds, which can affect protein structure and enzyme function.

herringbone A type of paving pattern in which *bricks* interlock at 90-degree angles, and which when laid flexibly distributes a point load. This is a suitable paving pattern for heavy industrial use, for example docks and warehouse roadways.

high-carbon steel A type of *steel* that comprises between 0.6 and 2.0 per cent carbon. It is the strongest steel but is also more brittle than other steels.

hoggin A mix of gravel and *clay* that acts as a binder. It is used as paving or sometimes as a fill material and is usually man-made, though naturally occurring self-binding gravels exist.

hot-rolled asphalt A commonly used road paving made of coarse aggregate and a mixture of *asphalt*, sand, and very fine filler material. It is rolled when hot, when it is therefore more free flowing and viscous. (also known as: hot asphaltic *concrete*).

hue The characteristic that distinguishes the primary colors red from yellow from blue. Hue can be viewed as the position on a color wheel.

hydraulic lime mortar A *lime mortar* that contains elements of clay or *silica*, which produce a di-calcium silicate and therefore allow the mortar to set under water or in waterlogged soils.

hydrocarbon An organic compound of hydrogen and carbon, such as coal and petroleum, and a constituent of synthetic plastics.

hydroseeding A planting technique in which a *slurry* of seed and mulch is sprayed onto a surface. Other ingredients can include fertilizer, tackifying agents, and color dye, and mulches can be paper or wood mulch mix. Hydroseeding is a way of economically seeding steep and inaccessible slopes. Often used for seeding grass, it is also used for general herbaceous, shrub, and tree planting and for planting herbaceous stolons and rhizomes.

hypabyssal A fine-grained *igneous* rock that has crystallized before reaching the earth's surface, for example *dolerite* or quartz porphyry.

igneous Rock formed by the cooling of hot melt or *magma* within the earth's crust, characterized by a small crystal size.

imprinted concrete A form of *stamped concrete*.

infiltration devices Infiltration drains (for example *French drains*) or *soakaways* that are designed to direct water into the ground.

iron Malleable, ductile, magnetizable metallic element with a melting point of 2,795°F. It is the most common metal on Earth and oxidizes to form rust when exposed to air.

iron pyrites A crystalline *iron* sulphide, also known as fool's gold.

ISO International Organization for Standardization.

joint The meeting of two components. Components can be connected by shaping them (e.g. tongue-and-groove boarding), or may be fastened, or sealed with a weld or adhesive. *Brick* joints are made using *mortar*.

jointing The process of filling the joints of *brick*work and blockwork with wet mortar.

joist A *beam* or horizontal member used to support floors or roofs. It can be of wood, *concrete* or of *steel* (for example an RSJ, or rolled-steel joist). Joists run from wall to wall,

wall to beam or beam to beam.

Kentish rag A very hard, compact gray-white *limestone* from mines in Kent, England, traditionally used in rubble walls in London.

kiln drying The drying or seasoning of *lumber* using heated air.

knot The place in a tree trunk where a side branch has grown and disrupted the grain of the *lumber*. Loose or dead knots reduce the strength of lumber while live or sound knots do not.

lake asphalt Naturally occurring *asphalt*.

laminated glass A material made of layers of toughened *glass* bonded together with *PVB* under heat and pressure. This strengthens the glass, spreads impact loads, and ensures that when broken the glass "crazes" and does not fall apart. It is used as a safety glass and also for sound insulation.

landing A platform in between two flights of steps.

lashing A cord or rope fastening, typically for wood components.

layered stone A stratified stone, such as *slate*.

lead A soft, rust-resistant metal with a low melting point, traditionally used in paints, garden ornaments, and flashing. Owing to its toxic nature, its use today is restricted.

lead glass A variety of *glass* with a *lead* constituent, which increases its brightness.

levee A *dike* or earth bank built alongside a river to limit flooding.

life cycle analysis (or assessment) The measurement of the full environmental cost of a product, component or project from raw material to final disposal in terms of the consumption of resources and energy and waste produced.

lime mortar Lime *putty* mixed with sand to the ratio of 1 part putty: 3 parts *sand*. Lime mortar is weak and permits movement and flexibility in a structure.

lime wash A wash or hydrated-lime and pigment mix that is painted onto a *finish*, *harling*, *masonry*, and *lumber* and which penetrates the material. Usually lime wash contains *calcite* crystals, which give a bright finish.

limecrete A lime *concrete* made of *aggregate*, sand, and natural hydraulic lime rather than *cement*. The material "breathes" and is permeable.

limestone A *sedimentary* rock composed mainly of calcium carbonate and formed by marine or lacustrine deposits.

live load A load that is temporary or that may be removed, for example snow, vehicles, or rainwater.

low-carbon steel *Steel* with less than 0.15 per cent carbon, suitable for wire and thin plating.

lumber Wood prepared for use in construction.

lumber durability The natural durability of solid wood depends upon the species and upon the presence of heartwood or the less durable *sapwood*. For example, chestnut is classed as a durable lumber but is usually available in the form of small logs with a large sapwood content, which easily decay. Preservative treatment modifies natural durability.

machine-pressed brick Dry-pressed *bricks* made from clay with a small amount of water. The bricks are shaped in steel molds under pressure applied by an overhead steel plunger, which provides the brick with cohesion in lieu of sufficient water for plasticity.

magma Hot, viscous molten rock found deep below the earth"s surface.

malleable cast iron A form of *cast iron* consisting of white iron reheated and used in thin-section casting.

marble A *metamorphic* rock formed of *limestone* that has been hardened and changed by geological pressure and heat. It is typically used as a prestigious building and facing stone and as a paving in non-frosty areas, and is often beautifully patterned, for example Carrara marble.

martensitic stainless steel *Stainless steel* containing a maximum of 14 per cent chromium and with the lowest corrosion resistance of all steels. Hard and brittle, it is used for knife blades and wear-resistant fittings.

masonry A load-bearing structure made of *brick* or stone, often held together by *cement*.

mass i) An object or body with substance and form. ii) A quantity of a matter in a body measured by weight, for example in pounds.

mass concrete Unreinforced *concrete* used for its compressive strength.

mastic i) A permanently plastic or flexible material used as a sealant and as an *expansion joint*. ii) A plastic or flexible material, for example *mastic asphalt*.

mastic asphalt A polymer-modified bound *asphalt* with small or sand-sized *aggregate* (smaller than ⅜ in diameter). It is used for paving (which is often sand-finished), flat roofs, and interior floors.

matrix A mass of fine-grained rock.

mechanics The study of the action of a force on a mass.

medium-carbon steel *Steel* that contains 0.2 to 0.6 per cent carbon, suitable for use as a structural steel and for casting.

metamorphic Rock which has been changed in structure or composition by heat, pressure or chemical action. For example, *slate* is formed from *clay* by geological pressure and heat.

mica *Iron*, magnesium, and *aluminum* silicates.

mild steel *Steel* containing between 0.15 and 0.25 per cent carbon. Used as a structural steel, it is strong and suitable for rolling and welding but not for casting.

miter joint An angled corner joint in which both pieces of wood are cut at 45-degree angles, thereby hiding the end grain.

modular wall A wall made of interconnected units, usually of *precast concrete*.

moisture-proof course A waterproof barrier to stop moisture penetration from the ground or from water on top of a wall. A mositure-proof course is typically made of bituminous material, *aluminum*, *lead*, or, traditionally, of *slate*.

molecule A unit in which two or more atoms are chemically combined, for example oxygen (O_2) is two atoms, and water (H_2O) is three atoms. It is the smallest particle of matter that can exist in a free state.

monolithic paving An undifferentiated surface material, for example *asphalt* or *cast-in-place concrete*.

monomer A simple *molecule* that can be linked with other monomers to form a *polymer*.

mordant solution A solution (often phosphoric acid-based) used to degrease and etch metal, particularly galvanized *steel* and *aluminum*, as preparation for a primer.

mortar A mixture of lime (for example *lime mortar*) or *cement*, sand, and water used for jointing *bricks* and stonework, for laying floor tiles and as a *finish*.

mortice (or mortise) and tenon joint A joint in which a hole is cut in the piece into which a protruding "haunch" of wood can fit and be glued. The joint can be strengthened by the use of *dowels* across the joint.

mulch A protective layer placed on the *soil* around plants or over seeds. Mulches retain water, protect from frost, and reduce weed competition. Mulch is often an organic material such as straw, bark chippings, or leaves, but other mulches include gravel and glass chippings, and proprietary *geotextiles*.

nail A pointed metal spike fastener with a flat head, which is hammered into components, especially wood, to fix them together.

needle-punched Mechanically oriented and interlocked fibers in a textile.

neoprene rubber A synthetic rubber developed by DuPont in 1931.

newton (N) The force required to move a *mass* of one kilogram at an acceleration rate of one meter per second squared.

non-hydraulic lime Calcium oxide (*quicklime*) that has been slaked with water to produce calcium hydroxide and has then matured for two or three months.

non-ferrous A metal with no *iron* content, for example *aluminum*, *copper*, or *lead*.

nozzle fountain A spout that controls the shape of a fountain.

nut A square or hexagonal metal fixing with a threaded hole used to secure a *bolt*.

olivine An olive green, silicate mineral rich in magnesium and *iron*.

oolitic limestone *Limestone* formed of sand-sized, white, rounded egg- or pearl-shaped particles with *cement*.

organic solvent A carbon-based solvent used

as a thinner in paints or in preservatives.

overburden The material, such as soil and *subsoil*, that lies above the economically valuable rock in a quarry.

overflow An outlet for excess water in a water feature such as an artificial pool or channel.

p.c. See *precast*.

paint binder The adhesive film-forming component of paint, which binds *pigments*. Binders include synthetic or natural resins such as *acrylics*, polyurethane, *polyester*, *epoxy*, and melamine resins and oils.

paint solvent Solvents that adjust the curing properties and viscosity of paint, which are volatile and evaporate during drying. Examples of solvents include water, alcohol, petroleum distillate, and white spirit.

panel pin A round, lightweight *nail* used in cabinet-making.

particulate Minute airborne (or waterborne) particles. Airborne particulates are of environmental concern because they affect lung function.

passivation (i) The chemical removal of *iron* compounds from the surface of a metal with a mild oxidant. For example, *stainless steel* is treated with citric oxide or a nitric acid solution to ensure a continuous protective film of chromium oxide on the surface. It is often a preparatory process in conjunction with *electro-polishing*.
ii) A preparatory treatment of one material to render it "passive" in relation to another material.

patten Ramped steps.

paver A unit or block used in paving, for example *concrete* blocks, *bricks*, or stone blocks.

pebbledash A wet *finish* with small pebbles that is thrown at the wet *cement* surface to be rendered.

PEFC Program for the Endorsement of Forest Certification schemes (formerly The Pan European Forest Certification System). PEFC endorses national sustainable lumber certification systems. It began in 1999 and now operates in 35 countries including those in Europe, Africa and Asia, as well as in Russia, Australia, Brazil, and the USA, and covers 546 million acres of forest (2010 figure). PEFC certification embraces *ATFS*, *CSA* and *SFI* systems.

peg A *dowel*.

permafrost Permanently frozen *subsoil* found in polar regions.

perpend A vertical *joint* in *brick*work.

PFA Pulverized fuel ash (also known as *fly ash*). A fine ash by-product of coal-fired electricity power stations, it can be used in the manufacture of *cement* and *concrete* and, when pelleted, as a lightweight *aggregate*.

pH A measure of the acidity and alkalinity of a material (such as soil) or liquid ("p" stands for potenz (power) and "H" stands for hydrogen). The pH scale ranges from 0–14 (7.0pH is

neutral). Acidic soils are usually in the range of 5–7pH and alkaline soils are usually 7–8pH. The pH scale is the logarithm of the reciprocal of the hydrogen ion concentration. Note that this is a logarithmic scale and so, for example, pH 4 is ten times more acidic than pH 5.

phenols Hydroxil group chemical compounds. They are acidic and found naturally in plants (for example, wine contains phenols), and may be germicidal.

phosphor bronze A *copper*–tin alloy to which phosphorus has been added (to avoid copper oxide formation), which increases rust resistance and strengthens the *bronze*.

photocatalytic concrete A self-cleaning *concrete* made with the white pigment titanium dioxide (TiO_2) in a water-based binder, which promotes the oxidization of pollutants, notably nitrous oxide.

pier A (usually projecting) column placed at regular intervals in a wall, and which strengthens the wall.

pig iron Smelted *iron* cast in the form of ingots or pigs (so called because of the resemblance of the shape of the molds to piglets feeding off a sow).

pigment Natural or synthetic solids which, when added to paint or a material such as a plastic, changes that material's color. Pigments modify reflected or transmitted light as the result of light wavelength absorption. In paints, pigments are mixed into a medium such as oil. Many pigments are metal oxides.

pile A column-like structure of *concrete*, *steel*, or *lumber* that is driven or cast into the ground and may resist lateral loads (for example, a sheet-pile canal wall) or vertical loads (for example, a building or other structure).

pile foundation A *slab* of *concrete* buried below the frost line, which acts as a foundation to support a wall.

pisé See *rammed earth*. Also known as pisé de terre or *cob*.

pitch-faced A natural, rough, quarried rock finish, a synonym of *rock-faced*.

pitching Paving comprising long river stones as opposed to round *cobble* stones, and laid flexibly.

plastic A synthetic *polymer* made from organic materials such as *hydrocarbons*, for example *PVC*, which has been molded on formation.

plasticity index The measure of the ability of soil to expand and contract.

plasticizer (i) A concrete or mortar *admixture* used to increase the plasticity of a mix so that it flows more easily. (ii) A non-volatile substance that is mixed with paint or varnish to improve flexibility. (iii) Substance added to a plastic to make it more soft and flexible.

plate lumber connector A flat or angled thin metal plate used to join two pieces of wood with the use of *bolts*.

plutonic An intrusive *igneous* rock formed deep under the earth's surface, which cools

slowly and is marked by large crystals, for example *granite*.

pointing The process of raking out a mortar joint in *brick*work to a depth of about ¾ in and then filling it with a fine pointing *mortar*.

polished A stone finishing process in which fine abrasives are used to produce a high gloss, which reveals the stone's natural pattern and color. It is suitable for stones with a high mineral content and a tight structure.

poly- A prefix meaning many or much, used in chemistry for *molecules* consisting of many smaller molecules, for example *polyester* or polythene.

polyester Synthetic resin in which the *polymers* are linked by esters; used especially in fabrics.

polyethylene A *thermoplastic*, used in cold-water pipes, tanks, and plastic bags, popularly known as polythene. There are two main types: high density (HDPE), which is more commonly used in construction, and low density (LDPE).

polymer A synthetic material formed by a process of molecular linkage by which large chains of *monomers* form a *molecule* with a repeated structural unit. Examples include *plastics*, *resins*, *rubber*, and other *elastomers*.

polyphenols A group of chemical substances found in plants, which is generally divided into *tannins* and phenylpropanoids (such as lignins, flavonoids, and condensed tannins). Polyphenols protect some *lumbers* (for example red cedar, redwood, and oak) from insect attack.

polypropylene (PE) A chemical-resistant *polymer* used as a pool liner. The joints require specialist site-welding.

polyurethane foam Type of foam made of polyurethane—a permanently elastic *polymer* joined by urethane—and used as a *expansion joint* filler.

polyvinyl chloride (PVC) A material used as a pool liner, it can be reinforced with nylon.

porphyry An *igneous* rock with large crystals set within a *matrix* of smaller crystalline material.

Portland cement A standard *cement* (so named because it was thought to look like *Portland stone*) made of *limestone* and clay heated to 2,642°F and then ground. Modern Portland cement has a large calcium silicate component.

Portland stone A fossil-filled *limestone* from quarries on the Isle of Portland, a peninsula in Dorset, England. It is used for building, notably in London, and also for making fine *cement*.

post A vertical support or structure of wood, *concrete* or *steel*, usually thinner than a *column*.

post and beam A concrete *beam* supported by *piles*. Together they act as a foundation support for a wall.

powder technology Technology used to form difficult-to-melt metals such as tungsten. It enables the economical shaping of small parts and also allows the incorporation of non-metals, such as graphite (a lubricant), into a metal.

pozzolan A material (for example, vitreous siliceous materials) which, when combined with calcium hydroxide, forms calcium silicates.

pozzolanic concrete A type of *concrete* made with the addition of a *pozzolan*. The original pozzolanic concrete (from Pozzuoli in Italy) used volcanic *silica* dust and set hard under water.

precast Term used to refer to *concrete* that has been factory-manufactured or cast away from the final construction location.

prescribed-mix concrete A *concrete* for which the purchaser determines the composition, usually because of a wish for a special effect or a uniformity of appearance (as in exposed *aggregate* finishes).

pressed-plate forging A form of metal *forging* in which the die presses or forms the whole component relatively slowly (as opposed to forming just the edges of a component in drop-hammer forging).

pressure impregnation The application of a preservative to wood by sucking out air under a vacuum and then flooding the wood with the preservative under pressure. Tanalizing is a proprietary pressure impregnation process using the product Tanalith, a chromated copper arsenate preservative.

primer A preparatory coating used before painting. Primers assist better adhesion of the paint, protect the component that is being painted, and improve paint durability. Because primers are not the final layer they can be better devised to fill and adhere to the material being painted. Primers are used on porous materials such as wood and *concrete* in order to fill and make the material less absorbant.

primary forest Ancient forest (also known as old-growth forest) that has been relatively untouched by man, with a rich habitat and ecology.

puddled clay A traditional pool liner. It is made by placing a layer of clay about 3 in thick over the bed of a pool and using sheep or cattle to pound the clay together, which forces out air bubbles and ensures a seal.

puddled iron A late eighteenth- or nineteenth-century process that involves stirring or "puddling" molten *iron* to remove impurities. It is used for producing bar iron for *wrought iron* or *steel* from *pig iron*.

pulverized fuel ash See PFA.

Purbeck limestone A fossil-filled *limestone* from quarries at Purbeck, Dorset, England.

putty i) A doughlike *cement* made by mixing linseed oil and calcium carbonate used in traditional construction and often nowadays superseded by *butyl rubber* and *silicone*.
ii) A fine lime *cement* used as a finishing coat on plaster.

PVB Polyvinyl butyral *resin*. It is prepared from polyvinyl alcohol and used as a laminar binder for laminated glass and as a primer and paint for metals.

quarry tile A clay floor *tile* made of ordinary kiln-fired clay. Quarry tiles are hard-wearing but porous and are therefore not frost resistant so should not be used externally in areas subject to ground frost.

quartz A crystalline form of *silica* (*silicon* dioxide).

quicklime Calcium oxide, a highly alkaline, hygroscopic, grayish-white material.

raked joint A *brick joint* in which a layer of *mortar* is raked out, creating a strong shadow. This type of joint tends to promote rainwater penetration and consequently frost damage.

rammed earth Material made from layers of mud rammed within a *formwork* (also known as *pisé* and *cob*).

ramped steps A ramp interspersed with steps at regular intervals (also known as a *patten*).

rayon A wood pulp- and cotton-based synthetic fiber made of cellulose.

reaction The force of opposition to an applied force.

rebate joint Method of joining in which one piece of wood is placed in a "rebate" or notch in the other piece, which allows *nails* and *screws* to be used on both pieces to create a stronger corner joint.

recycle To re-use materials in a new situation or a new product, for example, bricks and paving stones can be re-used for walls and paving, or may be broken down and re-used as *concrete aggregate*.

recycled glass Material usually made by crushing bottle glass. It is used in *asphalt* as a *roadstone* in road construction, as a *mulch*, and for paving bedding sand.

reinforced soil retaining wall A wall type, developed in France as *terre armée*, consisting of galvanized *steel* strips arranged horizontally and fronted with *precast concrete* or *gabion* structures. *Geosynthetic* fibers are now also used.

renewable Term for a natural resource that can replenish itself.

resin Solid or semi-solid viscous substance obtained either as exudation from plants, such as pine trees, or synthetically prepared by polymerization. It is used in waterproofing, paints, binders, and adhesives.

resin-bound asphalt Asphalt with a binder of *polymer resin*, which is clear and shows the color of the *aggregate*. Polymer resins used include polyurea and *epoxy*.

retention basin A dry or wet basin that stores surface water run-off until streams or drains can cope with storm demand. If permanently wet (that is, with a pool at the bottom), the storage capacity is limited to the volume above the permanent water level.

reverberation time The length of time in which a sound persists after the sound source has stopped. A long reverberation will sound soft, full and echo-like. A short reverberation gives a harder sound.

rigid construction A construction that is inflexible, for example paving that has been laid *mortar* jointed on a *cement* bed on *concrete*, or *brick*work that has been laid with cement mortar joints.

rigid paving A type of paving that has been made on site using a rigid or relatively inflexible material, or that has been made of units laid on an inflexible foundation such as *cast-in-place concrete*.

rip-rap Large quarried rocks placed on river banks and in coastal defences to protect against water erosion.

riser The vertical part of a step.

rivet A smooth cylinder or rod with a curved head used for fastening metal parts. Once fastened, the rivet's protruding end is flattened by hammering to ensure a permanent fixture. They are traditionally used in *lumber* joinery (for gates, doors, and locks) with metal plates and were frequently used in metal construction for ships, *steel* building frames, and boilers until the latter part of the twentieth century. They have now largely been replaced in metal construction by *welding*.

roach stone A type of *Portland stone* full of shell fragments. It is resistant to weathering and hence used as a building stone.

rock-faced A natural, rough, quarried rock finish, the synonym of *pitch-faced*.

rolling A method used mainly with *steel*, which can be hot or cold rolled. Hot rolling involves rolling white hot ingots through rolling mills which successively reduce and change the cross section of the metal and increase the length to produce either flat steel plate (in flat rolling) or standard structural *beam* sections (in profile rolling).

roundwood Wood in its natural shape with or without bark. It is used for *lumber* posts and may be used structurally.

rubbed brick Soft *brick* that has been shaped or rubbed down to form very fine joints, for example in archways.

rubber A natural or synthetic *elastomer* or elastic material. Natural rubber comes from the latex of tropical trees, while synthetic rubber includes *neoprene*.

rubble *Masonry* built of rough, unshaped stones.

rust The oxidized form of *iron* or of *ferrous* metals, typically it forms a red brown powder or crust on a ferrous component which in time delaminates. Wet and salty conditions exacerbate rusting.

saddleback A *brick* or *block* that has been shaped as a semi-circle for use as a wall topping.

sand Particles or grains of inert impermeable rock granular material. Grains may be *sharp sand* or soft (i.e. rounded). *Silica* sands, especially quartz, are the most common and other sands include the white *limestone* sand of tropical beaches and black volcanic basalt.

sand-blasted A dull, non-glossy finish achieved by blasting air and sand across the surface of a stone.

sand-faced brick Type of *brick* made by pressing clay into a mold sprinkled with *sand*.

sandstone A *sedimentary* stone formed from grains of *quartz* that are naturally cemented.

sap The fluid consisting of water, sugars, and mineral salts which circulates in the vascular systems of plants, including shrubs and trees.

sapwood The outer part of a tree trunk, excluding the bark, where the wood is growing. It is softer than *heartwood*, and contains *sap*.

saw-cut paving Unit paving cut with a saw (usually a diamond-edge saw). It can be used with *concrete* and *brick pavers* and stone *slabs*.

sawn stone Stone that has been cut with a diamond saw. This process usually produces a smooth, saw-cut marking, but finish can vary depending on the saw used.

saw-pulled A fine, straight, strong chisel pattern that has been made vertically across a stone surface using a saw. Saw-pulled stone looks more regular and machine-finished than *batted* stone.

scarf joint A joint made by cutting the ends of the pieces to be joined into long, complementary shapes. These may be simple, angled planes or may be shaped to interlock. This type of joint is used when the *lumber* elements are shorter than is required.

schist A *metamorphic* rock with a leaf-like structure formed from *clay*.

screw A metal rod fastener with a helical screw thread and a slotted or incised head. It can be withdrawn and re-used.

sealant A sealing compound made of a sticky liquid, which is placed in a joint where it then stiffens. It is used for fixing glazing and *pointing*, and in *expansion joints*. Materials include *acrylic*, *butyl*, polysulphides, polyurethane, and *silicone* sealants.

secant bored piled walls Method of retaining wall construction in which primary "female" concrete *piles* (usually un-reinforced) are interspersed with secondary "male" piles, which are inserted overlapping in order to intersect and form a more water-resistant construction.

sedimentary A type of rock that has been laid down in layers from pre-existing rocks, or from organic matter or by precipitation in water; examples are *sandstone* and *limestone*.

self-weight The weight of an object or structure.

semi-dry laying Method of laying unit paving on a semi-dry mix of *cement* and *sand*, which is then sprayed with water to wet the cement.

sett A cube or rectangular-shaped stone block, usually hewn or sawn, and used as a paving stone. Setts are usually made of *igneous* stone, such as *granite* or basalt, but may also be made of a hard-wearing *limestone*.

SFI Sustainable Forestry Initiative, a US and Canadian sustainable lumber certification system. It operates the SFI 2005–2009 Standard, which covers 178 million acres (2009 figure).

shale A loose, *metamorphic* rock formed from *clay*.

shank The straight, unthreaded part of a *nail*, below the head.

sharp sand *Sand* with angular grains.

shear strength The measure of the maximum strength of resistance of a *soil* or ground material to lateral loading or *shear stress*, at which point the plastic yielding (deformation) of the soil occurs.

shear stress A force that tends to push the layers of an object laterally. If left free to move these layers will slide under such a force.

sheet piling An interlocking *pile* of *steel*, reinforced *concrete* and *lumber*, designed to resist lateral loading. Steel sheet piling typically has a Z or a U profile in plan. It is often used for canals and river banks, foundations, and temporary deep *trench* construction.

shellac A natural *resin varnish* that is soluble in alcohol. It is not used for outdoor surfaces. The source of shellac resin is a brittle or flaky secretion of the female lac insect, found in Asia.

sherardizing A method of metal protection using *zinc*. The object to be protected is placed in a sealed container with zinc dust or zinc vapor and heated at 716°F. The two metals bond, forming *alloys* and an external layer of pure zinc in the form of a tenacious, corrosion-resistant coating. This treatment tends to be more durable than *galvanizing*.

shim A thin and often tapered or wedged piece of material (for example wood, metal, or stone) used to fill small gaps or spaces between surfaces or objects. Shims are used for support, to adjust components to fit, or to provide a level surface.

shot sawn A rough combed stone finish made by *gang saw*ing with chilled steel shots (small, beadlike objects).

shotcrete Sprayed wet-mix *concrete* or placed dry-mix concrete, which is then sprayed with water to wet it. Wet-mix concrete or a *sand* and *cement* mix is sprayed through a hose and nozzle using compressed air. Sometimes the spayed concrete is reinforced by pre-fixed wire mesh reinforcement. This technique is used for tunnel lining and steep rock slope reinforcement. See also *gunnite*.

shrinkable clay A type of *clay* with a high variation in moisture content which is therefore highly susceptible to movement. Highly plastic wet clays have a very fine particle size and so expand and shrink as they absorb and lose water.

shrink–swell capacity The measure of the extent to which a *soil* will expand when wet and compact when dry, especially significant in *shrinkable clay*.

silica Silicon dioxide (SiO_2), a major constituent of the earth's crust. Silica include quartz and flint, ingredients of *glass*.

siliceous sandstone Silica-rich *sandstone*.

silicon The most common metalloid or semi-metal material. Like water, silicon expands when it freezes because it has a density higher in its liquid state than in its solid state. Silicon is a constituent of *silicone*. Silicon, in the form of *silica* and silicates, is made into *glass*, *cement*, and *ceramics*.

silicone Synthetic *polymers* composed of *silicon*, carbon, hydrogen, and oxygen. Heat-resistant, nonstick, and rubber-like, they are commonly used in *sealants*, adhesives, and insulation.

silt Small *soil* particles.

sinkhole A hole or underground chamber down which a stream passes or is "swallowed." It is a feature characteristic of *limestone*.

slab A flat piece of paving stone or *concrete*.

slaked lime *Quicklime* mixed with water to produce calcium hydroxide (used in *lime putty*).

slate A *metamorphic* rock formed from *clay* that has been hardened and changed by geological pressure and heat. Typically it has a layered structure that may be split and is available in thick (*slab*) or thin forms.

sleepers Cross supports for railroad rails, which can be made of *lumber*, *concrete*, *steel*, or *polymer* (also known as: railroad tie).

sleeve joint An overlapping *joint* like a sleeve that is particularly used in tubular components such as handrails.

slop molding *Brick*-making technique in which the mold is wetted to prevent the damp bricks from sticking. Slop molding produces a very wet brick which has to be dried for several days before firing.

slurry A semi-liquid mix of solid particles and liquid, for example *cement* and water.

slurry wall A reinforced-concrete wall constructed by filling a trench with *bentonite clay* slurry (to stop it collapsing). *Steel* reinforcement is then lowered into the trench and the clay slurry is displaced by *concrete*, which is injected using a *tremie pipe*.

smelting Method of extracting a metal from an ore by heating and melting the ore.

soakaway A hole filled with stones into which drainage water is directed.

sod construction Wall and roof construction using cut slabs of grass.

sod wall A wall made of cut slabs of grass.

softwood Wood from *gymnosperm* trees.

soil The loose ground material above solid

rock, which includes the *topsoil* in which plants grow.

soil cement A mix of soil and *Portland cement* used in road and steep slope construction.

soil reinforcement A system of reinforcing *soil* strength so that it can bear a greater load or resist slope erosion. Methods include adding lime to soil in order to dry it out, installing a plastic or composite webbing layer (*geogrid*) or by planting methods including *hydroseeding*.

soldering A process of joining two metal components by melting a filler metal (such as a *lead-based* alloy) at a low temperature (below 840°F). Soldered joints are not strong, and should not be used in load bearing elements or with components under stress. Non-lead-based solder fillers should be used where there is access for children.

soldier-piled walls Wall construction method in which H-shaped steel columns are driven into the ground at 6–13 ft intervals and connected by *precast concrete* planks. In the past *lumber* posts were similarly driven into the ground and connected by horizontal lumber *baulks*.

spalling The *delamination* and falling away of a finish from a wall.

sparrow-pecked An even stone finish achieved with a fine chisel.

specific gravity The ratio of the density of a material to water.

splash-back Discoloration caused by rainfall splashing and staining the lower part of a wall with dust, *clay*, or loose material found at the foot of the wall.

split A stone finish formed by splitting a rock along its natural cleavage lines, which is, for instance used on *slate* and *sandstone*.

spot levels Elevation measurements shown as points, usually on a regular grid and relative to a datum, either on a site or a national mapping datum.

sprig A small *nail* without a head, used largely to fix *glass* in place.

sprig joint See *sleeve joint*.

stack bond A *bond* in which *brick*s are laid side by side with no interlock strength. It is used as a paving bond or for cladding.

stain A suspension or solution of a dye or *pigment* in water, alcohol, or petroleum distillate, or a finishing agent (such as *shellac*, lacquer, *varnish*, polyurethane, etc.) used on wood. Two types of colorants are used: pigments and dyes. Dyes are microscopic crystals that dissolve in the vehicle, while pigments, which are much larger, are suspended. Stains have less hiding power than paint, permit water vapor movement and give less protection.

stainless steel A highly corrosion-resistant *iron alloy* with a shiny surface, typically with 10–20 per cent chromium. A film of chromium oxide on the surface provides corrosion protection.

stamped concrete *Cast-in-place concrete* into which a pattern has been embedded by placing a mold over it before it has cured. Wet-mix concrete with air-entraining agents is used to ease leveling.

standard A technical publication with precise criteria that is used as a rule, guideline or definition.

standardized prescribed-mix concrete A *concrete* mix prepared on site and based on published *standards*.

staple A U-shaped round-wire *nail* with two points, used to hold a wire in place. Staples may be insulated for use with electrical wire.

statics The study of the action of a force on a fixed *mass*, a branch of mechanics.

steel An *alloy* of iron with 0.07–1.7 per cent carbon as well as other metals. It is stronger in tension than *cast iron*.

steep A traditional wood-preservative treatment in which *lumber* is soaked in water and preservative solution for a period lasting from several days to several weeks.

stock brick A term originally used to refer to a *brick* that has been hand-made on a stock mold (a plate raised to create a *frog* in the brick). The term is now applied to both hand-made and machine-made standard bricks that are found in one particular area.

stone mastic asphalt A road paving developed in Germany in the 1960s for roads in residential areas. It has a high content of coarse *aggregate* that interlocks with voids, which are filled with a *mastic* of *bitumen* with added filler and fibers for stability.

stretcher The long side of a *brick*.

stretcher bond A *brick bond* consisting entirely of the *stretcher* face of the brick that is therefore only as wide as one *header*. It is the commonest twentieth-century bond because of its use in *cavity walls*.

strainer post A reinforced or extra heavy fence *post*, often cross-braced by a diagonal stay, that is used in a post-and-wire fence against which the wire can be tightened. Strainer posts are usually placed at each end of a length of a post-and-wire fence and at corners.

string course A projecting course or line along the face of a wall that throws off rainwater and casts a shadow.

struck joint A *brick* joint that slopes inwards.

stucco A painted *finish*, traditionally of lime and *sand*, and in the twentieth century often of *cement* and sand or cement *lime mortar*. It is used to make a rubble or *brick* wall resemble stonework.

sub-base A layer of usually course granular material (or capping material) laid on top of the *sub-grade* laid directly below the road base.

sub-grade Term for the naturally occurring material beneath a road or pavement. It can also refer to imported fill material, for example for an embankment.

subsoil A layer of inorganic *soil* that sits below the *topsoil* and is less fertile than the topsoil.

SUDS Sustainable urban drainage systems—including green roofs, *retention basins* and *swales*—used to slow run-off from a built-up area in order to avoid flooding. It is necessary because building development renders permeable soil impermeable and hence *surfacewater run-off* is increased.

sulphate attack Damage to brickwork caused by sulphates in the *brick* reacting with tri-calcium silicate in *Portland cement*, which results in the crystallization and crumbling of bricks.

surfacewater Rainwater (and other precipitation) that collects on the ground as a pool, lake, stream, or river.

surfacewater run-off Water from run-off or surface drainage of an area when the soil is saturated to full capacity or drains are insufficient to take away water.

sustainability The conservation of ecological balance by avoiding the depletion of natural resources. To quote the UN Brundtland Commission of 1987: "Sustainable development is development that meets the needs of the present without compromising the ability of future generations to meet their own needs."

swale A shallow, grassed *ditch* designed to force water to flow slowly so that it is largely absorbed by permeable soil.

tack A short *nail* with a wide, flat head for stretching fabric onto *lumber*.

tactile paving Paving with a ridged, raised or blister-patterned surface that can be felt underfoot. It is designed to act as a hazard warning to pedestrians, including blind or visually impaired people.

tannin An acid–alcohol compound formed from gallic acid, which will attack metal fittings. It is found in oak.

tar oil An oil-borne wood preservative.

tension A stretching or pulling force.

terracotta A fine-grained, unglazed, relatively low porous and water-resistant *ceramic*, usually made in the form of hollow *clay* blocks.

Terram Trade name for a permeable, non-woven *geotextile* made of *polypropylene* and *polyethylene*.

terrazzo A mixture of *cement* and marble chips that is ground smooth to reveal the *marble*. It is used as a topping and usually separated by strips of metal or plastic to act as *expansion joints*. Terrazzo topping is laid ¾ in thick on a *concrete* base.

terre armée The French term for a *reinforced soil retaining wall*.

thermoplastic A type of plastic that softens in heat and hardens if cooled, for example *polypropylene*.

thermoset A plastic that, once cured, cannot flex or soften, for example *epoxy resin*.

tieback wall Another term for an *anchored wall*.

tile A small, thin, baked *clay slab* used in paving, walls, and roofing. Tile paving is normally laid on *cement* bed on *concrete* because tiles easily crack under point loads without support.

tooled Term applied to various patterned stone finishes achieved using *masonry* tools.

topsoil The top layer of *soil*. It has a mineral and organic content, a structure through which water and air can pass, and contains microfauna and flora. It is therefore unsuited for structural foundations.

torsion A twisting force.

toughened glass A safety *glass* produced by applying heat to sheet glass and then air-cooling it rapidly, which pre-stresses and toughens the material.

toxicity Poisonous nature.

tread The horizontal part of a step, which should be laid to ensure good drainage.

tremie pipe A pipe connected to a hopper through which *concrete* can be poured from a height or under water.

trench A long, narrow, usually temporary earth excavation, often with vertical sides that may need supporting by reinforcement.

tufa A *limestone* formed around hot calcareous springs.

two-pack Term for a paint, *varnish*, or glue in which the base and catalyst are supplied separately and only mixed just before application. *Polyurethane* adhesives and *epoxy* paints are often supplied in this way.

unit paving Paving made of *slabs*, *bricks*, *tile*s or other small components (as opposed to *monolithic paving* such as *asphalt*).

urban heat island A built-up area that is hotter than the surrounding countryside. The annual mean air temperature of a city of one million people or more can be 33.8– 37.4°F warmer than its hinterlands, according to the Environmental Protection Agency.

USDA United States Department of Agriculture.

varnish A hard, transparent protective finish or film used on wood or metal. Traditionally it is a combination of a drying oil, a *resin*, and a thinner or solvent. Varnish finishes are usually glossy but satin or semi-gloss sheens may be produced by the addition of "flatting" agents. For external work the most commonly used varnishes are phenolic varnish, *polyurethane*, and alkyd resin.

verdigris *Copper* oxide, with a distinctive green color.

vermiculated A *stone* finish with a wormlike pattern.

vernacular construction Traditional, indigenous construction using locally available materials.

virgin forest Another term for *primary forest*.

vitreous enamel A material made by fusing powdered *glass* to a substrate by firing, usually at 1,382–1,562°F. The powder melts and hardens to a smooth, durable, vitreous coating which is colorfast on metal, glass, or *ceramics*.

VOC Volatile organic compounds.

volatiles Natural or synthetic organic compounds (gases or liquids) that vaporize at normal temperatures. They may be found dissolved in water or may be trapped in *soil* or other solid substances. They are often harmful or toxic, for example methane and formaldehyde. Paint solvents are volatile and evaporate during drying.

vulcanization The process by which natural rubber is heated at a moderate temperature with the addition of sulphur, rendering the rubber harder, stronger, more elastic, and less sticky.

wane The irregular wavy surface of a tree trunk, with or without bark.

washer A circular plate of metal with a hole in the middle. It is used with a *bolt* and *nut* to spread the pressure of the fastening in order to prevent crushing of the component so fixed.

water bead A thin (usually round) strip of material such as *silicone*, used to seal edges of pools and to stop water penetration of fixing layers such as *cement*.

water table The underground surface or level below which the ground is saturated.

wearing course The surface course of *asphalt* paving which takes traffic directly and which is important in terms of appearance and adhesion or resistance to skidding.

weather struck joint A type of *brick* joint. It is recessed at the top, slopes outwards, and is flush at its base, which throws rain off and creates a shadow line.

weathering steel See *Corten*.

weir A low dam across a stream or water channel over which water flows.

welding A way of joining metals and *thermoplastics* in which the components are melted and then cooled and fused to create a strong joint.

wet laying Method of laying *unit paving* on a wet cement mix.

whitbed Strong, close-grained, bed of *Portland stone* with shells in layers. It is not as hard as *roach stone*.

white cast iron *Cast iron* with a low *silicon* content and no graphite.

white knuckle syndrome See *HAVS* (also known as white finger).

window cleaning strip A narrow path around a building to enable access for window cleaners. It also prevents *splash-back* from staining the lower part of the walls.

wire-cut brick A *brick* made by extruding a column of plugged clay and then slicing it into bricks using a set of evenly spaced wires before firing. The scraped pattern of the wire cut can often be seen on the brick.

wire nail A *nail* made from coils of wire, with a round *shank*. It is the characteristic twentieth-century nail.

wired glass A cheap type of *glass* formed by pressing two plates of semi-molten glass over *stainless-steel* mesh. It is used for factory roofs.

wood flour Pulverized wood, which ranges in fineness from dust to the size of rice grains. It is used in *wood–plastic composite*s and in some plastics such as Bakelite.

wood–plastic composite A composite material formed from *wood flour* or sawdust and a *thermoset* plastic such as *epoxy resin* or a *thermoplastic* such as *HDPE*.

wrot lumber *Lumber* with a prepared surface (wrot means wrought or worked).

wrought iron Purified *iron* with low carbon content that has been hammered under heat to change its molecular structure and then rolled to produce a laminated fibrous structure. Wrought iron has a greater tensile strength than *gray cast iron* and greater corrosion resistance than *steel*. It was the structural iron of the mid-nineteenth century before the general introduction of steel (the Eiffel Tower was built of wrought iron, or *fer puddlé*), and it was also the traditional blacksmith's metal used for gates and grills. Production ended in North America and most of Europe in the 1960s and 1970s.

zinc A rust-resistant metal used in *galvanizing* to protect *steel*. It is also a component of *alloys* (for example *brass* and solder).

Further reading

This is a bibliography of works used in the preparation of this book. Clearly it has a British orientation. Many other countries have equally useful publications and web-based resources, and this bibliography mentions some of the wealth from the USA and other countries. A useful introduction to the German literature can be found in Astrid Zimmerman's *Constructing Landscape* (2009), which is also a very useful follow-on to this book's introduction to the subject.

This book was inspired by Elisabeth Beazley's now out-of-print *Design and Detail of the Space between Buildings* (1960), re-published in 1990 as a new edition by A. and A. Pinder. Other books to recommend as progressions from our introductory volume include Everett's *Materials* in the Mitchell's Building Series. Berge's excellent *The Ecology of Building Materials* covers the sustainable aspects of construction and is written from a Scandinavian experience. Recommended US literature includes Ching's *Building Construction Illustrated*, Landphair and Klatt's *Landscape Architecture Construction*, Hopper's *Landscape Architectural Graphic Standards*, and Harris and Dines's *Time-Saver Guides for Landscape Architecture*.

Some publications are listed because they record historic or vernacular approaches to construction, such as Dobson's *A Rudimentary Treatise on Foundation and Concrete Works* (1850), the Road Research Laboratory's *Bituminous Materials* (1962), and Williams-Ellis's *Buildings in Cob, Pisé and Stabilized Earth* of 1947 (originally published in the 1920s).

Agate, Elizabeth and Brooks, Alan, *Waterways and Wetlands*, British Trust for Conservation Volunteers London, 2001, also available at http://handbooks.btcv.org.uk/handbooks/index/book/87 (accessed 25 March 2010)

Akbari, H., Surabi, M., and Rosenfeld, A., "Global cooling: Increasing World-wide Urban Albedos to Offset CO_2" in *Climatic Change*, vol. 94, nos. 3-4/June 2009, pp.275–286

Brooks, Alan and Adcock, Sean, *Dry Stone Walling*, British Trust for Conservation Volunteers, London, 1999; also available at http://handbooks.btcv.org.uk/handbooks/content/chapter/221 (accessed 25 March 2010)

Albion Stone, *Portland Stone technical manual*, Albion Stone, Nutfield, 2009, http://www.albionstone.com/AlbionStoneTechManual2_10.pdf (accessed 8 April 2010)

Allen, Geoffrey, et al, *Hydraulic Lime Mortar for Stone, Brick and Block Masonry*, Donhead Publishing, Shaftesbury, 2003

Barras, Colin, "How our green technology may rest on bacterial skills" in *New Scientist* (online version, 25 March 2009), http://www.newscientist.com/article/dn16841-how-our-green-technology-may-rest-on-bacterial-skills.html (accessed 9 March 2010)

Berge, Bjørn, *The Ecology of Building Materials*, second edition, Architectural Press, Oxford, 2009

Bevan, Rachel, and Woolley, Tom, *Hemp Lime Construction*, IHS BRE Press, Garston, 2008

Blockley, David, *The New Penguin Dictionary of Civil Engineering*, Penguin, London, 2005

Bradley, Simon, and Pevsner, Nikolaus, *The Buildings of England, London 1: City of London*, Yale University Press, London, 2002

Bradley, Simon, and Pevsner, Nikolaus, *The Buildings of England, London 6: Westminster*, Yale University Press, London, 2003

Brady, Nyle C., *The Nature and Properties of Soils*, Macmillan, New York, 1974

British Geological Survey, *Mineral Profile: Building and Roofing Stone*, November 2005, available as a pdf download at www.bgs.ac.uk/downloads/start.cfm?id=1407 (accessed on 25 March 2010)

British Geological Survey, *Mineral Profile: Building and roofing stone*, November 2005, available as a pdf at http://www.bgs.ac.uk/search/search.cfm?qFileType=&qCollection=&qSearchText=Building+and+roofing+stone&qSearchBtn (accessed 9 March 2010)

British Stainless Steel Association, *Specifying mechanically polished, brushed and buffed stainless steel finishes and their applications*, http://www.bssa.org.uk/topics.php?article=190 (accessed 25 March 2010)

Brooks, Alan and Adcock, Sean, *Dry Stone Walling*, British Trust for Conservation Volunteers, London, 1999, also available at http://handbooks.btcv.org.uk/handbooks/content/chapter/221 (accessed 25 March 2010)

Brown, William H., *The Conversion and Seasoning of Wood*, Stobart Davies Ltd., Hertford, 1988

Brunskill, Ronald and Clifton-Taylor, Alec, *English Brickwork*, Ward Lock Ltd., London, 1977

Chapman, Tim and Pitchford, Andrew, "Holding back the earth" in *The Architects' Journal*, vol. 208, no. 15, 22 October 1998, pp.70–71

Ching, Francis D. K., *Building Construction Illustrated*, John Wiley & Sons, Hoboken, 2003

Clifton-Taylor, Alec, and Ireson, A. S., *English Stone Building*, Victor Gollancz Ltd., London, 1983

Clifton-Taylor, Alec, *The Pattern of English Building*, Faber & Faber, London, 1987

Cobb, Fiona, *Structural Engineer's Pocket Book*, Butterworth-Heinemann, Oxford, 2004

Collins, Peter, *Concrete: The Vision of a New Architecture*, second edition, McGill-Queens University Press, Montreal, 2004

Corporation of London, Department of Planning and Transportation, *City Street Scene Manual Part Two*, London, 2005, p.7, published on the City of London website, http://www.cityoflondon.gov.uk/NR/rdonlyres/7F3DF93E-176F-4A32-BB1C-F0E6D3E55C2F/0/DP_PL_SS_manual2.pdf (accessed 9 March 2010)

Department for Transport, Guidelines on inclusive mobility, http://www.dft.gov.uk/transportforyou/access/peti/inclusivemobility (accessed 9 March 2010)

Dobson, E., *A Rudimentary Treatise on Foundation and Concrete Works*, originally published by John Weale, London, 1850, facsimile edition published by Kingmead Reprints, Bath, 1970

Everett, Alan, *Materials*, Mitchell's Building Series, Longman Scientific & Technical, Harlow, 1994

FAO, *Global Forest Resources Assessment 2005 Rome*, FAO Forestry Paper 147, Rome, 2006, p.11, available at ftp://ftp.fao.org/docrep/fao/008/A0400E/A0400E03.pdf (9 March 2010)

FAO, ISRIC and International Union of Soil Sciences, *World reference base for soil resources 2006*, World Soil Resources Report no.103, FAO, Rome, 2006, http://www.fao.org/ag/agl/agll/wrb/doc/wrb2006final.pdf (accessed 9 March 2010)

Finnish ThermoWood Association, *ThermoWood Handbook*, 2003, http://www.thermowood.fi/data.php/200312/795460200312311156_tw_handbook.pdf (accessed 9 March 2010)

Hammond, G., and Jones, C., *Inventory of Carbon & Energy (ICE)*, Department of Mechanical Engineering, University of Bath, UK, 2010, http://people.bath.ac.uk/cj219/ (accessed on 25 March 2010)

Hansom, O. P., *Adhesives for Wood*, TRADA, High Wycombe, 1987

Harris, Charles W., and Dines, Nicholas T., (eds), *Time-Saver Standards for Landscape Architecture*, McGraw-Hill, New York, 1988

Hastoe Housing Association, *Sustainable Homes: Embodied Energy In Residential Property Development, A Guide for Registered Social Landlords*, 1999, http://www.sustainablehomes.co.uk/upload/publication/Embodied%20Energy.pdf (accessed 25 March 2010)

Hendriks, C. A., Worrell, E., de Jager, E., Blok, K., and Riemer, P., *Emission Reduction of greenhouse gases from the cement industry*, Greenhouse gas control technologies conference paper 2004, International Energy Agency, Greenhouse Gas Program, http://www.wbcsd.org/web/projects/cement/tf1/prghgt42.pdf (accessed 9 March 2010)

Highways Agency, *Design Manual for Roads and Bridges: Volume 7, Pavement Design and Maintenance*, 2009, http://www.standardsforhighways.co.uk/dmrb/vol7/section2.htm (accessed 9 March 2010)

Highways Agency, *Specification for Highway Works,* 2009, series 600, table 6/1: Acceptable Earthworks Materials: Classification and Compaction Requirements, pp.31–37, www.standardsforhighways.co.uk/mchw/vol1/pdfs/series_0600.pdf (accessed 9 March 2010)

Hill, P. R., and David, J. C. E., *Practical Stone Masonry*, Donhead Publishing, Shaftesbury, 1999

Holloway, L., (ed.), *Polymers and polymer composites in construction*, Thomas Telford Ltd., London, 1990

Holmes, Stafford, and Wingate, Michael, *Building with Lime*, Intermediate Technology Publications, Bourton-on-Dunsmore, 2002

Holtz, R. D., *Geosynthetics For Soil Reinforcement*, Ninth Spencer J. Buchanan Lecture, 9 November 2001, Texas A & M University, College Station, TX, https://ceprofs.civil.tamu.edu/briaud/Buchanan%20Web/Lectures/Ninth%20Buchanan%20Lecture.pdf (accessed 9 March 2010)

Hopper, Leonard J., (ed.), *Landscape Architectural Graphic Standards*, John Wiley & Sons, Hoboken, 2007

Houben, Hugo, and Guillaud, Hubert, *Earth Construction: A Comprehensive Guide*, Intermediate Technology Publications, Bourton-on-Dunsmore, 1994

Interpave, *Permeable Pavements: Guide to the Design, Construction and Maintenance of Concrete Block Permeable Pavements*, sixth edition, 2008, available at http://www.paving.org.uk/permeable.php (accessed 5 April 2010)

Interpave, *Understanding Permeable Paving*, second edition, 2009, available at http://www.paving.org.uk/permeable.php (accessed 5 April 2010)

Jackson, Neil, and Dhir, Ravindra K., *Civil Engineering Materials*, Palgrave Macmillan, Basingstoke, 1996

Keyworth, Brian, "Paints finishes and sealants" in *The Architects' Journal*, August 1999, pp.47–54

Kirkwood, Niall, *The Art of Landscape Detail: Fundamentals, Practices and Case Studies*, John Wiley & Sons, New York, 1999

Landphair, Harlow C., and Klatt, Fred, *Landscape Architecture Construction*, second edition, Prentice Hall, New York, 1988

Landscape Promotions Ltd, *External Works*, Endat Standard Indexes Ltd, Stirling, published annually, http://www.esi.info/landingPage.cfm/External-Works/_/N-g4

Levinson, R., and Akbari, H., "Effects of composition and exposure on the solar reflectance of Portland Cement Concrete," Lawrence Berkeley National Laboratory publication LBNL-48334, Berkeley, 2001, http://nlquery.epa.gov/epasearch/epasearch?typeofsearch=area&querytext=effects+of+composition+and+exposure&submit=Go&fld=heatisld&areaname=Heat+Island+Effect&areacontacts=http%3A%2F%2Fwww.epa.gov%2Fheatisland%2Fadmin%2Fcomments.html&areasearchurl=&result_template=epafiles_default.xsl&filter=samplefilt.hts (accessed 11 June 2010)

Livesey, Katie, *Replacing Other Construction Materials with Wood*, BRE, published on http://www.forestry.gov.uk/pdf/nee-climate-conf-livesey.pdf/$FILE/nee-climate-conf-livesey.pdf (accessed 9 March 2010)

Lloyd, Nathaniel, *A History of English Brickwork*, facsimile of 1925 edition, Antique Collectors' Club, Woodbridge, 1983

MacLean, James H., and Scott, John S., *Penguin Dictionary of Building*, Penguin, London, 1993

McDonald, Roxanna, *Illustrated Building Pocket Book*, Butterworth-Heinemann, Oxford, 2007

McMorrough, Julia, *Materials, Structures, Standards*, Rockport Publishers, Beverly, MA, 2006

Neve, Richard, *The City and Country Purchaser and Builder's Dictionary*, London, 1726; facsimile edition published by David and Charles Reprints, Newton Abbot, 1969

Pinder, A. and A., *Beazley's Design and Detail of the Space between Buildings*, E. & F. N. Spon, London, 1990

Pomerantz, M., Akbari, H., et al, "Examples of Cooler Reflective Streets for Urban Heat Island-Mitigation: Portland Cement Concrete and Chip Seals," Lawrence Berkeley National Laboratory LBNL-49283, Berkeley, 2003, available at http://escholarship.org/uc/item/53w2s92d (accessed 11 June 2010)

Reichel, A., Ackermann, P., Hentschel, A., and Hochberg, A., *Building with Steel: Details, Principles, Examples*, Birkhaüser, Basel, 2007

Road Research Laboratory, *Bituminous Materials in Road Construction*, HMSO, London, 1962

Ross, P., Mettem, C., and Holloway, A., *Green Oak in Construction*, TRADA, High Wycombe, 2007

Shadman, Asher, *Stone: An Introduction*, Intermediate Technology Publications, London, 1996

SI Metric, *Density of Materials—Bulk Materials*, 2009, http://www.simetric.co.uk/si_materials.htm (accessed 25 March 2010); a website of metric/systeme internationale conversion tables run by Roger Walker

Simpson, F. Gerald, and Richmond, I. A., "The turf wall of Hadrian, 1895–1935" in *The Journal of Roman Studies*, vol. 25 (1935), pp.1–18, published online at http://www.jstor.org/pss/296549 (accessed 25 March 2010)

Smith, R.A., *Flexible paving with clay pavers*, BDA Design Note 9, Windsor, Brick Development Association, 1988, available as a pdf at http://www.brick.org.uk/_resources/DN9_Flexible%20Paving%20with%20Clay%20Pavers_Oct%201988.pdf (accessed 5 April 2010)

UNECE/FAO, *Forest Products Annual Market Review, 2008–2009*, Geneva Timber and Forest Study Paper 24, chapter 10, "Forest certification challenged by climate change and illegal logging concerns," pp.111–123, http://timber.unece.org/fileadmin/DAM/publications/Final_FPAMR2009.pdf (accessed 25 March 2010)

UNEP World Conservation Monitoring Centre, *CITES Species Database*, http://www.cites.org/eng/resources/species.html (accessed 25 March 2010)

US Department of Energy Building Technologies Program, *Building Energy Software Tools Directory*, http://apps1.eere.energy.gov/buildings/tools_directory/about.cfm (accessed 25 March 2010)

US Environmental Protection Agency, *Heat Island Effect*, http://www.epa.gov/heatisland/ (accessed 25 March 2010)

Vallero, Daniel, and Brasier, Chris, "Sustainable Design" in *The Science of Sustainability and Green Engineering*, John Wiley & Sons, Hoboken, 2008

John, Vanderley M., *On the Sustainability of the Concrete*, University of São Paulo, 2003, http://vmjohn.pcc.usp.br/Arquivos/On%20the%20Sustainability%20of%20the%20Concrete.pdf (accessed 25 March 2010)

VanGeem, M., *Albedo of Concrete and Select Other Materials*, Construction Technology Laboratories, 2002, http://www.lehighcement.com/Education/PDFs/Solar%20(Albedo%20from%20M.%20VanGeem)%200910021.pdf (accessed 25 March 2010)

Vitruvius Pollio, Marcus, *De Architectura*, in the edition *The Architecture of Marcus Vitruvius Pollio*, trans. Joseph Gwilt, Priestley and Weale, London, 1826; published online by Bill Thayer at http://penelope.uchicago.edu/Thayer/E/Roman/Texts/Vitruvius/home.html (accessed 25 March 2010)

Weston, Richard, *Materials, Form, and Architecture*, Laurence King, London, 2008

Wigginton, Michael, *Glass in Architecture*, Phaidon Press, London, 1996

Williams-Ellis, C., *Buildings in Cob, Pisé and Stabilized Earth*, Country Life, London, 1947; facsimile edition published by Donhead Publishing, Shaftesbury, 1999

Wilson S., Bray, R., and Cooper, P., *Sustainable drainage systems: Hydraulic, structural and water quality advice* (C609B), CIRIA, London, 2004

Woolley, T., Kimmins, S., Harrison, P., and Harrison, R., *Green Building Handbook*, Taylor and Francis, London, 1997, 2 vols

Zimmerman, Astrid, (ed.), *Constructing Landscape: Materials, Techniques, Structural Components*, Birkhaüser, Basel, 2009

Useful websites

Below is a list of websites of trade associations, research institutes, and some government agencies.

AASHTO American Association of State Highways and Transportation http://www.transportation.org/; nonprofit organization representing highway and transportation departments in the US and Puerto Rico. AASHTO also issues standards to the design and construction of highways, bridges, and other technical areas

ACI American Concrete Institute http://www.concrete.org/general/home.asp

ALSC American Lumber Standard Committee http://www.alsc.org/

ANSI American National Standards Institute Standards are downloadable from their website; http://webstore.ansi.org/

ASLA American Society of Landscape Architects http://www.asla.org/

ASTM International http://www.astm.org/; an international standards setting body

BIA Brick Industry Association http://www.gobrick.com/

Building Green An independent publisher providing information on green design; http://www.buildinggreen.com/

CIRIA Construction Industry Research and Information Association http://www.ciria.org (accessed 4 April 2010)

Department of Energy Information Bridge DOE Scientific and Technical Information http://www.osti.gov/bridge/index.jsp (accessed 5 April 2010)

EarthArchitecture.org http://www.eartharchitecture.org/ (accessed 25 March 2010); a website run by Ronald Rael, Assistant Professor of Architecture in the Department of Architecture, University of California, Berkeley

EPA Environmental Protection Agency http://www.epa.gov/ (accessed 4 April 2010)

SPI Plastics Industry Trade Association http://www.plasticsindustry.org/

Sustainable Building Association (AECB) http://www.aecb.net/ (accessed 4 April 2010)

US Steel http://www.ussteel.com/corp/index.asp

Appendix of tables and further information

Table 1. Embodied energy in kWh/metric ton from three sources (see page 10)

Material	Embodied energy in kWh/metric ton from three sources		
	Krogh and Hansen Danish Building Research Institute	Boonstra and Knapen, The Netherlands	CIRIA (Construction Industry Research and Information Agency) 1995
concrete	11	17	-
brick	60	-	76
softwood	144	306	195–250 (imported) 158 (indigenous)
cement	-	-	174 (wet-process kilns) 106 (dry-process kilns)
bitumen	278	-	-
glass	528	-	-
steel	834	473	-
plastics	2,224	2,029 (PVC pipes)	1,629 (PVC)

Source: adapted from Crane Environmental Ltd., *Embodied energy in residential property development, a guide for registered social landlords*, PP3/99 Sustainable Homes: no date

www.sustainablehomes.co.uk/upload/publication/Embodied%20Energy.pdf, p.8 (accessed 7 June 2010)

Table 2. Embodied carbon dioxide (eCO$_2$) and construction materials (see page 10)

Material	eCO$_2$ (lbsCO$_2$/ft^3)	eCO$_2$ (lbsCO$_2$/ton)
Sand		
General sand	0.9[7]	1.5[5]
Aggregate		
General aggregate	0.218[7]	2.5[5]
Asphalt		
Asphalt (road and pavement)	1.42[7]	70[5]
Bitumen		
General bitumen[5]	not available	240
Stone		
Slate (large database)[5]	not available	3–28
Limestone[5]	not available	8.5
Marble[5]	not available	56
Concrete		
Dense concrete aggregate block [2]	9.18	37.5
Aerated concrete block[2]	7.55	120
Generic lightweight aggregate block[3]	10.48	60
Brick		
Clay bricks includes transport to site	not available	101[4]
Bricks, old tech av.	63.73[7]	not available
Shingle		
General shingle[5]	not available	150
Lumber		
Lumber, sawn hardwood[5]	23.03	235
Lumber, sawn softwood[5]	11.55	220
Plywood[5]	24.85	375
Bitumen		
General bitumen[5]	not available	240
Iron		
General iron	not available	955
Steel		
Structural steel sections[6]	955.96	966
Polymer products		
PVC general	361.08[7]	1,205[5]
Epoxide resin[5]	not available	2,955
Aluminum		
Recycled aluminum	104.82[7]	835[5]
General aluminum (30% recycled)[5]	not available	4,120
Cast aluminum [5]	not available	4,140

* includes 1.56 lbs/ft^3 steel reinforcement

** includes 1.87 lbs/ft^3 steel reinforcement

*** includes 6.24 lbs/ft^3 steel reinforcement

Adapted, with additions, from: http://www.sustainableconcrete.org.uk/main.asp?page=230 (accessed 25 May 2010), Note: for further information refer to Geoff Hammond and Craig Jones, *Inventory of Carbon and Energy (ICE)*, University of Bath, version 1.6a: 2008, available online from www.bath.ac.uk/mech-eng/sert.embodied/ (accessed 7 June 2010). This is periodically updated to reflect latest research.

References:

1. The ECO$_2$ figures for GEN 1, RC32/40 and RC40/50 were derived using industry-agreed representative figures for cementitious materials, aggregates, reinforcement, admixtures, and an appropriate figure for water.

2. BRE Environmental Profiles database, Building Research Establishment (BRE), 2006.

3. Communication from the Environment Division, BREEAM Centre, Building Research Establishment (BRE), 2005.

4. Brick Development Association figure from http://www.brick.org.uk/industry-sustainability.html (accessed 25 May 2010)

5. Hammond, G. and Jones, C., *Inventory of Carbon & Energy (ICE)* version 1.5 Beta, 2008, Department of Mechanical Engineering, University of Bath, UK, http://people.bath.ac.uk/cj219/ (accessed 25 May 2010)

6. Amato, A. and Eaton, K. J., *A comparative environmental life cycle assessment of modern office buildings*, Steel Construction Institute, 1998.

7. Alcorn, Andrew, *Embodied Energy and CO$_2$ Coefficients for NZ Building Materials*, Centre for Building Performance Research: 2003, www.victoria.ac.nz/cbpr/documents/pdfs/ee-co2_report_2003.pdf (accessed 7 June 2010)

Table 3. Density of construction materials (see page 19)

Density is the mass in a given unit volume. In building construction materials (and according to ISO convention) it is usually measured in lbs/ft^3. The table below lists the density of commonly used materials, as well as that of a human being, for comparison.

balsa wood	10.61 lbs/ft^3
red cedar	24.34 lbs/ft^3
oak	36.83–58.05 lbs/ft^3
solid ice	57.24 lbs/ft^3
water	62.42 lbs/ft^3
human being	62.42 lbs/ft^3
glass (broken/cullet)	80.53–121.11 lbs/ft^3
earth (if moist)	90.02 lbs/ft^3
brick (common red)	119.9 lbs/ft^3
concrete	140–148 lbs/ft^3
aluminum	159.8–164.8 lbs/ft^3
limestone	166.12 lbs/ft^3
granite	167.99 lbs/ft^3
cast iron	424.5–486.93 lbs/ft^3
rolled steel	490 lbs/ft^3
stainless steel	466.96–499.4 lbs/ft^3
zinc	445.4 lbs/ft^3
cast lead	707.93 lbs/ft^3

Source: http://www.simetric.co.uk/si_materials.htm (25 May 2010)

Table 4. Table of basic concrete admixtures (see page 46)

Type	Air entrainers	Accelerators		Retarders	Water reducers	Plasticizers	Bonding agents	Water repelents	Pigments
		setting	setting and hardening						
Action	forms small bubbles	rapid setting	increased setting and hardening	delayed setting and hardening	increased workability		increased bond strength	reduced permeability	color
Purpose	increased frost resistance, e.g. for road building and for filling trenches and excavations	repairs	cold season work and rapid removal of formwork	hot season work	easier workability or higher strength		patching and repairs	to prevent absorption of rainwater	visual
Constituents	foaming agents, e.g. wood resin or detergent	very alkaline solutions	calcium chloride or calcium formate	lignosulphonic or hydroxylated -carboxylic acids with cellulose or starch	lignosulphonic or hydroxylated -carboxylic acids	formaldehyde condensates or modified lignosulphates	polyvinyl acetate or acrylic	metallic soaps or mineral and vegetable	natural and synthetic materials oils

Table 5. Table of standard brick sizes (see page 53)

Dimensions given are nominal; they include the thickness of the mortar joint. The actual physical dimensions of a brick would be smaller. When the brick is laid the mortar brings it to the size of the module. For example, a "standard" brick intended to be laid with $3/8$ in mortar joints might have actual dimensions of $3\frac{3}{4}$ in x $1\frac{7}{8}$ in x $7\frac{5}{8}$ in, while a standard brick for $1/2$ in joints might be $3\frac{3}{4}$ in x $1\frac{3}{4}$ in x $7\frac{1}{2}$ in.

Name	Joint thickness	Actual dimensions in inches
Standard	$3/8$ in	$3\frac{5}{8}$ x $2\frac{1}{4}$ x 8
	$1/2$ in	$3\frac{1}{2}$ x $2\frac{1}{4}$ x 8
Engineer standard	$3/8$ in	$3\frac{5}{8}$ x $2\frac{3}{4}$ x 8
	$1/2$ in	$3\frac{1}{2}$ x $2\frac{13}{16}$ x 8
Closure standard	$3/8$ in	$3\frac{5}{8}$ x $3\frac{5}{8}$ x 8
	$1/2$ in	$3\frac{1}{2}$ x $3\frac{1}{2}$ x 8
King	–	$2\frac{3}{4}$–3 × $2\frac{5}{8}$–$2\frac{3}{4}$ × $9\frac{5}{8}$ –$9\frac{3}{4}$
Queen	–	$2\frac{3}{4}$–3 × $2\frac{3}{4}$ × $7\frac{5}{8}$ –8

Table 6. Table of standard international brick sizes (see page 53)

Standard brick sizes vary from country to country. The table below lists standard dimensions in nine countries.

Country	Metric	Imperial (where it is the basis of the brick size)	Notes
United Kingdom	215 x 102.5 x 65 mm	n/a	BS EN 771-3: 2003 "metric brick"
South Africa	222 x 106 x 73 mm	n/a	South Africa Bureau of Standards SABS 227-1986 *Burnt clay masonry units* "standard or imperial brick"
Australia	230 x 110 x 76 mm	9 x 4¼ x 3 in	Australian Standard AS3700 *Masonry structures* "standard metric brick"
The Netherlands	210 x 100 x 40 mm	n/a	Nederlands Normalisatie Instituut NEN 2480:1976
France	220 x 105 x 60 mm	n/a	Norme Française P. 13.304 *"brique pleine"*
Germany	240 x 115 x 71 mm	n/a	DIN 105 NF "Normal format"
Spain	250 x 120 x 52/60/75 mm	n/a	UNE 67019-96 *"formato metrico"*
Italy	250 x 120 x 60	n/a	UNI EN 772 NF *"Normalformato"*

Table 7. List of useful metal trade organizations and websites (see pages 64–73)

US Aluminum, http://www.usalum.com/

Arcelor Mittal, http://www.arcelormittal.com

Cast Metals Federation, http://www.castmetalsfederation.com/home.asp

Castings Technology International, www.castingsdev.com

Paint Research Association, http://www.pra-world.com

Tata Steel, www.tatasteel.com

US Steel, http://www.ussteel.com/corp/index.asp

(All websites correct 25 May 2010)

Table 8. Table of hardwood species and their properties (see page 74)

Hardwood species

Latin name	Common name	Uses	Advantages	Disadvantages	Color
Lovoa trichilioides	African walnut	High-class furniture, sometimes used as a teak substitute	Attractive, available in larger sizes	Can be difficult to plane and finish	Bronze yellowish-brown with irregular dark lines
Khaya ivorensis	African mahogany	Store fittings, furniture, and veneers	Available in wide and long boards, easy to work, fairly strong	Warps, hardness varies	Pink to reddish brown
Pericopsis elata	Afrormosia	Sills, gates, doors, stairs, and floors	Works well, durable	Stains in contact with iron and moisture	Yellow to dark brown
Latin name	Common name	Uses	Advantages	Disadvantages	Color
Fagus sylvatica	Beech	A very hard wood used for furniture, floors, veneers, and wooden toys	Tough and very strong, the close grain withstands wear and shocks	Not suitable for outside work because it is not durable to moisture, changes it is difficult to work and warp	White or pinkish
Ulmus campestris	Elm	Turnery, garden furniture if correctly treated with preservative, some domestic furniture	Elastic, tough, durable, does not split easily, medium weight, good for use under water	Will warp unless well seasoned, no longer easily available	Light reddish brown
Quercus robur	European oak	Boat building, garden furniture, quality furniture and gate posts	Strong and durable, easier to use than beech	Heavy and expensive, it is prone to splitting; because of tannic acid content it can corrode iron and steel fixings, so use wood dowel (or stainless-steel) fixings	Light to dark brown and gray when weathered
Shorea pauciflora	Meranti	A mahogany substitute, used for furniture and interior joinery, can be used outside if correctly preserved	Cheaper than mahogany	Does not polish as well as mahogany	Dark red or yellow
Tectona grandis	Teak	Ships' decks, garden furniture, and veneers	Naturally resistant to moisture because of its oil content, does not corrode iron and steel fittings, hard and strong	Difficult to glue because of the oil content; it blunts tools very quickly	Golden brown
Milicia excelsa	Iroko	Boat-building, domestic flooring and furniture, piling and marine work	Dense graining and high oil content make it quite durable for external use; heartwood is very durable and is resistant to termite and marine borer attack, good nailing and gluing characteristics	Works fairly easily with hand or machine tools, but with some tearing of interlocked grain; occasional deposits of calcium carbonate severely damage cutting edges, moderate steam-bending properties; may cause dermatitis when working with wet wood	Yellow but darkens to a richer brown
Vitex agnus-castus	Vitex	Decking, boat building, posts and piles	Durable	Hard, fairly heavy, steam-bending properties	Olive gray weathering to silver gray

Source: Based on http://www.design-technology.org/CDT10woodsproperties.htm (accessed 25 May 2010) with amendments and additions by the authors.

Table 9. Table of softwood species and their properties (see page 74)

Softwood species

Latin name	Common name	Uses	Advantages	Disadvantages	Color
Araucaria angustifolia	Parana pine	Staircases and furniture	The best quality internal softwood, attractive grain, available in long and wide boards, easy to work	Lacks toughness, tends to warp and can be expensive	Pale yellow with attractive streaks
Picea sitchensis	Sitka spruce	General outside work	Resistant to splitting, easy to work	Small hard knots, not durable	Plain creamy white
Pinus sylvestris	Scots pine	Suitable for all types of inside work, used for wood turning; can be used outside with suitable preservative	Cheap and readily available, easy to work and finishes well, durable	Knotty	Cream to pale reddish brown
Pseudotsuga menziesii	Douglas fir	External construction, ladders and masts	Water resistant, knot free, durable, and easy to work	Splits easily	Attractive reddish brown
Thuja plicata	Western red cedar	Cladding for the outside of buildings	Resistant to insect attack, weather and dry rot because of natural preservative oils, knot free, durable, and easy to work	More expensive than red or whitewood, not strong	Dark reddish brown turning to silver on exposure

Table 10. National Grading Rule lumber classes (see page 74)

Lumber class	Grade name
Light framing (2–4 in thick, 4 in wide)	Construction Standard Utility
Structural light framing (2–4 in thick, 2–4 in wide)	Select structural 1 2 3
Studs (2–4 in thick, 2–4 in wide)	Stud
Structural joists and planks (2–4 in thick, 6 in and wider)	Select structural 1 2 3
Appearance framing	Appearance

Table 11. Levels of treatability, durability, and ease of preservation (see page 83)

Levels of treatability	
Easy to treat	sawn lumber can be penetrated completely and without difficulty by pressure treatment
Moderately easy to fairly easy to treat	usually complete penetration is not possible, but after two or three hours of pressure treatment, lateral penetration of more than $\frac{1}{4}$ in can be reached in softwoods, and in hardwoods a large proportion of the vessels will be penetrated
Difficult to treat	three to four hours of pressure treatment may not result in more than $\frac{1}{8}$–$\frac{1}{4}$ in lateral penetration
Extremely difficult to treat to virtually impervious to treatment	little preservative absorbed even after three to four hours by pressure treatment; both lateral and longitudinal penetration minimal

Table 11 continued. Table of lumber durability classes:

A selection of lumbers from BS EN 350-2:1994, *Durability of wood and wood-based products. Natural durability of solid wood. Guide to the principles of testing and classification of natural durability of wood.*

Latin name	Common name	Natural durability		Treatability
		against fungi: 1 = very durable 2 = durable 3 = moderately durable 4 = slightly durable 5 = not durable	against insects and marine borers: D = durable M = moderately durable S = susceptible SH = heartwood known to be susceptible V = species high level of variability N/A = insufficient data	1 = easy to treat 2 = moderately easy to treat 3 = difficult to treat 4 = extremely difficult to treat
Softwoods			Anobium — termites	
Picea sitchensis	Sitka spruce	4–5	S — S	3
Pinus nigra	Austrian pine	4	S V — S V	4
Pinus pinaster	Maritime pine	3–4	S — S	4
Pinus sylvestris	Scots pine	3–4	S — S	3–4
Taxus baccata	Yew	2	S — N/A	3
Thuja plicata	Western red cedar	2	S — S	3–4
Hardwoods				
Acer pseudoplatanus	Sycamore	5	S — S	1
Aesculus hippocastanum	Horse chestnut	5	S — SH	1
Carpinus betulus	Hornbeam	5	N/A — S	1
Castanea sativa	Sweet chestnut	2	S — M	4
Eucalyptus marginata	Jarrah	1	N/A — M	4
Fagus sylvatica	Beech	5	S — S	1 (4 for red heartwood)
Fraxinus excelsior	European ash	5	S — S	2
Ocotea rodiaei	Greenheart	1	N/A — D	4
Milicia excelsa	Iroko	1–2	N/A — D	4
Tieghemella heckelii	Makoré	1	N/A — D	4
Quercus robur	Common oak	2	S — M	4
Quercus rubra	American red oak	4	N/A — S	2–3
Robinia pseudoacacia	Black locust	1–2	S — D	4
Tectona grandis	Teak	1	N/A — M	4

Note: *Anobium punctatum* is the common furniture beetle.

The European Norme BS EN 350 also gives a separate table of species suitable for consideration due to their resistance to marine borers:

Latin name	Common name	Durability class (as above)
Pericopsis elata	Afrormosia	M
Lophira alata	Azobé	M
Dicorynia guianensis	Basralocus	D
Nauclea diderrichii	Bilinga (Opepe)	M
Ocotea rodiaei	Greenheart	D
Entandrophragma cylindricum	Sapelli	M
Tectona grandis	Teak (Asian origin)	M

General note: When selecting from these lumbers be aware of the current CITES endangered species list.

Table 12. Types of plastic and their uses (see pages 89–91)

Name	Type	Properties and uses
ABS (acrylonitrile butadiene styrene)	thermoplastic	Tough, high-impact strength; boat hulls, model car bodies, car dashboards, telephones, safety helmets, electrical appliances
Acrylic (polymethyl-methacrylate)	thermoplastic	Hard, but brittle, durable outdoors, good electrical resistance but splinters and scratches, can be clear, translucent or opaque, wide range of colors available; display signs, machine guards, bathtubs, rooflights, windows, illuminated signs (the original plane canopy glazing in the 1930s and 40s); transparent forms are marketed as "Plexiglas", "Lucite," etc.; paints
Cellulose acetate	thermoplastic	Eyeglass frames, cutlery handles, chisel/screwdriver handles
Epoxy resin (epoxide, ER)	thermoset	Low shrinkage rate, high strength if reinforced; adhesives, castings, printed circuit boards (PCBs), surface coatings, and used in composite materials such as GRP and carbon fiber
Melamine formaldehyde (melamine methanal, MF)	thermoset	Tough, fire-resistant surface, used in thin laminate form for boards, e.g. chipboard, tableware, electrical insulation, synthetic resin paints; "Formica" is a well known laminate surface
Nylon (polyamide)	thermoplastic	Hard, tough, rigid, heat-resistant, self-lubricating, high melting point (374–662°F); usually white or off white; curtain rail fittings, combs, gear wheels, bearings, hinges, clothing; also available in oil-impregnated forms
PET (polyethylene terephthalate)	thermoplastic	Soft drink bottles (up to 2 liters)
Phenol formaldehyde (phenol methanal, PF, phenolic resin)	thermoset	Strong and rigid, heat resistant; usually black or brown; used for dark-colored electrical fittings and parts for domestic appliances, high-strength fabrics, bottle tops, kettle/iron/pan handles; original trade name is "Bakelite"
Polycarbonate	thermoplastic	Riot shields, safety glasses, machine guards, light diffusers, skylights
Polyester resin (PR)	thermoset	Brittle unless laminated to form GRP, when it is strong; used for casting, encapsulating, car bodies, boat hulls, pool liners
Polypropylene (polypropene, PP)	thermoplastic	Strong and tough, chemical resistant, melting point of 320°F; containers, bottle crates, medical equipment, syringes, food containers, nets, storage boxes, chair shells, car bumpers; usually pale pink or off white but can be pigmented
Polystyrene (expanded, PS)	thermoplastic	Very light, buoyant, stiff and hard; comes in thin sheets; inexpensive packaging, good sound and heat insulation; ceiling tiles, electrical equipment cases; available in wide range of colors
Polystyrene (high-impact, HIPS)	thermoplastic	Low-cost and disposable items produced by vacuum forming or injection molding, internal secondary glazing, toys, model kits, refrigerator linings; trade name "Styrofoam"
Polythene (high-density polyethylene, HDPE)	thermoplastic	Tough, flexible and soft, good chemical resistance, good electrical insulator, attracts dust unless anti-static; bottles, pipes, bowls, milk crates, buckets
Polythene (low-density polyethylene, LDPE)	thermoplastic	Flexible and soft, good chemical resistance, good electrical insulator; packaging film, shopping bags, toys, detergent bottles, dip coating
Polyurethane (PU)	thermoset/ thermoplastic	As solid: skateboard wheels, shoe soles, for buoyancy in boat hulls. As foam: sponges, cushioning. As liquid: varnish
PTFE (polytetrafluoroethylene	thermoplastic	Low-friction applications, non stick coatings (eg. Teflon), mechanical pipe joint sealing tape
PVC, plasticized (polyvinylchloride)	thermoplastic	Good acid and alkali resistance; leathercloth, dip coating, hosepipes, electrical wiring insulation, vinyl wallpaper, toys, dolls, footballs
PVC, rigid (polyvinylchloride)	thermoplastic	Stiff, hard, and tough at room temperatures, good acid and alkali resistance; rainwater goods, air and water pipes, chemical tanks, shoe soles, shrink and blister packaging, floor and wall coverings
Urea formaldehyde (urea methanal, UF)	thermoset	Electrical fittings, domestic appliance parts, textiles, wood adhesives

Table 13. Table of wood adhesives (see page 191)

Table of wood adhesives

Key to applications:
S surface or edge
C close contact joints
G gap filling joints
SJ structural joints

Types		thermosets	thermoplastics	Solvent or emulsion-based elastomer	Natural
General purpose					
urea formaldehyde (UF)	amino-plastic	S, C			
melamine urea formaldehyde (MUF)					
phenol formaldehyde (PF) resorcinol formaldehyde (RF)	phenolic	G, SJ			
polyvinyl acetate (PVAc)			S, C		
Special purpose					
contact				S	
hot melt			S, C		
epoxy		G			
Other					
synthetic			S, C, G, SJ		
natural					S, C, G, SJ

Adapted from O. P. Hanson: *Adhesives for Wood*, TRADA:1987

Index

Picture credits

Apart from those images listed below, all photographs are by
the authors. All line drawings are by Jamie Liversedge.

Front cover image based on a plan of the Bali Memorial, Perth,
Australia, by Donaldson + Warn (drawing by Laurence King Publishing)

46 top right RIBA Library Photographs Collection

51 bottom left Jade Goto

71 right Colin Westwood/RIBA Library Photographs Collection

78 top © Juan Carlos Reyes/FSC

93 © Martin Bowker

97 CDTS Ltd

167 Atelier Dreiseitl GmbH

184, **185** and **186** Photographs of nails, screws, and bolts by Andy Maby

Authors' acknowledgments

The authors acknowledge the support, help, and indeed patience of our editor Liz Faber; our book designer, John Round; Tessa Clark, who proofread the text; Srijana Gurung, production controller; and Philip Cooper, our commissioning editor at Laurence King. We also acknowledge the many contractors, suppliers and manufacturers, craftsmen, engineers, and designers we have worked with over the past 40 years on projects worldwide, and who have shown us that there is invariably more than one answer to any construction question.